MANAGING YOUR
GOVERNMENT
CAREER

MANAGING YOUR
GOVERNMENT
CAREER

Success Strategies That Work

Stewart Liff

AMACOM

American Management Association

New York • Atlanta • Brussels • Chicago • Mexico City • San Francisco
Shanghai • Tokyo • Toronto • Washington, D.C.

Special discounts on bulk quantities of AMACOM books are
available to corporations, professional associations, and other
organizations. For details, contact Special Sales Department,
AMACOM, a division of American Management Association,
1601 Broadway, New York, NY 10019.
Tel: 212-903-8316. Fax: 212-903-8083.
E-mail: specialsls@amanet.org
Website: www.amacombooks.org/go/specialsales
To view all AMACOM titles go to: www.amacombooks.org

*This publication is designed to provide accurate and authoritative
information in regard to the subject matter covered. It is sold with the
understanding that the publisher is not engaged in rendering legal,
accounting, or other professional service. If legal advice or other expert
assistance is required, the services of a competent professional person
should be sought.*

Library of Congress Cataloging-in-Publication Data

Liff, Stewart.
    Managing your government career : success strategies that work /
Stewart Liff.
        p.   cm.
    Includes index.
    ISBN-13: 978-0-8144-1099-8
    ISBN-10: 0-8144-1099-5
    1. Civil service positions—United States.   2. Career
development—United States.   I. Title.

    JK716.L68   2009
    351.73023—dc22

                                                    2008044716

Printing number

10   9   8   7   6   5   4   3   2   1

This book is dedicated
to my brother, Michael Liff, whose smile
lit up every room that he entered.

Contents

PART 2   GETTING OFF TO A GOOD START
(SURVIVING) 57

PART 3   PLOTTING YOUR CAREER
(THRIVING) 139

Preface

THIS BOOK IS INTENDED as a companion piece to my last book, *Managing Government Employees: How to Motivate Them, Deal With Difficult Issues and Produce Tangible Results* (AMACOM, February 2007). Whenever I gave presentations about that book, people remarked that it was about time someone wrote a book dealing with the problems that are unique to the government. It seems that the book has struck a nerve, and I continue to hear that officials in different sectors of the government are using it to help them manage their employees.

For example, *Managing Government Employees* is the one book that the state of New Jersey recommends for all candidates who are taking the Sheriff's Promotional Exam. I am truly grateful for the reaction to this book, since my goal in writing it was to improve the way government is managed.

After completing it, I had no intention of doing a follow-up book. However, since the first book was written from a "top-down" perspective and many people were urging me to write one from a "bottom-up" point of view, I finally decided to tackle the subject of *Managing Your Government Career*.

This book is organized into three parts. Part 1 addresses whether working for the government is right for you and, if it is, how to get into the government. Part 2 discusses how to get off to a good start, build a good relationship with your supervisor, and develop some perspective. The last part is for people who have been with the government for a while and are trying to make the most of their career. It is the most philosophical of the three parts, and it talks about looking down the road, deciding whether management is right for you, balancing your work and family lives, and personal growth. Feel free to read the book from beginning to end, or to start with the part that best corresponds to the current stage of your career.

If there is one overriding theme of this book, it is you need to be in charge of both your career and your life. I firmly believe that the choices you make ultimately determine how successful you will be. Moreover, I also believe that the best way to make sound choices is by (1) being aware of the ramifications of those choices and (2) living your lives (business and personal) according to a consistent set of core values.

Of course, that is easier said than done, because life is not simple, and neither is working for the government. However, if you follow the guidance contained in this book, which is supplemented by many real-world examples, I am certain that you will have an excellent career and avoid the mistakes that so many other people have made and continue to make.

Stewart Liff

California
April 26, 2008

Acknowledgments

SO MANY PEOPLE WERE INVOLVED in helping me write this book that it is impossible to acknowledge everyone. However, I'd like to start off by thanking my editor, Christina Parisi, and the editor of my two previous books, Adrienne Hickey, for their support and confidence in me. I'd also like to thank Veronica Wales and Carol Thomas for the assistance they provided me in answering my technical questions.

As always, I'd like to acknowledge my four primary mentors, Joe Thompson, Tom Lastowka, Bill Snyder, and Paul Gustavson, as well as the many other people who have mentored me over the years, including but not limited to Pat McLagan, Peggy Hutcheson, Paul Draper, Karmie Kalmanowitz, Rick Nappi, Barry Jackson, Herman Greenspan, Dan Kowalski, Dan Bisgrove, John Coghlan, and Montgomery Watson.

A special thanks as well to Pamela A. Posey, D.B.A., for everything she has taught me over the years.

To my government friends such as Dennis Kuewa, Gloria Young, Grant Singleton, Pat Amberg-Blyskal, Ed Russell, Lynda Russell, Susan Fishbein, Bob Dolan, Ben Weisbroth, Paul Koons, Ken Clark, Michele Kwok, Mike Harris, Julius Williams, Debbi Greitzer, Bob Epley, Steve Simmons, Jenn Kler, and many others I did not mention: I want you all to know that I appreciate your service to this country and am honored to have you as part of my life.

I'd be remiss if I didn't also thank the following outstanding physicians for their assistance in helping me recover from my personal trials and tribulations: Dr. Robert Carroll, Dr. Robert Bray, and Dr. Sanjay Khurana.

I would never have been able to write this book without the loving support of my family. As always, a deep, heartfelt hug to my parents, Pearl and Hal; my mother-in-law, Jaffa; my brother, Jeff; my three children, Rob, Jen, and Marc; and my nephew, Matt.

Lastly, I would like to thank my fiancée, Lisa, for putting up with me through the past 16 months. She has truly been a gift, and I look forward to spending the rest of my life with her.

MANAGING YOUR
GOVERNMENT
CAREER

PART I
GETTING IN
(ARRIVING)

CHAPTER 1

Should I Work for the Government and if So, Where?

THIS BOOK IS DESIGNED to assist current and future government employees in developing the best possible career with respect to self-fulfillment, overall growth, and personal happiness. It is based on my more than 32 years of experience in government, along with my interactions with thousands of government employees, some of whom had exciting and satisfying careers, while others had, quite frankly, miserable and disappointing careers that left them angry and cynical.

I spent the first part of my career in human resources management (HRM), starting as a personnel management specialist trainee and eventually moving up to run a national HRM program serving about 13,000 employees. During this time, I had the opportunity to learn the civil service personnel systems that are the framework for how people advance in government, and I will share that knowledge with you.

However, before we get started on learning the ins and outs of the government's HRM systems, it is important for you to decide whether the government is in your future. This is a key decision that you need to make up front, because you do not want to languish in a system that is not a good fit for you. At the same time, there is nothing wrong with going to work for the government, getting some needed experience there, and then making the transition to the private sector, if that is a better fit for you. The key is to have at least some sense of where you are going, since if you don't know where you are going, you'll never get there.

Is the Government Right for You?

Like everything else, working for the government has its pluses and minuses. Before you decide to work for the government, it is important that you know what you are getting into, as the government is certainly not the right place for everyone. Let's examine some of the advantages of working for the government (regardless of whether it is at the federal, state, or local level[1]).

Advantages of Working for the Government

ADVANTAGE: HELPING YOUR FELLOW CITIZENS

You have the opportunity to make a difference. Every organization in government is designed to help our citizens. This may involve defending our country from terrorists, serving our nation's veterans, protecting the environment, collecting taxes, managing immigration, educating our children, maintaining our libraries, fighting fires, or improving public health. Regardless of which branch of government you work for, you have the opportunity to help people and make a difference.

Imagine if you were part of the team that sent Neil Armstrong to the moon or helped the *Apollo 13* astronauts return to earth. Now imagine that you are helping to prevent a recurrence of the 9/11 disaster, trying to combat global warming, fighting an infectious disease, aiding soldiers who are returning from Iraq or Afghanistan, or aiding victims of a major hurricane, fire, or flood. Government employees have the chance to make a difference on a daily basis . . . and they do.

Looking back on my government career, there is no doubt that being able to make a difference was definitely the highlight. Working with the dedicated employees of the U.S. Department of Veterans Affairs (VA) New York Regional Office (RO) to improve the way that veterans' benefits were administered was an exhilarating and fulfilling experience. For example, we changed the way in which claims were processed from an assembly-line approach to a team-based, veteran-focused process. We also changed the way in which we paid our employees and developed VA's first balanced scorecard. While we eventually received Vice President Gore's first Hammer Award for reinventing government, and I actually got to meet him in the process, what was most meaningful to me was working together with great people to improve the lives of America's heroes.

ADVANTAGE: JOB SECURITY AND SUPPORT

The government offers more job security than the private sector for a number of different reasons. The government is funded by taxes and does not require making a profit, so it will always exist in some shape or form. Moreover, for the most part, unlike their counterparts in the private sector, government employees don't have to worry about corporate mergers, jobs moving overseas to low-cost areas, and other such threats. However, it should be noted that in recent years, there has been a drive to contract out some government work that is not inherently governmental,[2] and there is always the risk of consolidation.

In the unlikely event that a government job is abolished or transferred to another location, government employees still have strong protections. In the federal government, this type of situation is usually referred to as a reduction in force, or RIF. A myriad of procedures are in place to ensure that if a RIF occurs, employees are given appropriate credit for veterans' preference, time with the government, excellent performance, and other such factors. Moreover, once an employee is in danger of losing her job as a result of a RIF, the government takes a series of actions to ensure that the employee is protected to the maximum extent possible.[3]

Many state and local governments take a similar approach. For example, in the state of New York, if an employee loses his job as a result of a RIF,

> Every effort is made to avoid any employees losing State employment by reviewing their seniority rights and eligibility for transfer or reassignment and determining their "bumping" and "retreat" rights. Reemployment lists can provide job opportunities to competitive, non-

competitive, and labor class employees before and after they are laid off.[4]

Government employees also work within a system that enables them to appeal their removal,[5] which makes it difficult and costly for their supervisors to fire them. In the federal government, employees can appeal the loss of a job to the Merit Systems Protection Board (MSPB) or file a grievance that can be decided by an arbitrator.

Many city and state governments provide their employees with similar protections. For example, in the city of Seattle, the Civil Service Commission "provides timely reviews of employee appeals regarding disciplinary actions and the administration of the City's Personnel system."[6]

In the event that you get into some sort of trouble in government, you generally have a union available that will represent you at no cost. In the federal government, "78 unions represent 1.1 million . . . civilian workers. . . . The unions range from the tiny 13-member Sport Air Traffic Controllers Organization to the American Federation of Government Employees, which represents 600,000 employees. . . . In addition, four major unions represent most of the 800,000 workers at the Postal Service."[7]

Unions also represent government workers at the state and local levels. For example, AFSCME, the American Federation of State, County and Municipal Employees, has about 1.4 million members nationwide. AFSCME represents a variety of service and health-care workers, including nurses, emergency medical technicians, bus drivers, and librarians.[8]

At virtually any level of government, employees also have the opportunity to complain about most issues affecting their employment either through the negotiated grievance procedure (where the union generally represents them if they are in the bargaining unit) or through the agency's internal grievance procedure. Moreover, employees also have the right to file equal employment opportunity (EEO) complaints for acts of prohibited discrimination, where they are also entitled to a representative of their choice.

During my career, I never had the need for representation, since for the most part I was treated fairly and reasonably. However, on two occasions, I was concerned about losing my job, once because the organization that I was working for at the time was being downsized, and once because the organization faced the possibility of having its mission transferred to another location. In the first situation, I was able to switch to another agency in the same general area. On the second occasion, the mission was not actually transferred, although I was concerned about this happening for many months.

Had I actually lost my job on either occasion, I knew that my organization would follow the government's priority placement program strictly and that I was likely to find another job within a reasonable period of time. Knowing this was very comforting during these periods of uncertainty.

ADVANTAGE: BENEFITS

The federal government offers an incredibly attractive array of benefits to its employees. To name just a few:[9]

- Its health insurance program offers you choice and flexibility along with a substantial employer contribution to premiums. Moreover, employees can pay both their share of premiums and out-of-pocket costs with pre-tax dollars.

- Its leave program provides time off to take care of personal, recreational, and health-care needs. In addition to 10 paid holidays, employees accumulate 13 days of sick leave and from 13 to 26 vacation days each year, depending on their length of service.

- To help employees manage their responsibilities outside of work and enhance their peace of mind, federal agencies may provide options including flexible work schedules and telework; child-care and elder-care resources; adoption information and incentive programs; child support programs, including subsidies and dependent-care flexible spending accounts; and employee assistance programs.

- The government's three-part retirement program includes a social security benefit, a 401(k)-type plan, and a defined-benefit component based on years of employment and salary history.

- Employees can choose among several options for life insurance coverage.

- The government offers the largest group long-term care insurance program in the country. New employees can apply by answering just a few simple questions.

- Other programs include incentive awards, employee development programs, student loan repayment programs, and retention allowances.

The overwhelming majority of state and local governments offer similar benefits packages. For example, the following are some of the benefits that the state government of Ohio offers to its employees:[10]

- Ten paid holidays.
- Child care. Its Child Care Voucher Program provides cash grants once a year for work-related child-care expenses.
- Commuter choice. The commuter choice plan allows state employees to save money by paying for eligible transportation expenses, such as parking and transit passes, using pretax dollars.
- Credit union.
- Deferred compensation. The limits of this program are set by the IRS.
- Dependent-care assistance.
- Disability, worker's compensation, and unemployment benefits.
- Employee assistance program.
- Flexible spending account.
- Health benefits:
  Benefits comparison chart and guide
  Dental coverage for bargaining-unit employees
  Dental coverage for exempt employees
  Health-care benefits
  Health-care benefits phone numbers
  Long-term care
  Mental health and substance abuse
  Prescription drug benefits
  Vision coverage for bargaining-unit employees
  Vision coverage for exempt employees
- Leave donation program.
- Life insurance.

My government benefits were extremely helpful to me and my family throughout my career and into retirement. For example, my health insurance covered the births and care of my three children, I went through a total of eight surgeries (two for my sinuses and six for my back), and my wife battled cancer. Despite all of these happy, painful, and difficult events, our out-of-pocket costs were always relatively minimal because of the generous health insurance plan offered by the government. To put this in perspective, during the last five months of 2005, I had two back surgeries and my wife underwent brain surgery. Without health insurance, we would have been liable for about $500,000 in health-care costs. However, because we had such excellent insurance, we had to pay only about $6,000.

ADVANTAGE: CAREER GROWTH

The federal government has roughly 2,700,000 employees,[11] not counting military personnel. There are about 87,900 government units in the United States and about 19 million public employees.[12] Obviously, given the sheer scope of the positions available, there are enormous opportunities for career growth in government. Moreover, with the class of 1973 continuing to retire, there are many openings, and many more can be expected in the coming years.[13] As an illustration, "The Social Security Administration . . . is one of many agencies faced with the prospect of losing more than half of its employees by 2010, including a large number of the organization's leaders."[14]

To provide a sense of the range of opportunities available, as of November 6, 2007, the USAJOBS web site,[15] which is the official site of the federal government, listed 59,072 vacancies. Those jobs ranged from entry-level positions to high-level positions paying more than $100,000 per year. In addition, 119 of these jobs were classified as being in the senior executive service (SES). "Members of the SES are in the key positions just below the top Presidential appointees. SES members are the major link between these appointees and the rest of the Federal work force. They operate and oversee nearly every government activity in approximately 75 Federal agencies."[16] The federal government had 7,868 permanent SES positions in fiscal year 2004/2005.[17]

The minimum rate of basic pay for SES positions in 2007 was $111,676. The maximum rate of basic pay was $168,000, not counting bonuses.[18] While the pay of these positions will never impress a high-rolling stockbroker on Wall Street, it is still high enough to attract plenty of people.

To compare this to but one city government, as of the same date, the city of Los Angeles was recruiting for 621 positions, with salaries ranging from as low as $7.50 an hour for a neighborhood worker to a high of between $113,426 and $170,138 for a chief nursing officer. Clearly, government at any level offers plenty of career opportunities.

However, not only do governments offer many opportunities to advance, they also offer a number of programs that make it easy for certain categories of people to get in, get ahead, and/or be retained. For instance, since the Civil War, veterans have been given some degree of preference in appointments to federal jobs in recognition for their contributions to and sacrifices for this country.[19]

When an agency advertises job vacancies through the U.S. Office of Personnel Management or locally through direct hiring authority, applicants are rated on the basis of their knowledge, skills, and abilities. They receive points for related education, experience, special skills, awards, and written tests if required. The agency must then select from the top-rated eligible applicants, who are ranked on a scale of 70 to 100.

For most positions, qualified veterans with a compensable service-connected disability of 10 percent or more are placed at the top of the civil service examination list. Five-point preference is given to those honorably separated veterans who served on active duty in the Armed Forces. Ten-point preference is given to those honorably separated veterans who (1) qualify as disabled veterans because they have served on active duty in the Armed Forces at any time and have a present service-connected disability or are receiving compensation, disability retirement benefits, or pension from the military or the Department of Veterans Affairs, or (2) are Purple Heart recipients. The selecting official may not pass over an eligible candidate with veterans' preference, however, and appoint an eligible candidate without preference who is lower on the list unless the reasons for passing over the veteran are appropriate.[20]

Eligible veterans receive many advantages in federal employment, ranging from preference for initial employment to a higher retention standing in the event of a RIF. However, veterans' preference laws do not guarantee veterans a job, nor do they give preference in internal agency actions such as promotion, transfer, reassignment, and reinstatement.

Many state and local governments also provide preference to veterans in one form or another. For example, the state of South Dakota ensures that "applicants eligible for veteran's preference will receive an interview for positions they apply for."[21] In Utah, "Any officers, agents or representatives of the state . . . who willfully [fail] to hire a military veteran shall be guilty of a misdemeanor."[22] In Texas, the law requires that "State agencies must practice veterans' preference until they have reached 40% veteran employment."[23]

The city of North Miami provides veterans with five- or ten-point preference as appropriate.[24] In the city of West Sacramento, "an applicant who qualifies for veterans' preference and successfully places on an eligibility list for initial entrance into employment with the city shall be advanced one rank on the final eligibility list."[25]

Another category of individuals that governments provide assistance to is people who have disabilities. The federal government stipulates that "people who are disabled and have a certification letter from a State Vocational Rehabilitation Office or the Department of Veterans Affairs may apply directly to agencies for noncompetitive appointment through the Schedule A hiring authority."[26]

Other governments have similar approaches. For example, the U.S. Equal Employment Opportunity Commission surveyed the best practices of four states (Florida, Maryland, Vermont, and Washington) "that promote the hiring, retention, and advancement of individuals with disabilities in state government jobs."[27] In its "Interim Report on Best Practices for the Employment of People with Disabilities in State Government,"[28] the EEOC identified the following best practices:

- The states surveyed include individuals with disabilities as part of their diversity programs and their targeted outreach and recruiting efforts.
- Vermont provides for a "must interview" to anyone with a disability who meets the minimum qualifications for a state job.

- Washington passed legislation creating a supported employment program for individuals who need on-the-job training and long-term support to work successfully.

- Maryland and Vermont have tracked information related to the provision of reasonable accommodations that could be used to assess the effectiveness of their reasonable accommodation procedures.

- In 2004, Florida established the Agency for Persons with Disabilities and Maryland elevated its former Office on Individuals with Disabilities to cabinet-level status. These legislative and executive actions send a clear message "from the top" that people with disabilities are a state priority.

- Florida has secured a waiver from the Social Security Administration, enabling it to move persons with developmental disabilities into jobs without immediately jeopardizing their eligibility for Medicaid and Social Security Income benefits.

- Vermont has participated in a pilot project to establish "disability program navigators" at four state One Stop Career Centers established under the Workforce Investment Act to help people with disabilities access these services more easily.[29]

Both applicants for government jobs and qualified employees who have disabilities are covered by the Rehabilitation Act of 1973, which protects them from employment discrimination based on disability. The substantive employment standards of the Americans with Disabilities Act, 42 U.S.C. Section 12111, et seq., require federal employers to provide reasonable accommodations to qualified individuals with disabilities so that they can enjoy the benefits and privileges of employment equal to those enjoyed by similarly situated employees without disabilities.[30]

This means that the federal government is obligated to reasonably accommodate the needs of disabled people through such approaches as making existing facilities accessible; restructuring jobs; utilizing part-time or modified work schedules; adjusting or modifying tests, training materials, or policies; providing qualified readers and interpreters; acquiring or modifying equipment; and/or reassigning an individual to a vacant position for which the employee is qualified, as long as it would not impose an undue hardship on the organization.[31]

Governments at every level also try to attract students into their systems. For example, the federal government uses its Studentjobs.gov[32] web portal to provide information on thousands of federal government job opportunities. A no-cost site, it provides information on multiple employment opportunities for students at the high school, college, and postgraduate levels.

The federal government hires students through several programs. The Student Educational Employment Program consolidated 13 student hiring authorities into one program with two components. Students may be hired under these programs if they are working at least half-time for a high school diploma or general equivalency diploma (GED), a vocational or technical school certificate, or a degree (associate, baccalaureate, graduate, or professional).

The first component, the Student Temporary Employment Program (STEP), introduces students to a work environment and teaches basic workplace skills. Approximately 46,307 students participated in this program in 2005. The second component, the Student Career Experience Program (SCEP), provides experience related to the student's academic and career goals. Roughly 16,786 students participated in this program in 2005.

Participants in the SCEP program may qualify for conversion to a permanent appointment. Appointments to jobs under STEP are temporary, and there is no conversion to permanent status under this program.

Another program is the Presidential Management Fellows Program. This program is targeted toward graduate students who want to enter management in the federal government. Entry into this program is very prestigious and is recognized throughout government. It offers entry-level professional positions that provide experience in a wide range of public management issues and have career progression potential. Candidates receive two-year appointments, with most positions being located in the Washington, D.C., area. Upon completion of the program, fellows are converted to permanent positions if their performance is satisfactory.[33]

Outstanding scholars with a college grade-point average (GPA) of 3.5

or above on a 4.0 scale or who graduated in the upper 10 percent of their graduating class can apply for more than 100 positions with simply an application based on their scholastic achievement, proof of their GPA, and their work experience. They can be hired on the spot at Office of Personnel Management (OPM) college fairs or by agencies under the Outstanding Scholar Program.[34]

Many state and local governments offer similar programs for students, although these programs are not nearly as formal or as extensive as the federal government's. For example, the state of Illinois provides the following internships:[35] (1) the Curry Internship, offered by the governor's office (summer internships with the state for college juniors, seniors, and graduate students), (2) the Dunn Fellowship, offered by the governor's office (one-year fellowships with the state for college graduates), (3) the Pollution Prevention Internship (summer internship with the Illinois Environmental Protection Agency), and (4) the Governor's Environmental Corps (summer internship with the Illinois Environmental Protection Agency). Indiana offers the Governor's Public Service Summer Internship Program,[36] which is designed to introduce bright and motivated college students to the operations and officials of state government. Under this program, interns are given the chance to work with state officials and participate in a Speakers Series that features elected officials, agency directors, and other government representatives.

Many local governments also offer opportunities for students. For example, the city of Boston offers a variety of internships for students. As of November 9, 2007, the Design and Construction Unit of the Parks and Recreation Department was seeking an intern with an interest in library sciences, historic landscape preservation, and/or document conservation to assist in the organization and protection of these resources. Meanwhile, at the same time, the city of Manhattan Beach, California, was looking for an "Administrative Intern for the Department of Finance in the Information Systems Division."[37]

I entered government service in 1974, shortly after graduating from college. I had a degree in fine arts with a minor in education, but it was extremely difficult to find a teaching job because of the Vietnam War.[38] I eventually went to work for the federal government as a personnel management specialist trainee making $8,055 per year. I steadily worked my way up, changing jobs and agencies on several occasions. Eventually, I became a senior executive with the U.S. Department of Veterans Affairs.

At the time of my retirement, I was making about $145,000 per year plus bonuses. Not bad for a guy who entered the working world without a marketable skill.

As you can see, there are many reasons why people want to work for the government. In a recent MSPB Survey, "When asked the single most important factor in coming to work for the government, the top response for new hires younger than 30 and the 30-and-older hires was the same: job security."[39]

An MSPB Survey in 2005 found that "federal employees are committed . . . agencies are successful . . . the current workforce has the necessary skills . . . employees generally believe that they are treated fairly in employment matters . . . employees essentially trust their supervisors . . . [and] employees are satisfied and secure."[40] Clearly, despite the negative image of government employees that some people have, the government continues to be a highly desirable employer.

Disadvantages of Working for the Government

While working for the government is both attractive and a good fit for many, it is not for everyone, and it certainly has its downsides. Let's examine a few of them.

DISADVANTAGE: PAY GAP

In many cases, the government does not pay as much as the private sector. "The pay gap between private and public sector employees seems to be a given. Just this week, 10 congressmen made their case for a higher 2007 civilian pay raise than President Bush has requested by citing a 30 percent private-public gap reported by the Bureau of Labor Statistics."[41]

Actually, the data on this alleged gap vary and are often contradictory. The determining factors seem to be who is conducting the study; what their agenda is, if any; what is being compared; and what is being studied. That having been said, for some types of jobs, the private sector clearly pays more than the public sector; in other cases, the opposite is true; and in many cases, they pay about the same. What is certain is that the actual situation is much more complex than many might think.

A 1998 study by the Congressional Budget Office (CBO) found that

> The government offers about 22 percent less pay than the private sector for similar jobs. The memorandum noted, however, the wide variation in how federal and private-sector salaries compare. Higher-skilled professional, administrative, and technical jobs generally show the greatest pay disadvantage relative to the private sector. Some lower-skilled and clerical jobs, however, show little or no pay disadvantage.

> Such variations . . . make generalizing about the federal compensation package difficult. . . . For federal jobs with pay near the level of their private-sector counterparts, an advantage in benefits could put the value of the full pay and benefits package at or above the private sector's. But this analysis shows that not all federal employees have an advantage in benefits. Differences in the value of benefits ranged from a federal advantage of 7.2 percent of pay to a federal disadvantage of 2 percent of pay.

> For the significant number of federal jobs with pay gaps near or above the national average of 22 percent, however, federal pay and benefits together would still be well below what large firms offer for similar jobs—even for federal employees with the largest relative advantage in the value of benefits.[42]

A later study by the CBO

> reinforce(d) a long-standing concern about the federal pay system: it allows no variation in pay raises by occupation, with the potential result that employees in professional and administrative occupations may receive smaller pay raises than those needed to match private salaries for similar jobs, and employees in technical and clerical occupations may receive pay raises that are higher than those needed to match salaries in the private sector.[43]

A study by the Center for State and Local Government Excellence shed some light on the difficulty of comparing government salaries with those in the private sector. It concluded, "Knowledge workers require specialized education, training or skills . . . the percentage varies among sectors, with 32.3 percent of private sector workers classified as knowledge workers, while federal, state and local sectors have 49.8 percent, 68.7 percent and 67.5 percent . . . of their workforce in occupations that fall into the knowledge worker category."[44] Thus, some of the disparity in pay may be due to the nature of government work compared to that of the private sector.

Another complicating factor at the federal level is the issue of locality pay. The cost of living varies significantly across the country, making it difficult to pay employees on an equitable basis. As a result, employees in certain geographic areas receive a locality adjustment tied to local labor markets. The adjustment is intended to reduce the differential between nonfederal and federal pay. "The locality adjustment, for example, increases federal pay in the Washington-Baltimore area by nearly 19 percent over the base General Schedule pay scale and counts toward pension credits."[45]

However, "the locality pay system has not been fully implemented, in part because of concerns about the methodology used to match federal jobs with comparable non-federal positions."[46]

One area that clearly is not in dispute, at least for the most part, is the gap between the salaries of federal government executives and those in the private sector. In the federal system, the top salaries are capped by law;[47] in the private sector, they are not.

A CBO study in 1999 found that, "Pay and benefits for federal executives generally fall well below those for executives in the private firms examined." As an illustration,

> The large firms in CBO's comparisons—including companies such as AT&T, Federal Express, and Dow Chemical—have the large, diverse operations and nationwide workforces typical of many federal agencies. Comparisons with those companies show that the compensation of private-sector executives is well above that of federal executives. That difference holds true for pay alone, pay and bonuses together, and total compensation (including benefits). For example, total compensation at the low end for one of the lowest-ranking private-sector

positions in the comparisons, deputy head of law, is more than 50 percent higher than the highest amount for federal executives.[48]

The same also held true for medium-large and medium-size companies.[49]

The study also compared SES pay to pay for executives in nonprofit organizations, who (1) often deal with issues similar to those dealt with by the federal government and (2) generally have much smaller operations than many federal agencies. It found that, "Comparisons show that compensation for executives of such organizations is much closer to that for federal executives than for executives in private firms."[50]

A later CBO study compared federal executive salaries only to those for top jobs at nonprofit organizations. It found that

> Federal executive pay is low compared with salaries for the top jobs at large nonprofit organizations. Such jobs and firms, however, may be an appropriate basis of comparison only for top-level federal executives. When CBO looked at other nonprofit positions and firms—which may more closely correspond to federal positions other than the top ones—it found that federal salaries were comparatively high. That analysis suggests that salary comparisons may vary by level of position—a finding consistent with the results of other analyses by CBO.[51]

While these studies cite only averages, in many cases, senior executives in the private sector earn incredible amounts of money that simply are not available to government executives at any level. For example, in the past two decades, "compensation for top executives in the United States . . . has soared, from 30 to 40 times average worker pay a generation ago to over 400 times average worker compensation today."[52] By contrast, in the federal government, the average pay for a senior executive is about two and a half times that of the average employee.[53]

Clearly, one disadvantage of working for government is that employees at the upper levels do not have the same opportunity to make money as their counterparts in the private sector do. That having been said, it is no secret that many people have used government service as a springboard to earning far more money in the private sector.

There are not a lot of data available that compare state and local

salaries as a whole to salaries in the private sector. Most of the data compare individual state or local salaries to those in the private sector. However, on balance, in many if not most cases, state and local salaries appear
to be more than competitive with those in the private sector. Where there
are disparities, as with the federal government, it is sometimes a function
of the work and education mix.

Let's look at a few studies at the state and local levels. In Michigan,
"the average Michigan state employee receives a salary and benefits package worth nearly $75,000. If Michigan private-sector employees received
the national average for fringe benefit compensation, their total 'pay'
would be $58,000."[54]

In Iowa, state and local government employees also earn more than
their private-sector counterparts, but when you "control for the average
education level . . . a different picture emerges. For all workers with a
bachelors degree or higher, the private sector was significantly more generous than the public sector. For those with less than a bachelor's degree,
the private sector paid significantly more than the local government
sector."[55]

In Oregon, "the study found that base salaries for some state jobs
seem to be at or above competitive levels offered by Oregon private employers and neighboring states. But some jobs—including those of college
professors, administrative managers and judges—provide salaries below
competitive levels."[56]

In Minnesota,

> As a group, state employees are paid more than private sector employ-
> ees because the state workforce contains a higher concentration of pro-
> fessional workers and a lower concentration of sales, craft, and
> assembly-line positions. According to data from the Current Popula-
> tion Survey, 37.5 percent of state employees work in professional occu-
> pations, for example, compared to 12.4 percent of private sector
> employees. In the private sector, a far higher percentage of workers are
> employed in sales, craft, or assembly line positions.[57]

In New York, the "statewide average salary for all jobs in the state
and local government sector is $45,956—only 87 percent of the private

sector's . . . average. . . . When average salaries are broken down . . . on a regional basis, a different picture emerges: in 51 out of 62 counties, government workers collect higher average salaries."[58]

On a personal note, while I certainly did quite well with the government, others I know who went to work in the private sector earned a lot more than I did. For example, one family member became the chief attorney for a high-powered company and earns about $500,000 per year. Two others opened up a small business and for many years grossed well over $1,000,000 per year. Unfortunately, in the case of the latter two individuals, their business eventually closed as a result of competition from larger companies, and they wound up losing their homes and declaring bankruptcy. Such is both the reward and the risk of working in the private sector.

As you evaluate so much complex and sometimes contradictory pay data, the bottom line is that you need to decide what is important to you. If pay is a driving force, you should target the organization and positions that will give you the biggest bang for the buck.

DISADVANTAGE: THE NATURE AND BUREAUCRACY OF THE GOVERNMENT AND FRUSTRATION

The sheer size and scope of government requires that there be a high degree of bureaucracy, which can be a turnoff at times. It can also make communication quite challenging. Moreover, the rigidity and complexity of the rules, coupled with a culture that far too often enables poor performers to skate by, can cause employees to seek greener pastures. Lastly, the competition for a piece of the pie (promotions, awards, and so on) and the myriad employee protections (EEO complaints, grievances, and so on) sometimes result in pressure to promote, reward, protect, or retain undeserving people. Let's see how these perceptions manifest themselves.

In 2006, the U.S. Office of Personnel Management conducted a human capital survey of its employees.[59] Over 90 percent of the employees felt that the work they were doing was important. Most of them were satisfied with the benefits, liked the kind of work they did, thought that the people they worked with were cooperative, and believed that their work group did quality work. Overall, 67.5 percent of those surveyed were satisfied with their job.

On the other hand, less than 50 percent of those surveyed felt that they had sufficient resources[60] to do the job and were satisfied with the information they received from management concerning what was going on in their organization. Moreover, only 42.2 percent had a feeling of personal empowerment with respect to work processes, and only 38.9 percent reported that creativity and innovation were rewarded.

With respect to a culture of performance, the scores were even worse. Just 29.7 percent felt that in their work unit, differences in performance were recognized in a meaningful way, and a mere 28.6 percent thought that steps were taken to deal with a poor performer who could not or would not improve. In addition, only 21.7 percent indicated that pay raises depended on how well employees performed their jobs.

I was unable to find any across-the-board surveys of state and local employees to get their sense of the culture of their organizations. This is undoubtedly because of both the sheer number of such organizations and the vast differences in their missions. To put this in perspective, "in addition to the 50 State governments, there [were] about 87,500 local governments in 2002. . . . These include[d] about 3,000 county governments; 19,400 municipal governments; 16,500 townships; 13,500 school districts; and 35,100 special districts."[61]

Some of the challenges of working in certain positions for these forms of government include the following:

> Different working conditions and schedules. Fire fighters' hours are longer and vary more widely than those of most workers. Many professional fire fighters are on duty for several days in a row, working over 50 hours a week, because some must be on duty at all times to respond to emergencies. They often eat and sleep at the fire station. Following this long shift, they are then off for several days in a row or for the entire next week. In addition to irregular hours, firefighting can involve the risk of death or injury. . . .
>
> Law enforcement work also is potentially dangerous. The injury and fatality rates among law officers are higher than in many occupations, reflecting risks taken in apprehending suspected criminals and responding to various emergency situations such as traffic accidents. Most police and detectives work 40 hours a week, with paid overtime

when they testify in court or work on an investigation. Because police protection must be provided around the clock, some officers work weekends, holidays, and nights. Many officers are subject to call any time their services are needed and are expected to intervene whenever they observe a crime, even if they are off duty.

Most driver/operator jobs in public transit systems are stressful and fatiguing because they involve dealing with passengers, tight schedules, and heavy traffic. Bus drivers with regular routes and subway operators generally have consistent weekly work schedules. Those who do not have regular schedules may be on call and must be prepared to report for work on short notice. To accommodate commuters, many operators work split shifts, such as 6 a.m. to 10 a.m. and 3 p.m. to 7 p.m., with time off in between.[62]

At times, I certainly found it challenging to work for the government. When I worked in New York, the local union seemed to feel that it was its mission to disrupt our operation as much as it could, so it would routinely file more than 100 grievances and unfair labor practice charges in a given year. Many times, I saw employees try to take advantage of their employment with the government by goofing off, working on personal business, or simply not trying very hard. On other occasions, I observed supervisors who were unwilling or unable to deal with difficult people, which frustrated me and others no end.

That having been said, I've heard similar complaints from many of my friends who work in the private sector. After all, people are people, regardless of the job they hold. However, I do believe that these issues are somewhat easier to address in the private sector because private-sector organizations usually don't have the same degree of bureaucracy or offer their employees the same amount of protection that the government does.

Being an innovative person, I found that the government's rules and regulations certainly made creativity a challenge. Any time I tried to implement a significant change, it had to go through so many layers of approval that I was often frustrated and had to find other ways to get things done.

Again, when considering whether you want to work for government, you need to understand the culture of government, the challenges of the level you are striving for, and the particular demands of the position(s) you are interested in.

DISADVANTAGE: THE ROLE OF POLITICS

The political nature of government can make working there uncomfortable. Since the highest leaders of government at every level are elected officials, and since elections occur on a regular and predictable basis, it is important to understand that management styles, philosophies, and approaches may change every few years. When elected officials take office, they quickly hire a group of political appointees to help them implement their agendas. These appointees recognize that they have only a limited amount of time in which to make a difference, since the next election is only a few years away. Moreover, they generally try to differentiate themselves from the last administration by (1) trying to implement the promises that resulted in a change in administrations and (2) attempting to justify why such a change was required.

Once the transition occurs, the new administration will examine what occurred in the last administration in more detail, requesting position papers, briefings, and other such material. It will then put its organization together and establish its own set of plans, which will inevitably result in a great deal of change and turmoil for the career civil servants.

From the civil servants' perspective, they will need to bring the political appointees up to speed, since, in most cases, the appointees will not be familiar with the day-to-day operations of the organization, and they are unlikely to have much technical or institutional knowledge. Moreover, the civil servants are the individuals who are responsible for implementing the changes, whether they agree with them or not.

In many cases, the new procedures may be diametrically opposed to the approach taken by the last administration. Having worked hard to implement that approach, the civil servants may now literally have to change course 180 degrees and follow the direction of a political appointee who does not really understand the organization that the civil servants have devoted their working life to.

In addition, if civil servants become too closely affiliated with one administration, they run the risk that the next administration may see them as the enemy and try to marginalize them. After all, the incoming leaders are likely to have a hard time believing that the same civil servants that carried out a different and sometimes conflicting agenda will energetically advocate theirs.

Meanwhile, from the elected officials' and political appointees' perspective, they have a limited window in which to implement the changes that have been promised to the electorate. They tend to be suspicious of the motives of the civil servants, knowing that they sometimes give lip service to the desires of political appointees. Let's be honest, some civil servants have been known to stall a political agenda, recognizing that they will eventually outlast the appointees.

The perspectives that I have just described are normal and are part of the American political process and the way that government works at every level. That having been said, this system can make things uncomfortable for government employees, particularly those who work at the headquarters level and have to deal directly with political appointees, and those individuals who are responsible for implementing the political agendas, such as senior executives and high-level managers.

The 2006 U.S. Office of Personnel Management Human Capital Survey[63] that I referred to earlier reflected some of this discomfort. For example, only 49.2 percent of those surveyed had a high level of respect for their organization's senior leaders, while only 48.7 percent felt that their organization's leaders maintained high standards of honesty and integrity. Moreover, only 48 percent indicated that they could disclose a suspected violation of any law, rule, or regulation without fear of reprisal, and only 45.2 percent said that arbitrary action, personal favoritism, and coercion for partisan political purposes are not tolerated. Perhaps most disconcerting, only 37.8 percent believed that in their organization, leaders generated high levels of motivation and commitment in the workforce.

In contrast, employees seemed to have a much higher opinion of their supervisors. For example, 77.8 percent indicated that their supervisor supported their need to balance work and family issues, 64.1 percent said that their supervisor supported employee development, and 63.8 percent had trust and confidence in their supervisor. Overall, 66.2 percent reported that their immediate supervisor was doing a good job.

On a personal note, I experienced some of the same frustration with changes of administrations, although it certainly didn't happen with every change. Early in my career, I simply didn't feel much of an impact from the change because I was at a relatively low level. At other times, I worked with political appointees who understood the mission and were quite familiar with the organization, so it was relatively easy to work with them.

Undoubtedly, my best experience was working for a political appointee who was a former career civil servant. This individual understood every facet of the organization, was quite a visionary, and strongly supported innovation and creativity. This was a perfect fit for me, since I am a creative individual, and I flourished in this administration.[64] However, once a new administration arrived, some of the new people viewed me with suspicion, since I had been so closely affiliated with the previous administration. Moreover, since the new administration valued uniformity and consistency, my reputation for being a highly creative individual did not exactly endear me to it either.

As you can see, working for the government has its pluses and its minuses. It is clearly not for everybody (nor is working for the private sector). However, for those people who go into the government for the right reasons, and go into it with their eyes wide open, government service can prove to be an exciting, fulfilling, and rewarding career.

Federal Versus State and Local

Assuming that you've now decided to go to work for the government, the next question you have to ask yourself is, what part of the government do you want to work for? While there is no reason at this point to limit yourself to only one level of government (unless you have already made up your mind and have targeted a specific career), it is good to understand the advantages and disadvantages of each so that you can at least have some idea of where you want to develop your career. Accordingly, let's compare working for the federal government and for a state or local government in a number of different categories.

Pay and Benefits

The Center for State and Local Government Excellence examined reports by the Bureau of Labor Statistics and concluded,

> Federal and state workers earned 4.8 percent and four percent more respectively, than private sector workers, while local government workers earned seven percent less than a private sector worker. These sector differentials have been evident since the late 1990's. . . . The federal sector experienced the highest annual rate (4.3 percent) of increase in pay between 1997 and 2005. The average annual increase for state government and local government workers was 3.3 percent, while private sector workers' pay increased by 3.8 percent.[65]

While the federal government may pay a bit more than state and quite a bit more than local government as a general rule, that may not be the case in all situations. With so much data out there on comparative pay, it is important to remember that we are usually talking about broad averages, which can give a skewed picture. Moreover, government pay across the country varies greatly by locality (e.g., Alabama, with a much lower cost of living, is going to pay its government workers less than California or New York), making the development of broad, all-encompassing statements on the subject even more difficult. Lastly, because the mission of government at the state and local level is different from that at the national level, the occupations are often different as well, making comparisons even more tenuous. The bottom line is that all three levels of government pay a relatively reasonable salary, at least until you get to the very upper levels.

One way to decide which level of government works best for you with respect to pay is to first decide the career field you want to enter. With this approach, you may want to work at the level of government that has the greatest number of positions in your chosen career field. For example, teachers, firefighters, and police officers are more plentiful at the state and/or local levels, and those levels generally pay more and offer more opportunities than the federal level. Conversely, if you are interested in a career field that has more of a national flavor (environmental protection, defense, veterans' issues, or homeland security, for example), the federal government may be a better fit for you.

On the other hand, if you don't know what career field you are interested in, you should look at the pay at each level of government, as well as the other factors I will be discussing later in the chapter, to decide what level makes the most sense for you.

With respect to benefits, in general, all levels of government offer a strong series of benefits.

> Most federal employees hired on or after January 1, 1984, are automatically covered by the Federal Employees' Retirement System (FERS), a three-tier retirement system encompassing benefits provided by Social Security (tier one), the Basic Benefit Plan (tier two), and the Thrift Savings Plan (tier three). . . .
>
> About 14 million state and local government workers are covered by a retirement system. About 95 percent of the participating employees are in defined benefit plans. These plans vary from state to state, but in general they promise employees specific retirement benefits based on age, years of service, and salary level.[66]

As discussed earlier, all levels of government generally offer competitive health insurance plans. While comparative data on this subject are not readily available, since there is so much variance at the state and city levels, an earlier study did indicate, "The federal government continues to hold a leadership position among employers in adopting managed competition principles. . . . State and local government workers fall somewhere in the middle. . . . strong financial incentives and the provision of information for informed choice are not as pervasive among these employees as in the federal program."[67]

I could go on and on trying to make nuanced comparisons of the pay and benefits at the federal, state, and local government levels, but ultimately, I think each individual will have to decide for himself, especially since each level offers a relatively strong, although somewhat different, package. The factors that I will describe in the rest of this chapter will also be important to most people, since I think the differences in these areas are more pronounced.

Location

One of the biggest and most significant differences in working at the federal, state, or local level of government is simply the location of the work. Obviously, most local jobs (in or near the city you live in) are located within commuting distance of your home. Many state jobs are located within commuting distance as well, as are plenty of federal jobs. However, if you look down the road, the issue of location becomes tricky, depending upon which level of government you work in.

If you work for a local government, you know that you will probably never have to move in order to move up. Virtually all of the available jobs are going to be located at least somewhat close to where you live. Moreover, if workload consolidations occur, they are still likely to occur within a reasonable distance from your home, so you can be reasonably certain that as long as the local government's finances are in decent shape, you will not have to uproot your family. This is an important consideration for many people, especially those with two-income families; to me, it is one of the greatest attractions of working for local government.

Another advantage of working for local government is that in many cases, you will be serving the people who live in your hometown. Whether you work as a police officer, firefighter, bus driver, librarian, or teacher, it is always nice to know that you are helping people who live in the area where you grew up.[68]

Working for the state offers some of the same advantages as working for the city, since you will never have to make a cross-country move in order to get promoted or avoid being laid off. In addition, you will have the opportunity to help the people who live in the same state as you. From this perspective, working for the state is more like working for the city than like working for the federal government.

That having been said, there are some significant differences, both on the plus side and on the minus side of the ledger. On the plus side, state governments tend to employ a lot more people than city governments, so they generally offer more opportunities for advancement. For example, according to the 2002 Census,[69] state governments employed 4,223,000 employees, while local governments employed 11,379,000 employees. At first blush, it may appear that local governments actually employ more people than state governments, which they do in the aggregate. However, when you realize that there are more than 87,000 local governments and only 50 state governments, a different picture emerges. A state government is generally much larger and employs more people than a local government, and therefore, on a systemwide basis, potentially offers more opportunities.[70]

The downside of working for the state is that at some point you may have to move to reach your full career potential. Since jobs are located throughout the state and generally are not limited to one area, you may have to relocate, particularly to the state's capital, where agencies' headquarters are normally situated, if you want to realize your full career potential.

The federal government obviously has the largest number and variety of positions, employing, as stated earlier, about 2,700,000 people. It offers many career choices and a wide variety of opportunities. For people who like to move, it has jobs around the country and, in many agencies, around the world. In my case, I worked in a variety of different agencies, including the Department of Defense, General Services Administration, Federal Energy Administration, and Department of Veterans Affairs, including both the Veterans Health Administration and the Veterans Benefits Administration. I worked in three boroughs of New York, as well as in Roanoke, Virginia; Washington, D.C.; Atlanta; and Los Angeles. Moreover, in my official capacity, I traveled to about 40 states, including Hawaii.

Some people spend their entire career with the federal government working in just one state, but those people who aspire to senior-level positions in the federal government generally have to move, which often means at least one tour in Washington, D.C. In certain cases—for example, when entering a Senior Executive Service Development Program— they may even have to sign a mobility agreement pledging to move whenever they are directed to do so.

Part of the problem with mobility is that you may have to move from a low-cost area, such as Muskogee, Oklahoma, or Waco, Texas, to a much higher cost-of-living area, such as Washington, D.C., in which case you will quickly experience sticker shock. In other cases, you may have to sell your home in order to take another job at a time when the real estate market is on the decline. For example, a couple I know recently sold their home in California because he was selected for a higher-level position in Providence, Rhode Island. Since the California real estate market was depressed at the time, they sold their home for roughly 20 percent less than they had purchased it for.[71] For a more detailed discussion of the issue of mobility, see Chapter 8.

The point is that in deciding which branch of government to work for, you need to be aware of and take into consideration all of these potential scenarios. That having been said, you do not have to feel that you are limited to only one level of government. That type of thinking probably made more sense prior to 1984, when the federal government operated under what was known as the Civil Service Retirement System (CSRS). "CSRS was designed as a stand-alone program to provide a means for employees to survive after they retired from government. CSRS was supposed to serve career civil servants who entered federal service at a young age and remained onboard for a full career."[72] Under this program, your retirement was based on (1) the average of your highest three consecutive years of salary and (2) your length of service.

The retirement system changed for new employees in 1984[73] with the introduction of the Federal Employees Retirement System (FERS). "FERS has its roots in 1983 changes to Social Security mandating that all federal employees hired after that year would be subject to Social Security tax withholding, and would later receive benefits from the program. FERS was designed to be compatible with private sector retirement plans."[74]

The idea here was that this compatibility would enable agencies to attract employees from the private sector and would allow federal employees to move to positions outside of government. This is because if FERS employees were to leave the federal government prior to retirement, they would still retain their social security benefits and be able to roll over their thrift savings plan accounts into 401(k) plans. They would also be able to draw a separate pension if they had completed at least five years of federal service.

Given the advent of FERS, it makes sense, at least in many cases, to consider switching from the state or local government to the federal government and vice versa when there is a career opportunity. After all, in most cases, you bring both your social security and your thrift/401(k) benefits with you. The potential downside is that when you change levels of government, you may have to begin at the first step of your pay grade, which, in general, you would not have to do if you simply switched agencies within the same level of government.[75] Moreover, you may lose a certain part of your retirement pension, depending upon the policy of the particular government that you are working for.[76]

Since the retirement plans and pay policies vary among both state and local government entities, I cannot give you a hard-and-fast rule about transferring across levels of government. However, if you take the information given here into account, you will be able to ask the right questions and make a decision that is right for you.

Conclusion

Working for the government is a personal choice that has both advantages and disadvantages. However, there is no doubt that for many people, it has proven to be a satisfying and fulfilling career. It is my hope that the information presented in this chapter will help you make a more informed choice regarding your career aspirations. If you conclude that working for the government is for you, move on to the next chapter, as it will explain how to get into government and find the job and career path that will meet your needs.

CHAPTER 2

How Do I Get In?

THE FIRST STEP in beginning your government career is to get in. That is the hardest part of the process, and it can be so frustrating that people often give up and never make a really good faith effort to secure such a job. It is frustrating because so much paperwork (often electronic) is usually involved and because people's initial experiences often prove to be unfavorable. This can happen because someone may not get selected for the first few jobs that she applies for as a result of the sheer number of applicants or because others have veterans' preference and she does not; or because she may simply be found to be unqualified, not know why, and be unable to speak with a human resource specialist about the process.

Until you get into the system on a permanent basis, which means that you do not have to compete with members of the public for internal positions, you are simply on the outside trying to get in. However, once you get in, the rules are simpler, and moving either laterally or upward in your career becomes much easier.

Let's look at what happens under both scenarios. In the federal government, when an agency is looking to fill a job from the outside, the Office of Personnel Management (OPM) (or an agency equivalent under delegated examining authority) issues a vacancy announcement to the public; OPM also notifies state employment service offices. The examining office then determines the candidates' qualifications and rates and ranks them according to job-related criteria. Veterans' preference applies in this situation, and those veterans who are entitled to preference have five or ten extra points added to their passing score. This list of eligible candidates, or certificate, is then given to the selecting official, who must select from the top three interested candidates.[1]

When positions are filled from inside the federal government, selecting officials generally choose someone from an agency-developed merit promotion list, reassign a current agency employee, or transfer an employee from another agency. Veterans' preference usually doesn't apply, nor does the agency have to select from the top three candidates.[2] Moreover, the paperwork involved is minimal compared to the procedure required for outside applicants.[3]

So what is the best way to get into the government? The answer is that it depends upon your own personal situation, including your qualifications, your background, your career goals, and your expectations. Let's examine this topic in more detail.

How to Get a Government Job

A number of people come into the government in a temporary capacity. The advantage of this approach is that you have a job, at least for a while, and you get your foot in the door, i.e., a government employer gets to know you and, if it likes you, may work with you on perfecting your application for a permanent job. The downside, however, is that a temporary appointment generally does not bestow any civil service eligibility on you, so when this ends, you are out of a job and will have to compete with everyone else for a permanent position. Moreover, you usually do not receive benefits.

I do not recommend entering the government on a temporary basis, for the reasons just stated. To me, you are better off securing a permanent position and then working your way up within the system.

From my perspective, there are three broad ways to enter the government.[4] The first route is for people who enter the government in a clerical, minor technical, or simple blue-collar capacity, with the goal of getting a government job and taking advantage of the benefits. Some of these individuals stay in such positions for their whole career, either because they are satisfied and do not wish to take on a more challenging job or because their knowledge, skills and abilities, and/or personality prevent them from moving up. Other individuals see these positions as an opportunity to get their foot in the door, with the eventual goal of moving into the type of position described in the next paragraph.

Many, if not most, people come into the government via the second route, which is in a trainee capacity, i.e., expecting to learn a career that will provide them with growth opportunities. These are your personnel specialists, claims processors, public contact representatives, budget analysts, passport specialists, health-care specialists, police officers, firefighters, and so on. These individuals often come into the government as part of a class of new employees, with the understanding that they are not technical experts at the time and with the expectation that they will receive one or more years of training that will prepare them to become journeymen in their chosen career field.

The third broad way in which people come into the government is in a technical or managerial capacity above the trainee level (accountant, property manager, librarian, doctor, nurse, attorney, scientist, engineer, high-level manager,[5] and so on). These individuals already have the knowledge, skills, and abilities required for higher-level work because of their education, and experience, or a combination of these.

In planning your government career, it is important that you take a good, hard look at yourself and decide which route best fits you. If you don't have much education and your skills are not particularly marketable, the first route may be your best bet to get in. The level of government you choose to enter should be a function of the factors described in the previous chapter. Once you get in, you can improve your credentials by attaining valuable experience. Moreover, there is nothing to stop you from going back to school and increasing your education. On the other hand, if you have some college, or, better yet, a college degree, and/or some general work experience with a reasonable track record, you will probably want to secure a trainee position in a career field that makes sense for you.

If you are not sure of your career field, the best thing to do is to apply for any trainee position that has upward mobility, as long as it is in a career that might be of interest to you. If you do this, and you participate in several interviews, you will get exposure to different career fields and organizations, which will help you narrow down what you want to do and for whom. Moreover, once you get started, if things don't work out to your satisfaction, you will at least have begun to develop a track record and will already be in the system, which means that it will be relatively easy for you to switch government jobs, at least within the same levels of government.[6]

If you are among those taking the third route (both qualified and looking for a higher-level technical or managerial position), you want to scan the announcements at all levels of government, unless a specific level clearly makes the most sense (e.g., many accountants like to start out working for the Internal Revenue Service because it offers good career potential and the experience is valued by private-sector companies). When you do this, learn as much as you can about the organizations you are applying to, so that if you have more than one job offer, you will be in a position to make an informed choice. One long-term consideration should be the number of jobs (not vacancies) that the organization that you are applying to has. The total number of jobs in the organization is often a good indication of the likelihood of upward mobility.

Scanning Job Announcements

Assuming that you have a rough idea of the category of job you are going to apply for, along with the level(s) of government and the locations you are interested in, it is time to begin looking at job announcements. For the federal government, the best place to start is at the USAJOBS web site, http://www.usajobs.opm.gov/, which is the official site of the U.S. federal government and is intended as a one-stop source for federal jobs and employment information.

At the state and local levels, you will need to look at the entity's individual human resources web sites. Fortunately, you can find simple links to these web pages on the Internet. For example, "The State and Local Government on the Net"[7] web site provides access to the web sites of thousands of state agencies and city and county governments. Its directory contains all the web sites in a given state, from a state's home page or governor's site to the sites of the smallest counties or townships. "About.com: Job Searching"[8] contains links to all the state job banks along with information on city and county jobs.

Let's look at a few job announcements in the federal government. Note that these announcements were listed on the USAJOBS web site as of November 27, 2007, and were located in the Philadelphia metropolitan area:

CASH CLERK (VETERANS AFFAIRS, VETERANS BENEFITS ADMINISTRATION)

Cash Clerks work on a part time schedule. Cash Clerks are responsible for the receipt, processing, and depositing of payments received for the National Service Life Insurance program. The payments . . . [more]

Vacancy Ann.#:	310-08-03
Who May Apply:	Public
Pay Plan:	GS-0530-03/03*
Appointment Term:	Permanent
Job Status:	Part-Time
Opening Date:	11/19/2007
Salary:	From 11.62 to 15.10 USD per hour

* *Note:* GS means that the job comes under the federal government's General Schedule pay system, 530 represents the occupational series of the job, and 03 represents the pay grade.

As I scanned this announcement, the first things I noted were that (1) it was a relatively low-paying job, (2) it was part-time, and (3) it was permanent, which is a good thing for the reasons discussed earlier. Obviously, you should apply only if the job and the organization are attractive to you.

Once I followed the link for "more" at the end of the job description, I quickly learned that there were five vacancies, which is also good because (1) by sheer numbers, the more vacancies there are, the greater your chances of getting in, and (2) the more vacancies there are, the less likely it is that veterans with preference will block you on the civil service register.

From my perspective, for people who are taking the first broad route (those with relatively little education and experience), this is an excellent job to apply for. True, the pay is relatively low, but that eliminates a lot of the competition. Moreover, you can work your way up the pay schedule fairly quickly,[9] so you need to think about this as a short-term investment in a long-term career.

Also, do not get turned off by the fact that the job is only part-time. That will also screen out a number of candidates who otherwise might apply. Once you get into the government on a permanent basis, within a short period of time, you can request to become full-time or apply for other jobs that are full-time. Again, it is much easier to navigate through the system once you are in than when you are outside.

Another thing to look at on vacancy announcements is the qualifications requirements. Given the fact that this is a relatively low-level job, most people will probably meet the requirements, which can be found under "Qualifications and Evaluations" once you click on the link for "more":

> You can qualify if you have six months of general work experience that shows your ability to perform progressively more complex, responsible, or difficult duties; and that shows your ability to learn the specific work of this job.
>
> OR, you can also qualify if you have successfully completed one year of education above the high school level. Education must have been obtained in an accredited business, secretarial or technical school, junior college, college or university. One year is defined as 30 semester hours, 45 quarter hours or the equivalent.
>
> OR, if you do not meet in full, the experience or education substitute, you may qualify based on an equivalent combination of experience and education.[10]

Assuming that you meet these requirements and are interested in the position, simply follow the instructions under "How to Apply" and submit your application.

Let's now take a look at a different opportunity.

GENERAL SUPPLY SPECIALIST (DEFENSE LOGISTICS)

Vacancy Ann.#:	DTC-08-496
Who May Apply:	Status Candidates
Pay Plan:	GS-2001-07/11
Appointment Term:	Permanent
Job Status:	Full-Time
Opening Date:	11/20/2007
Salary:	From 37,723.00 to 49,040.00 USD per year

This job starts at a higher level and has promotion potential to the GS-11 level ($55,829 to start in the Philadelphia wage area as of January 2007),[11] so at first blush it is very attractive. Moreover, the agency is advertising for seven vacancies, so that is also a big plus.

Obviously, the qualifications requirements for this position are more restrictive[12] than those for the first job we reviewed. However, even if you meet these requirements, note the following statement under "Who May be Considered":

> **Current Appointable Employees of Defense Logistics Agency within the local commuting area only, VRA,[13] DVAAP Eligibles,[14] and persons eligible for appointment under the Persons with Disabilities Program. Applicants with disabilities seeking employment under Special Appointing Authorities approved by OPM (reference OPM Web Site: http://www.opm.gov/disability; for eligibility requirements for disabled veterans reference: http://www.opm.gov/veterans/html/vetguide .asp). ALL APPLICANTS MUST BE WITHIN THE LOCAL COMMUTING AREA.[15]**

What this is saying is that only certain categories of veterans, disabled individuals, and employees who are already in the Defense Logistics Agency will be considered. If you fit into one of those categories, meet the qualification requirements, and are interested in the organization and the position, by all means apply. However, if you do not, you will not be considered for this job, so do not waste your time in applying.

Here is an opportunity that may be a better fit for some people.

INTERNAL REVENUE AGENT

What is the Internal Revenue Service (IRS)? The IRS is a bureau of the Department of the Treasury and one of the world's most efficient tax administrators. Yearly, the IRS collects more than $2 tri . . . [more]

Vacancy Ann.#:	08PH3-SBE0088-512-5-11
Who May Apply:	Public
Pay Plan:	GS-0512-05/11
Appointment Term:	Permanent
Job Status:	Full-Time
Opening Date:	11/26/2007
Salary:	From 28,862.00 to 79,590.00 USD per year

This is an excellent opportunity for many people coming out of college who have a business or accounting background. They agency is willing to hire people at the GS-5, 7, 9, or 11 level, depending upon the person's qualifications.[16] It is a permanent position, and there are many vacancies, as you will quickly learn when you click on "more." The key for this job is your education, as you have to meet the following requirements to be considered eligible:

> To be minimally qualified, you must meet the basic qualifications as defined in A, B, or C and D below.
>
> A. Bachelor's or higher degree in accounting from an accredited college or university that included at least 30 semester hours (45 quarter hours) in accounting or 24 semester hours in accounting and an additional 6 semester hours in related subjects such as business law, economics, statistical/quantitative methods, computerized accounting or financial systems, financial management or finance. OR
>
> B. A combination of experience and education at an accredited college or university equivalent to a four year degree that included courses equivalent to a major in accounting, i.e. at least 30 semester hours in accounting or 24 semester hours in accounting and 6 semester hours in related subjects as described in A above. OR
>
> C. Certificate as a Certified Public Accountant (CPA) obtained through written examination in a State, territory or the District of Columbia. AND
>
> D. You must possess the following professional accounting knowledges: Knowledge of Principles of Accounting; Knowledge of Intermediate

Accounting; Knowledge of Cost Accounting; Knowledge of Advanced Accounting; and Knowledge of Auditing.[17]

For those of you who have the required background, this is an excellent opportunity. For those of you who do not, and are looking for a different type of career that requires a more general background, the following job might be a good fit:

PASSPORT SPECIALIST[18]

Relocation Expenses May be Paid. Salary may vary depending on location please see below: Many locations have locality pay rates . . . [more]

Vacancy Ann.#:	PHJL-07-143476S0
Who May Apply:	Public
Pay Plan:	GS-0967-05/07
Appointment Term:	Permanent
Job Status:	Full-Time
Opening Date:	6/12/2007
Salary:	From 30,386.00 to 48,933.00 USD per year

This job is permanent and will be filled at either the GS-5 or the GS-7 level, and if you were to click on "more," you would learn that there are many vacancies and promotion potential to the GS-11 level.[19] Moreover, the qualification requirements are more inclusive:

To qualify for the Passport Specialist, GS-5, you must meet one of the following criteria.

A. Three years of experience, one [of] which was equivalent to the GS-4 level, in work such as a law clerk, claims clerk, contact representative, or voucher examiner that involved interpreting and applying laws, rules, and regulations and dealing effectively with individuals to secure their compliance with applicable laws. OR

B. Successful completion of a full 4-year course of study in any field leading to a bachelor's degree. OR

C. Combination of education and experience. If you do not qualify based on education or experience alone, you can combine your education and experience by converting each to a percentage and then adding the percentages. To calculate this, determine your total qualifying experience as a percentage of the experience required; then determine your education as a percentage of the education required; then add the two percentages. The total percentages must equal at least 100 percent to qualify.[20]

This is a very good opportunity for people who are looking for trainee positions but do not yet have a specific skill. Moreover, if you live in a different part of the country, relocation expenses may be authorized, which is quite unusual. If you later decide that this is not the career for you, you should be able to move into another career field with a minimum of difficulty.

Now let's look at an example for people who are taking the third route.

PUBLIC AFFAIRS SPECIALIST (DEFENSE LOGISTICS AGENCY)

Vacancy Ann.#:	DSCP-08-445
Who May Apply:	Public
Pay Plan:	GS-1035-11/11
Appointment Term:	Permanent
Job Status:	Full-Time
Opening Date:	11/20/2007
Salary:	From 55,829.00 to 72,579.00 USD per year

This position has only one vacancy, so from that perspective it is not overly attractive. However, it is a permanent position that is being filled at the GS-11 level. This means that relatively few people are likely to apply and be found eligible, because the qualification requirements are pretty stringent at that level:

Applicants must possess one year of specialized experience that equipped the applicant with the particular knowledge, skills and abilities to perform successfully the duties of the position, and that is typically in or related to the position to be filled. To be creditable, specialized experience must have been equivalent to at least the next lower grade level (GS-09).[21]

Obviously, if you are a veteran, you are in a better position to compete for this position than if you are not a veteran. However, even if you are a nonveteran, if you are interested and qualified for this type of position, or for another technical position such as a nurse, economist, or accountant, it is definitely worth your while to apply for it. That is because many more people meet the qualification requirements for the lower-grade positions than for the higher-grade, more complex jobs.

Let's now look at a few announcements from the state and local levels. The state of Pennsylvania issued the following announcement:[22]

> Pennsylvania State Government is recruiting candidates for Limited Term Clerk and Limited Term Clerk Typist positions with the Commonwealth's clerical pool. Successful candidates enjoy full-time work in a series of temporary assignments in state agencies located in the Harrisburg metropolitan area.
>
> The hourly rate is $8.22 (Clerk) and $8.70 (Typist) with regularly scheduled raises. These positions frequently lead to permanent full-time employment with benefits.[23]
>
> Typists must also pass a typing test with a minimum speed of 40 words per minute.

As stated earlier, I normally do not recommend applying for a temporary job with the government unless you are simply looking for a temporary job or have no other opportunity. However, it is clear from this announcement that this is a good opportunity because it is likely to lead to a permanent appointment. Accordingly, if you are taking the first route and can type 40 words per minute, this is a good opportunity to get your foot in the door, show what you've got, and get a job that enables you to grow.

Here's another announcement from the state:[24]

CORRECTIONS OFFICER TRAINEE

Employment Opportunities	Excellent employment opportunities at the State Correctional Institutions (SCI) at Chester and SCI-Graterford
Starting Salary	$29,815 annually
Minimum Requirements	You must pass the test. [Note: This is a written test]

This type of job is clearly not for everybody. For example, to get in,

You must agree with the 6 conditions of employment listed below. By submitting an application, you are indicating your willingness to:

1. Attend and complete a five-week training program at the Training Academy in Elizabethtown. (You must successfully complete all phases of training, including firearms proficiency, to continue being employed.)
2. Work "locked inside" a facility while unarmed and be exposed to the danger of physical harm.
3. Accept the possibility that you may have to use physical force during inmate disturbances.
4. Work on any shift, work in all areas of the institution as assigned, and occasionally work overtime as required by operational necessities and emergencies.
5. Work on weekends and holidays which occur during your normal work schedule.
6. Report for work under adverse weather conditions. Days off for adverse weather will not be approved.[25]

Again, this type of work is not for everyone. However, if it appeals to you, it is a good opportunity because (1) many people will not apply as a result of the nature of the work, (2) the qualifications are not particularly difficult to meet, and (3) hundreds of positions are filled each year, meaning that you will have an excellent chance of getting in and getting ahead.

At the local level, the city of Philadelphia often has many job opportunities. One of their announcements is for a laborer, which pays $28,335 to $30,636 per year.[26] Unlike most government jobs,

there is no previous experience or training required to apply for a laborer. However, to be hired for laborer positions, candidates are required to:

- Pass a drug test, a physical capability test and a medical exam.
- Be willing to perform physically exerting work, often in unpleasant environmental conditions.

• Be a Philadelphia resident for one year prior to hire.
• Be ranked on the Laborer civil service hiring list as described below.[27]

Note: Rank on the hiring list is determined by computer random lottery.

The announcement did not list the number of vacancies, but it is likely that there is more than one, given the nature of the work. This is clearly a good opportunity to get into the government for someone who has limited education and/or experience and does not want to work at a desk job. It is a bit more of a crapshoot than other government jobs, however, because candidates are ranked at random, but it is definitely worth applying for if you are taking the first route.

Most of the jobs that the city of Philadelphia was recruiting for at the time of this writing were for people who would be taking the third route. The announcements were for such positions as industrial electrician, mechanical engineer, electrician, carpenter, and certified registered nurse practitioner. Let's take a look at one such position: A librarian 2, which pays $43,305–$51,960 per year. This is a permanent position that requires "Possession of a fifth year degree from an accredited school of library science; and one year of librarian experience."[28] Since this position is announced on an open continuous basis (meaning that there is no closing date and applications will be accepted indefinitely), it is likely that there will be at least several vacancies throughout the year. Accordingly, this is an excellent opportunity for people who possess these qualifications.

While the city of Philadelphia was also looking for trainees, these trainees were generally required to already have expertise in specific areas. For example, the trainee positions the city was recruiting for included auditor trainee, city planner trainee, information technology trainee, and social worker trainee. There is no reason to apply for a position of this type unless you meet the qualifications, which are pretty specific when compared to more general trainee positions.

The bottom line is that regardless of the level of government, the vast majority of people come in through one of the three routes I discussed earlier. The key is to be able to scan the announcements, quickly understand which ones are a good fit for you, and put your energy into applying for those particular jobs. This approach will clearly give you the best bang for your buck.

Your Application

Gathering Records

Once you've identified one or more jobs that you are interested in applying for, it is time to prepare your application(s). The first thing you need to do is gather the appropriate records. They generally fall into up to four categories: (1) your work history, (2) your education, (3) your veterans' preference, if applicable, and (4) information regarding a disability, if any. Let's look at these four categories and see why they are so important.

WORK HISTORY

You need this information so that you can prepare your résumé/application form.[29] Your work history is normally used to determine if you have the qualifying experience for the position to which you are applying. A résumé/application form should include the names of your previous employers, the dates of employment, the name(s) and phone number(s) of your supervisor(s), a detailed description of your duties and accomplishments, and a list of any special qualifications that you may have (licenses, certificates, and other such material), which you should have on hand. Your résumé/application should also contain information regarding your education and whether you are claiming veterans' preference, but we'll discuss that in more detail in the next few paragraphs.

I strongly recommend that you add two additional pieces of information to your work history descriptions: (1) the salary you earned at each position held, and (2) for jobs that are related to, but not within, the same career field as the position you are applying for, a breakdown of the percentage of time you spent on each of the key tasks of the job.

You should give your salary because when staffing specialists review your qualifications, they often have to determine whether you have specialized experience at a certain level. For example, in the announcement for the Public Affairs Specialist, GS-11, described earlier in this chapter, candidates were required to have one year of specialized experience that was equivalent to at least the next lower grade level (GS-9). This is easy to determine if you work for or previously worked for the federal government, since your résumé/application would show the grade levels of all of your government jobs. However, if you have not worked for the government, the easiest way that a staffing specialist can make this determination is by comparing the salary of your previous jobs with the salary of the government's grade levels.

Showing the percentage of time spent on key tasks is also important, because this will enable you to receive maximum credit for your experience. For example, let's say that you are applying to become a Human Resources Management Specialist, GS-201-7, with the federal government. To meet the minimum qualifications for this job based on experience, you need at least one year of specialized experience equivalent to at least the GS-5 level.[30] Such experience must have

> equipped the applicant with the particular knowledge, skills, and abilities to perform successfully the duties of the position, and that is typically in or related to the work of the position to be filled. To be creditable, specialized experience must have been equivalent to at least the next lower grade level in the normal line of progression for the occupation in the organization.[31]

Now let's say you owned your own small business, so that most of your time was spent on growing the business, increasing sales, negotiating contracts, and other such tasks. At first blush, you would not seem to have the necessary experience. However, let's assume that you owned the business for five years and made about $60,000 per year, and that 20 percent of your time had been devoted to recruitment, selection, training and development, employee relations issues, benefits, and incentive awards—all of which are human resources tasks and responsibilities. Under this scenario, you might meet the minimum qualifications, since you could be credited with one year of specialized experience at or above the GS-5 level (5 years × 20 percent = 1 year). Since your average income was $60,000 per year, your experience, if applicable, would be deemed to be at or above the GS-5 level.

EDUCATION

If you plan to use your education as a basis for qualifying for a particular position, you should gather these records immediately. There is no reason to wait until the last minute, then scramble to try to find a copy of them.

You should gather them now so that you'll have them and know exactly where you stand. Remember, if you are going to use your education as a basis for your qualifications, at some point you will probably be required to provide proof.

VETERANS' PREFERENCE

If you are a veteran, you are going to want to claim all of the preference to which you are entitled. That may be five or ten points, depending on your disability and the way the government entity handles veterans' preference. Your best bet is to claim the preference on your résumé/application, have a copy of your Department of Defense Form DD-214, "Report of Separation from Active Duty" (for 5-point preference), and complete Standard Form-15, "Application for 10-Point Preference," if you are claiming 10 points.

If you are applying for a state or local job, read its regulations, since they do not always follow the lead of the federal government. For example, in the state of Pennsylvania, "veterans, qualified widows and widowers of veterans and spouses of disabled veterans who pass civil service appointment tests, *receive ten points* added to their final score. They must pass the test before points are awarded."[32] Unlike the federal government, however, Pennsylvania does not offer five points for some categories of veterans. Like the federal government, it accepts the DD-214 as proof of service, but the federal government accepts this only for a five-point preference.

DISABILITY

Should you have an employment disability, you need to be aware that

> The federal government has special appointing authorities for persons with disabilities. To be eligible for these . . . appointments, a person must meet the definition for being disabled. The person must have a severe physical, cognitive, or emotional disability; have a history of having such disability; or be perceived as having such disability. The person must obtain a certification letter from a State Vocational Rehabilitation Office or the Department of Veterans Affairs to be eligible for appointment under these special authorities.[33]

Do not wait to find a job you are interested in. If you are disabled and you meet these criteria, get your certification as soon as possible.

Again, state and local governments also provide services to people with disabilities, but those services vary by entity. For example, in Pennsylvania, people with disabilities who need assistance in filling out an application or in taking a state test may contact the Test Administration Division for assistance. All information regarding a candidate's disability is kept confidential.[34]

The city of Philadelphia takes the same approach by advising applicants to request accommodation for a civil service examination through contact with the EEO/Affirmative Action Unit of the Personnel Department.[35] However, neither of these entities appears to offer special hiring authorities in the same way that the federal government does.

Submitting Your Application

Before you submit an application for a job in the federal government, you will need to review the application procedures carefully. Generally, you will have to mail or fax your résumé or apply online through USA-JOBS, depending upon the announcement's instructions. As discussed earlier, you can also submit OF-612 in lieu of a résumé. Along with your résumé/application form, you are often required to submit appropriate documentation. For example, if you are using education to qualify, you may be required to submit copies of college transcripts or a course listing that identifies for each course completed the college or university, the number of semester or quarter hours earned, the grade received, and your grade-point average.

All of this information will be used to determine whether you meet the minimum requirements for the job.[36] If you do not, you are ineligible for further consideration. Therefore, it is crucial that you write a good, solid application the first time, since you rarely have the chance to rewrite it or have it reviewed a second time.[37]

I strongly advise you to customize your résumé/application form to the job that you are applying for, since staffing specialists do not have the luxury of spending a lot of time reviewing each application—they often have to review dozens, if not hundreds, of applications. Let me be clear: I do not mean you should lie or misrepresent your experience and/or education. However, you should make sure that your résumé/application form emphasizes the information that is most likely to support your qualifications for the job. That may mean changing a few words here or there, so that the reviewer clearly understands that you have the requisite background. The point is that you must take the time to sell yourself as best as you can, while at the same time being honest and up front.

Along with your résumé/application form and supporting documentation, for most jobs, you will also have to submit a supplemental statement of your qualifications.[38] This is so that you can be assigned a rating and ranked against other people who are found eligible, with the candidates receiving the highest scores being referred to the selecting official. Obviously, the higher your score, the better your chances of getting referred for consideration by the selecting official.

Let's take a look at what is required for a Veterans' Services Representative (VSR), GS-0996-7,[39] as described in Veterans Benefits Administration Job Announcement Number: VB162131:

> Your rating will be based on an evaluation of your experience, education, training, and responses to the Supplemental Qualifications Statement (SQS) items and questions contained below as part of this announcement. Your application cannot be assigned an eligible rating without a completed SQS, and you must answer all of the required items and questions contained in the SQS, especially the questions contained in the Occupational Questionnaire, otherwise your application will be rated ineligible. PLEASE FOLLOW ALL INSTRUCTIONS CAREFULLY. Qualified candidates will be assigned a score between 70 and 100, not including additional points that may be assigned for veterans' preference.
>
> Your qualifications will be evaluated on the basis of your competencies in the following areas: ability to interpret and analyze material and make well-justified decisions from the analysis; skill in writing that reflects organization of subject matter and support for your position and conclusions; ability to effectively communicate orally; ability to

effectively work with others in a team environment; and ability to determine priorities and successfully balance conflicting demands.

All told, the SQS contains 156 questions that applicants are required to complete. A few of those questions are listed here:

25. Have you received a grade of B or above on essays or reports written for high school classes?

26. Since high school, have you received a grade of B or above in writing courses (for example, composition, creative writing, journalism, etc.) or on essays, reports, or term papers written for school courses that were not focused on writing skills (for example, history, geography, psychology, etc.)?

27. Have you successfully done work of an emergency nature that required you to be flexible about being on call, working for indefinite periods of time, etc. (for example, worked as a criminal investigator, emergency medical technician, firefighter, etc.)?

28. Have you successfully done work that regularly required you to determine resource requirements or monitor the use of resources (for example, staff, space, equipment, supplies, materials, etc.)?

29. Have you successfully determined space layouts or assignments for equipment, furniture, displays, etc.?

30. Have you successfully completed a long-term project outside of work where you were solely responsible for doing the work (for example, completed a thesis, wrote a book that was published, prepared a horse for competition that won a ribbon, restored an antique car, etc.)?

31. Have you successfully done work that regularly required you to make quick decisions where the consequences were critical (for example, worked as a 911 operator, on an ambulance squad, etc.)?[40]

As you can see, these questions are quite detailed and, when taken as a whole, provide a good way to evaluate every applicant relative to the job requirements and to one another. To get the highest possible score, you need to answer each question as best you can, while ensuring that you do not shortchange yourself in the process. The fact that so much time must be spent in putting your résumé/application form together, gathering supporting documents, and completing the SQS highlights why developing job-scanning skills is so important—you simply don't have the time to apply for every possible job that you are interested in.

You also need to be aware that not every announcement requires you to complete a detailed series of multiple-choice questions. Sometimes, supplemental written statements of your knowledge, skills, and abilities (KSAs) are used instead. For example, applicants for the position of Information Receptionist (Office Automation) GS-0304–3/5[41] with the Department of Justice, Job Announcement Number: 08-WDPA-02, must address their KSAs in the following areas:

1. **Knowledge of office practices and administrative procedures. (Describe your experience performing duties, such as, mail, reception, filing, preparing time and attendance, or similar functions using guides and procedures).**

2. **Skill in answering a multi-line telephone system. (Describe your experience receiving telephone calls, forwarding calls, and maintaining telephone equipment).**

3. **Ability to organize and prioritize work to meet deadlines. (Provide examples of how you organize and prioritize work assignments to meet deadlines, and describe the work environment, for example, minimal disruptions, frequent interruptions).**

4. **Ability to communicate both orally and in writing. (Describe your experience providing information to callers, visitors, and coworkers, and describe your experience writing clear and concise messages).**

5. **Ability to use word processing software packages. (Describe your ability to use personal computers, types of software/hardware, types of documents prepared).[42]**

These types of KSA statements provide applicants with greater flexibility, as compared to a multiple-choice approach, since you have the chance to be more detailed and more specific. However, make sure that you write down all of your significant experience and/or education that relates to each KSA. The best way to do this is to address each KSA separately in one or more clear and concise paragraphs. If writing is not one of your strengths, ask someone who is skilled at writing to assist you. Also be aware that your experience and education are always subject to verification.

State and local governments take similar approaches, but again, read the announcements carefully, as there can be significant differences. For instance, in Pennsylvania, state jobs have qualification requirements that are similar to those of the federal government. However, unlike the federal government, Pennsylvania offers written tests for most positions at testing sites throughout the state.

Nevada also determines basic eligibility by reviewing the applicant's background and experience. However, it does rating and ranking in several different ways. For many jobs, it simply evaluates the candidate's application, which places added emphasis on putting together a first-class résumé/application form. For a few jobs, the state actually conducts a written test, while for others it has each candidate respond to a series of questions. For example, applicants for a Training Officer 2 position are asked to: "1. Describe any law enforcement experience [they] have to include any special assignments, training and education. 2. Describe [their] experience in planning, developing and conducting adult based training. [And] 3. Describe [their] experience with developing performance objectives, curriculum development and test validation."[43]

At the local level, the city of Philadelphia also establishes minimum requirements to determine basic eligibility. In terms of rating and ranking, it may give a written test, an oral performance test (primarily for blue-collar positions), and/or a simple evaluation of the applicant's training and experience, depending upon the position. As discussed earlier, it also rates and ranks laborer applicants by lottery.

The city of Baltimore evaluates candidates in a manner that resembles the federal government's approach. It sets minimum qualification standards, identifies any special licenses that may be required, and has candidates fill out a series of supplemental questions that it uses for rating and ranking purposes. Note that the number of questions can vary from as little as three to twenty-five or more, depending upon the position.

As you can see, while there are differences in the way in which government entities evaluate applicants, there are even more similarities. The key is to review every announcement that you are interested in carefully so that you know exactly what each organization is looking for; then put together a detailed, comprehensive, and professional package that addresses all of the important issues. By doing so, you will have the best possible chance of receiving a high rating and being referred to the selecting official.

A note of caution: You cannot control the number of people who apply for positions, nor can you control whether the applicants are veterans or not.[44] Realistically, there may be times when you do everything right, but you still do not get referred for consideration. The best way to address this issue is to apply for multiple positions, at different grade levels, in as wide a geographic area as makes sense for you. By doing this, you will create more opportunities for yourself and greatly improve the odds that you will eventually get selected.

The Interview

If you follow the advice contained herein, the time will almost certainly come when you will be contacted for one or more job interviews. Once that happens, you will need to continue to do your homework. Learn as much as you can about each organization that has contacted you for an interview. This is particularly easy when it comes to government employers. Simply go online and read the organization's web site. Learn about its mission, vision, and core values. Review its performance, outlook, and key issues. Determine what the job you are being interviewed for entails. If you do this, you will come to the interview confident in your understanding of what the employer is looking for. This alone will give you a leg up on the competition.

Another thing you should prepare for are potential questions from your interviewer. You can expect to receive some broad questions such as, "Tell me about you," "What are your career goals?" and "Why do you want to work for this organization?" However, these days, interviewers also tend to ask more detailed, performance-based questions that try to anticipate how you will perform in the future based on how you performed in the past. Accordingly, you can also expect such questions as, "Give me an example of a problem you encountered, and tell me how you overcame it," or "Tell me about a mistake you made at work and what you learned from it."

Be prepared to answer both types of questions, recognizing that the more specific you are about your past accomplishments, the more impressed your interviewer will be. In my experience, the best way to prepare for these types of questions is through review and practice. Review your résumé/application form and overall work history and make sure you have a number of examples that you can refer to during the interview. Better yet, participate in one or more mock interviews with someone who has interviewed other people. This type of practice will increase your confidence and reduce your stress level prior to the interview.

On the day of the interview, recognize that you will only have one chance to make a good first impression on the interviewer, so take advantage of that opportunity. Make sure you are well groomed, and, by all means, dress professionally. Remember, you want to come across as a serious individual who will be a team player.

When the interview begins, look your interviewer straight in the eye, smile, give him a firm handshake, and try to project an air of self-confidence. To the maximum extent possible, stay relaxed, since the calmer you feel, the better you will come across. Listen carefully to each question that is asked, making sure that you fully understand it. If you are not clear about the question, it is better to seek clarification than to answer the wrong question. Once you understand the question, take some time to think before answering. Keep your answers relatively concise and to the point, giving concrete examples whenever possible.

If you don't know the answer to a question, say so. It is much better to say, "I don't know," than to stutter and stumble, trying to sound like you know what you are talking about when you don't.

At the end of the interview, the interviewer may ask you why he should select you for the position. Consider this question in advance of the interview and make sure you can state your case as strongly as possible.

Once the interviewer has finished asking you questions, he will probably give you the opportunity to ask him questions. By all means, take advantage of this and ask some questions (you should prepare these in advance as part of your research). This will further show the interviewer that you have done your homework, demonstrate your interest in the position, and enable you to determine whether this organization is right for you. After all, while the organization is interviewing you as a prospective employee, you should be interviewing the organization as a prospective employer.

After the interview is over, it is generally a good idea to send a brief thank-you note to the interviewer, thanking him for his time, reiterating your interest in the job if you are still interested in it, and reminding him once again why you would be a good fit for the organization. This will keep you fresh in his mind and again let him know that you are a serious individual.

At some point, the organization will notify you of its decision. If you don't get selected, do not take it personally. Everyone fails to get selected at some point in her career. Perhaps you were not high enough on the list to be selected,[45] or perhaps others were simply better candidates. You usually do not know.

On the other hand, if you have the selecting official's phone number, it may be a good idea to contact him and see if there was anything you could have done better to improve your chances. Such insight is always helpful and will assist you the next time around.

If you are selected, congratulations on starting your career with the government! Find out when you will start, where and to whom you should report, and if there is any paperwork you will need to complete in advance of your starting date. If you have any questions or concerns at this point, this is also a good time to bring them up. For example, if you think the salary is a bit low, you might want to try to negotiate for a higher pay step. If you want to know when your health benefits will become effective, find out that answer before terminating your current benefits, if any.

If you are currently employed, notify your employer and give her the appropriate notice. If possible, try to take some time off before starting your government career, since you want to begin it feeling relaxed and refreshed.

PART 2

Getting Off to a Good Start

(Surviving)

CHAPTER **3**

In the Beginning

NOW THAT YOU ARE READY to begin your career, you obviously want to get off to a good start. Most likely, your first few days will involve paperwork and getting to know the organization and its people. After that, you will probably go into a training mode, unless you have been hired as a journeyman or a higher-level technical expert. Use this opportunity to make a good first impression and learn as much as you can.

Making a Good First Impression

The most successful career civil servants that I've come into contact with all started their careers on an excellent note and continued to move onward and upward. These individuals dressed for success; came to work on time and with a positive attitude; tried to learn as much as possible about the organization and its culture, history, and processes; and tried to absorb as much wisdom as they could from the most experienced, knowledgeable, and successful employees. Let's examine some of these strategies in more detail and see why they proved to be successful.

Appearance

"There is no official [federal] government wide policy about how employees are to dress, how their hair, beards, etc. should be worn, or what standards of rudimentary hygiene are to be maintained."[1] However, some government organizations do have a negotiated dress code policy. For example, in the last organization that I managed, jeans, T-shirts, baseball caps, and other such items were prohibited, except on our monthly "dress down" day. Men who met with the public were required to wear a business shirt and tie. Obviously, if you work for an organization that has a dress code, at a minimum, you must comply with it, although I personally would try to exceed it and dress as professionally as possible.

Many people have asked me, "How should I dress? Should I dress to impress, or should I dress to fit in?" To me, the answer to that question is in another question, "How do you want people to view you?" Do you want to be viewed as someone who doesn't really care, comes to work simply to collect a paycheck, and will do her 30 years so that she can collect her retirement?[2] If you come to work dressed as if you are going to the park or the movies, with the goal of simply fitting in with other employees, that is how management will probably view you, at least initially. That's not to say that this is a fair way of judging people, but my experience has taught me that the way you dress and carry yourself will go a long way toward shaping the way in which others view you. After all, the manner in which you dress is a conscious choice, and others will evaluate you based on the choices you make.

I remember being part of an organization where most people came to work in jeans and a casual shirt, except for one individual. At this time I was not a member of management, but I was privy to its thinking on many subjects. This person always came to work in a suit and tie and carried himself with a high degree of dignity and professionalism. I noticed that whenever his name came up, everyone in management spoke of him favorably and lamented the fact that others did not dress up to his standards. Simply by dressing professionally, this individual had helped to positively shape management's view of him.

The question that then arises is, how will your fellow employees feel if you dress better than they do? The answer is that most of them won't care, although a few vocal and perhaps cynical ones may not like it, since they may feel that you will make them look bad. If these individuals give you a bit of a hard time, simply tell them that you are new to the job, and you want to make a good impression. If they persist, ask yourself these questions: Do you really want to be friends with these people? Are they really interested in what is best for you, or are they simply using you in a political battle? And most importantly, if you have to choose, are you going to side with the most bitter and cynical members of your new organization, or are you going to do what you think you need to do to get ahead, which is to show management and your fellow employees that you are a serious professional?

I'm not suggesting that you start your career by trying to make enemies. Enemies never help. Moreover, in most instances, people will not think it a big deal if you dress for success. What I am saying is that sometimes you have to make choices, because you may get caught in the middle of conflicting agendas. If and when you face such a situation, particularly at the start of your career, when your reputation has not yet been formed, make sure that you analyze your options carefully. Look at them from several different points of view, and then do what you think is right and for the right reasons.

The same thing goes for your hair and your hygiene. Sure, it's good to be an individual and to express yourself in whatever way you see fit. Moreover, most government organizations do not have any written policies in this area because it is such a touchy and personal subject. However, also take into consideration the fact that you are now part of a team, and you need to behave accordingly. Furthermore, consider the attitudes of the people you will be working for and the way they will view you (either consciously or unconsciously) based upon the manner in which you present yourself. Like it or not, this will probably be a factor in people's first impression of you, and it could have an impact on your career prospects.

Concerning tattoos, "With a competitive job market, companies are recognizing the pressure to be more flexible regarding employee appearance. However, much of it has to do with the industry. . . . Rural areas tend to be less tolerant of body art than urban work areas."[3]

Since "new research finds 23 percent of college students have one to three tattoos, 51 percent are pierced beyond women's ears and 36 percent of 18- to 29-year-olds have tattoos,"[4] it seems pretty clear that tattoos are becoming more acceptable at work. However, the degree to which tattoos will be accepted in your particular government organization will ultimately be a function of its culture (which may be driven by its location) and the people you work for.

Attendance

All employees are expected to come to work on a regular basis. For people who are hoping to make a good first impression and learn as much as possible, that is even more crucial. If you cannot come to work as scheduled, you will be in trouble right from the start. You will be viewed as unreliable and may miss scheduled training classes, which means that you will quickly fall behind. This may require management to divert crucial resources away from direct labor in order to train you separate from other trainees, so that you can keep up. Naturally, this is not going to ingratiate you with anyone.

Everyone understands that people get sick from time to time. However, do not be the type of employee who misses a day here and a day there for personal business that could be handled at another time. Moreover, don't be the kind of person who misses work because of a minor cold or some aches and pains. This type of behavior will not go unnoticed and will anger both management and your peers, who expect you and want you to be at work. Remember, frequent unscheduled absences, whether they are caused by personal issues or by illness, will not be viewed favorably and will not enhance your career.

Another important reason why you shouldn't use much leave at the beginning of your career is that you will not have much. For example, the federal government allows you to accrue four hours of sick leave and four hours of vacation time per pay period (there are 26 pay periods in a year) during your first three years of employment. If during your first six months you are absent from work for 10 days because of both illness and vacation you would have a grand total of only three days of leave left (13 pay periods $\times$ 4 hours sick leave = 6.5 days; 13 pay periods $\times$ 4 hours vacation time = 6.5 days; 6.5 + 6.5 = 13; 13 − 10 = 3 days left). In the event that you then had a major illness or personal catastrophe, you would be left with virtually no leave to tide you over, which could prove to be a major financial drain. This is one more reason why you should not use leave unless it is absolutely necessary.

Along these lines, if you don't already have it, begin to develop self-discipline. Go to sleep on time, eat well, avoid smoking and drugs, drink alcohol only in moderation, exercise regularly, and maintain a proper diet. This will enable you to feel your best, make it easier for you to come to work on time and on a regular basis, and allow you to project an image of health and energy. People who have no specific illness yet are often lethargic and unfocused are generally viewed with suspicion, and for good reason. Who wants to work with someone who is always dragging and can't concentrate on the job?

Obviously, if you are sick, you should go to the doctor and get professional care, and the sooner the better. After all, no one is the picture of health at all times. The point here is that you need to take care of yourself so that you are at your best as often as possible. To a large extent, your health is a personal choice, and the better your health is, the better your attendance will be and the more successful you will be as an employee; and the more successful you prove to be as an employee, the greater your chances of reaching your full career potential.

Good attendance doesn't mean just coming to work; it also means coming to work on time. If you are periodically late, you will slow things down for everybody, and you will be watched more closely. That's the last thing that a new employee should want to see happen.

Better yet, try to come to work early every day. This will give you the opportunity to be relaxed, prepare for the day's challenges, and start the day on a good note. The best way to do this is to understand the traffic and/or mass transportation patterns in your area, plan for the unknown, and then leave home in plenty of time to get to work. Obviously, an occasional accident or mass transportation failure can cause anyone to be late. That's okay within reason. However, it is your responsibility to anticipate these types of problems and get to work on time each day. If you frequently arrive five or ten minutes late, leave home fifteen minutes earlier each day. Another alternative might be to change your starting time if that is feasible.

Remember, management didn't tell you where to live; you chose that location. Don't look for excuses for why you can't get to work on time, because if you can't make it, there are plenty of other people out there who will be happy to do your job and are able to be at work at the start.

At the end of the day, don't be the type of person who watches the clock and begins to shut things down well before the day is over. We've all seen that type of individual, because every organization seems to have at least one. Such a person is a cynic who is interested only in a paycheck, is anxious to get out of the office as quickly as possible, and has little pride in his work. For all intents and purposes, he is just going through the motions. On one level, this is a person to be pitied because he is miserable at work and no longer gives a damn. On another level, he is someone who commands virtually no respect. Remember, everyone knows who the people who run out the door at the end of their tour are. You do not want to be known as this type of employee, because bolting from the office every day is a career-limiting decision.

Give the government your best efforts during the eight hours it pays you for, and then go home. You owe it to the organization, its clients, and yourself. Be someone that everyone looks up to, not looks on with disdain.

Take the same approach on breaks and during lunch. Use that time to rest, relax, socialize a bit, and/or replenish yourself. However, do not abuse this time by returning a few minutes late. It will not go unnoticed, I assure you. Be an honest, straightforward, and reliable employee and everyone will recognize you as such.

Attitude

Dress is one way to make a good first impression, but it is certainly not the only way. Another way is with the attitude you bring to the job. People who come to work with a smile on their face, and who display a positive, upbeat attitude, almost immediately get noticed and create good first impressions. People who come to work in a bad mood, i.e., those individuals who bring their personal problems to the job or who always blame others for causing their problems, create bad first impressions that can come back to haunt them for quite a while. Let's look at a few examples.

I recall one individual who was a problem from the day she was hired.

She frequently missed work because of personal problems; did not pay much attention during training, and was often disruptive during class. As you can imagine, she had a hard time grasping the nuances of the job, but her attitude seemed to be that the government owed her a living.

As expected, management's antenna quickly went up when it came to this employee. While it made a good faith effort to try to turn her around, she was extremely defensive, and every counseling session turned into an ordeal. Everyone (including the other employees) knew that she was a problem, her reputation was quickly formed, and management eventually terminated her during probation.

Another employee we hired quickly proved to be a cynic. In his particular case, we could tell from his interview that he was not going to be a good fit with our organization. However, he was a disabled veteran who was at the top of the civil service register, so we had little choice but to hire him. If we did not, we could not hire the people below him on the list whom we really wanted.

The problem with this individual was that he viewed everything through a negative prism and let everyone know exactly how he felt. He had had a tough time in the military and he had an unhappy personal life, and this spilled over into all aspects of his life. Instead of seeing his new job as an opportunity to turn things around, he immediately saw it as one more bad break: He was working in another bureaucracy where he had to take orders from higher-ups whom he did not respect. People did not like associating with him, and he proved to be a drag on the organization. His reputation, which was initially formed during the interview, continued to go downhill, and management confronted him, which made him even more angry and cynical. Eventually, we had to terminate him.

A third trainee was bright, charismatic, and very handsome. Everyone was drawn to him because of his magnetic personality, and he knew it. However, over time, it became clear that he also had an ego to match. He started every day by putting his feet up on his desk and reading the newspaper. He tended to ignore others, and he didn't like to follow instructions. He was also dismissive of many of the women in the office. When management counseled him about his behavior, he became belligerent, and we eventually had to let him go.

Both good attitudes and bad attitudes can be contagious, and both draw the attention of others. Very quickly, everyone checks everyone else out, and reputations tend to be formed within a matter of a few weeks, if not days. People notice the employees who are eager to succeed. Most individuals, including members of management, tend to be drawn to these people because it's simply more enjoyable and rewarding to be around them.

A good example of this was a trainee class that was formed in 2001. This was the best class of trainees that I encountered in my career. In general, they were bright, energetic, highly inquisitive, and very hardworking. They fed off one another and constantly tried to push everyone to greater heights. Many of them were so good that they were a challenge for the class trainers to keep up with, because they asked insightful, well-thought-out questions. Meanwhile, the few trainees in the class who were not as gifted or as motivated looked bad by comparison, so they had to step things up just to keep their heads above water.

Management quickly became aware of this class's potential and gave many of them assignments of increasing complexity and responsibility. They all readily embraced these challenges. Within just a few years, many of them had moved into the supervisory ranks or important technical positions.

Learning

My desire to learn was certainly a big factor in the success I attained with the government. When I began my career as a personnel management specialist trainee, I tried to learn everything I could about the field. I spent hours reading the personnel manuals, the laws, the regulations, agency policies and procedures, and other such material. I even developed a catalogue of key decisions by the Merit Systems Protection Board (MSPB), the Equal Employment Opportunity Commission (EEOC), and arbitrators, so that I could see how everything fit together, and I tried to memorize as many of these decisions as possible. Sometimes I even studied this information at home, because I wanted to keep on increasing my knowledge base.

All of this work was grueling and at times a bit exhausting, but it gave me a competitive edge over everyone else because I was learning both the job and the system at a much faster pace. Moreover, it established my credentials as someone who was serious about learning the job and branded me as an up-and-comer.

Another thing you should try to learn is the history of your organization. This means learning about both the organization as a whole and the immediate component of it that you work for. You will quickly find that the more you know about the institution's history, the better you will be able to understand its culture and its decision-making processes. You will begin to understand that things happen for a reason, and you will not get as caught up in the gossip as others do because they do not understand the way things work and why. Knowledge is power in any organization, so by all means try to learn as much as you can.

I have found that in government, history truly repeats itself. The existing philosophy and approach invariably goes out the door when a new administration comes into power. However, if you look at this with a long view, you will find that in reality, there are only a few potential approaches (e.g., a centralized versus a decentralized approach). If you learn the history of your organization and understand its philosophical cycles, you will be in a better position to anticipate what the next change will be, recognize what that will entail, and be able to adjust accordingly.

One of my mentors, an individual by the name of Joe Thompson,[5] took an even broader interest in the history of the organization that I spent most of my career with (the Veterans Benefits Administration [VBA]). Joe researched the history of veterans' benefits and discovered that this was a time-honored tradition dating back to the Egyptians, Greeks, and Romans. He developed a series of information displays on the history of veterans' benefits that was prominently posted in VBA's central office, in a veterans' museum in New York, and in other parts of the country. He also developed a large booklet detailing the history of the VBA.[6]

His work triggered a much greater national interest in the history of veterans' benefits and resulted in the use of this material at all orientation sessions for new VBA employees. It also greatly influenced many younger employees within the VBA, including myself, leading us to take greater pride in our mission and to learn more about the history of our organization.

When I've watched groups of trainees in action, they've generally fit into three categories: (1) people who never asked any questions, (2) people who asked some questions, and (3) people who asked many questions. The first group tended to be the most worrisome. Sure, you might find the occasional individual who didn't ask many questions because he was unusually sharp and didn't need to. However, individuals like this were invariably the exceptions to the rule. The people I was most concerned about were the ones who didn't ask questions either because they didn't care or because they knew that they were in over their heads, so they did not ask anything in order to try to stay under the radarscope. Ultimately, despite their best efforts, these people did get noticed, in most cases did not learn the job properly, and were eventually dealt with by management, either through more intensive training or through termination.

Trainees in the second category tend to be your normal, everyday, run-of-the-mill trainees, who come to work, ask a reasonable number of questions, learn the job, and move on to successful careers. There is nothing wrong with these folks, and they do just fine.

For my money, though, I prefer the third category of people, i.e., those individuals who are highly motivated and tend to pepper their trainers with complex questions, ask for extra reading assignments, and so on.[7] These individuals establish from the get-go that they will be forces to be reckoned with, because they quickly demonstrate that they want to know more than the average trainee. These people get noticed quickly because of their energy, intellect, and drive, and before too long they become identified as future stars.

Another thing that successful people do at the start of their careers is to learn from the wisest and most successful employees. They recognize that by "sitting at the feet of the organization's masters," they can learn valuable lessons that other employees who are less motivated and curious will never fully grasp.

For example, when I first started my career, I identified several individuals who were universally recognized as experts in various branches of personnel. I tried to suck as much information as I could out of their brains so that I could greatly reduce my learning curve. Interestingly, while they were all acknowledged experts, few people had ever tried to learn from them on a systematic basis. What they constantly found was that people would ask them questions on technical issues, but would rarely spend time trying to learn the big picture. I found that to a person, they were more than willing to share their time with an eager trainee and pass on their well-earned knowledge and wisdom.

One of those individuals, a rather crotchety type, used to playfully complain that as a trainee, not only did I want to learn what the rules were, but I also wanted to learn the history of the legislation behind the rules and the congressional intent behind that legislation. To a large extent, this was true, because I found that the more I understood about how everything fit together, the better I was able to do my job—and that the better I did my job, the stronger my reputation. Over time, because I learned so much, so quickly, management was impressed and considered me to be an up-and-comer. This caused other people to come to me for advice and assistance, which further enhanced my standing in the organization.

Fitting In

My comments about dress notwithstanding, it is always good to try to fit in with the organization you are working for. Everyone wants to make friends and to feel that she has people she can talk to and even socialize with. There is absolutely nothing wrong with that. Making friends comes easily to some folks, but not to everyone. One of the best ways to make friends is take advantage of all of the activities offered by your organization.

This means that you should attend all of the office events that you can possibly get to, including lunches, dinners, picnics, after-work drinks, and other such occasions. The reason these events are so helpful is that they provide you with an opportunity to get to know people on a more human level. Once you do this, you will learn what makes each person tick, people will get to know you on a deeper level, and you will build allies for the future. Do not underestimate the importance of building allies because you never know who will be your boss down the road, nor do you know who will be in a position to either help or hurt your career.

A good rule of thumb in this area is that you can never have too many allies.

Along these lines, do not limit the number of allies you build based on their level within the organization. Obviously, you want to build allies among your peers and the people above you, and the best way to do this is through your day-to-day interactions with them, as well as at social events. Take the time to say hello to everyone you see, since a few well-chosen words of interest will go a long way toward building relationships. While most people won't be able to help you right away, it's always worth the minimal investment in time and energy because you never know when you will need a friend.

Getting to know members of management can be a bit trickier because of the nature of their role in the organization; by definition, they are often required to be a bit distant from the troops. That having been said, in my experience, there are three ways to get to know the people above you.

The first way is through your day-to-day interactions, which include the way you do your job. Obviously, your supervisor and the people above him will know you, or at least know of you. The second way is through the social activities I described earlier. Again, these are wonderful opportunities to get to know people when their guards are down and good chances for them to get closer to you as well. You can learn how they got ahead, the career paths they chose, the experiences they had, and other such information. You can also learn about the mistakes they made so that you can avoid repeating them.

This is also your chance to get to know the people above you on an individual level, so that you can know what motivates them, what they look for in rising stars, what to stay away from, and so on. Conversely, they can learn more about you: what your unique talents are, what drives you, how you view the world, what you are looking for, and so on. The more they see you as an individual and get to know you as such, the more they will look out for your interests. That is simply human nature.

The third way to get to know members of management is to stop by their offices during slow periods and simply talk to them or give them the opportunity to talk to you. Managers often are under so much pressure and have so much stress that they enjoy the chance to talk to someone and either vent or discuss a nonwork subject. This type of one-on-one connection is a golden opportunity to cement your relationship with someone above you, to share your insights, to advance your agenda, and/or to learn more about what the person is thinking. It is also a chance for you to build trust, which is always crucial when developing allies. In my experience, the best time to approach people under this scenario is either at the beginning of the workday or at the end, when they are not as focused on work.

I would like to inject one note of caution if you decide to take this approach. If you do this every day, virtually without fail, you run the risk of being viewed as a "brownnoser." In other words, people may believe that you are doing this simply because you are trying to curry favor with management. If this happens, you can lose a substantial number of allies and lose credibility at many levels. The point is that while you definitely want to build a strong relationship with members of management, you should do it judiciously, because for every action there is a reaction.

While you should be courting your peers and the people above you, you should also remember to get to know the people below you. First of all, it's the right thing to do. Everyone is a person, is interesting in her own right, and is worth getting to know.

On a more selfish level, many of these individuals are probably influential in their own right, since they often have access to some powerful people. They are more likely to advocate your cause to these individuals if they know you, like you, and respect you. Also, just because these individuals are below you now doesn't mean that they will always be there. For example, I once knew a woman who served as a secretary to the director of a VA hospital that I was working for. She was a smart, friendly individual, and we had a good working relationship. I eventually left that hospital and moved to the benefits side of the Department of Veterans Affairs. Years later, I found out that she became a hospital network director, which means that she supervised a network of VA hospitals. This only goes to show that you never know.

While cultivating relationships is important, you have to be careful about what you say. Especially at the beginning of your career, you do not really know the person you are speaking to: what his agenda is, who he is friends with, and who his enemies might be. As a result, you need to watch what you say and make sure that you do not say anything that could come back to haunt you. Feel free to discuss your personal interests, such as your family life, sports, the arts, and travel. Ask the person you are talking to about his interests as well, so that you get to know him as a person. Also feel free to discuss the technical parts of the job and to ask about how things are done and why.

At this point, I would avoid controversial subjects such as politics, both national and office, until you are certain about where the person you are talking to is coming from. For example, if you make an adverse comment about the president and/or his policies to a listener who is a strong advocate of the president, she may immediately view you in a negative light and share your views with others who think the same way she does. All of a sudden, you may have developed a series of enemies without even knowing it.

I also suggest that you refrain from comments on such controversial issues as gay rights, abortion, and religion. Again, you never know whom you are speaking to and what he believes in. For example, I recall an individual who once made an offhand comment about gays to his boss, who turned out to be a homosexual. Obviously, such a comment, as innocent as it might have been, did not exactly ingratiate him with his boss.

By all means do not make adverse comments about a fellow employee to another until you really get to know that individual. Again, for all you know, that individual may be friends with the person you are criticizing, and may pass along your comments without your knowledge. Remember, for all intents and purposes, you are never "off the record" on the job, so act accordingly.

Be very careful about making jokes, especially until you get to know the people and learn the culture. They can really come back to haunt you in ways that you can't possibly anticipate. While there is nothing wrong with a mild joke that doesn't seem to offend anyone, remember that you are probably working in a very diverse and multigenerational organization, so people may interpret what you say through different filters. What's funny to one person may be offensive to another, so think before you speak.

Never tell ethnic jokes or jokes of a sexual nature, because they are always unacceptable in the workplace. These types of jokes by definition are offensive and can result in an EEO complaint that can be quite damaging to your career. For example, an African American employee kept referring to other African American coworkers using an ethnic slur. From his perspective, it was common practice on the street for African Americans, particularly males, to use this term to refer to each other. However, another African American employee who had overheard his language was offended and complained to management. Management investigated; ultimately concluded that this term was offensive, regardless of who used it; and took disciplinary action against this employee.

In another example, one of our male employees had a habit of complimenting certain female employees on the size of their hips. Most of them brushed off the "compliment," but one of them did not and complained to management that she found his comments to be both inappropriate and offensive. An investigation ensued, and other women came forward and acknowledged that he had made similar comments to them, and that they had been bothered by these comments but had decided not to make a ruckus. Action was taken against this employee that damaged his career, and he was required to attend a class on how to avoid committing sexual harassment. All of this could have been prevented had he simply kept his mouth shut.

That having been said, I am not suggesting that you be so concerned about every word you say on the job that you go into a shell and say nothing. That would truly lead to a pretty miserable existence. What I am saying is that you should be careful, think before you speak, and slowly open up to people only after you get to know them and decide whom you can trust and whom you can't. In my experience, that is the best way to act.

Also recognize that sometimes you may act appropriately and still do something that hurts you, at least in the short run. For example, when I started my second job with the government, my boss took me out to lunch. When he asked me what I wanted to drink, I replied, "A Diet Coke." He rolled his eyes at my selection and then ordered a strong alcoholic beverage. The next day, I found out that he was insulted that I had not ordered something stronger than a Diet Coke, which apparently labeled me, at least in his eyes, as some kind of a wimp. Obviously, this bothered me greatly, and I wondered if I had already ruined my career at that organization. Fortunately, my action did not have any long-lasting impact, as I received several promotions and rewards before moving on. The lesson here is that everything you do and say can be used against you; but that doesn't mean that it will be. Do not let each incident that upsets someone bother you. If you do something wrong, learn from it. If you do not, simply move on.

Office Romance

Be very careful about becoming involved in an office romance, as it can place you in a very uncomfortable position. That having been said, in general, there are no prohibitions against office romances in the government, especially at the beginning of your career, when you are not in management.[8] Later on, if you do become a member of management, be extremely careful about becoming involved with one of your subordinates, as that could easily make both you and your organization liable to a charge of creating a hostile atmosphere.[9]

Attitudes regarding office romances seem to be shifting, with "the stigma associated with workplace romance . . . fading [according to SHRM survey research specialist Michael Parks]. 'Over the past four years, it appears that employees have become more open-minded about relationships between their colleagues,' he surmised."[10]

During my career, I've seen dozens of office romances blossom, with many of them leading to marriage. In fact, an American Management Association survey found that, "44 percent of managers who dated someone from work said their relationships led to marriage."[11] It's also been my experience that most of the romances that did not result in marriage ended rather benignly. However, on occasion, I've also seen office romances turn ugly and the aftermath have a severe impact on the careers of all involved.

For example, on one occasion, a man and his wife were working in the same government office. He then became involved with another woman in the office, which created quite a stir, as you can imagine. Things became even more complicated when he eventually divorced his first wife and married the new woman. Hard feelings ensued all around, and people were forced to choose sides. With all of the turmoil that had been created, the couple eventually decided that the best thing for them to do was to transfer to new jobs in a different city.

In another case, two newly hired employees became romantically involved to the point that her parents flew in to meet him. However, prior to the meeting, he called her up and abruptly terminated the relationship. As you can imagine, she became distraught and shared her anger about him with their coworkers, which proved embarrassing to him. Eventually, at an office basketball game in which they were both playing, she intentionally tripped him in front of their peers. Shortly thereafter, he took the path of least resistance and transferred to another office.

My point here is not to discourage you from engaging in an office romance, especially if you are single. What I am saying is that if you become involved with someone at work, go into the relationship with your eyes wide open, be aware of the risks, and handle the situation with as much discretion as possible.

Personal Business

Keep your personal business to yourself. That's why it is called "personal." To the maximum extent possible, do not let it bleed into your business life, because if you let it do so, it can truly have an adverse impact on your job. A good rule of thumb in this area is that when you come to work, "check your problems at the door." This means not making personal phone calls during work, not using the government's computer systems to conduct your own affairs, not paying your bills while on the job, not complaining about your problems to your coworkers, and so on. Let's look at how doing any of these things can shape your reputation and hurt your career.

Personal Phone Calls

Generally, Federal employees may use government office equipment for authorized purposes only . . . limited personal use of the govern-

ment office equipment by employees during non-work time is considered to be "authorized use" of Government property . . . if the use
does not interfere with official business and involves minimal additional expense to the Government. This limited personal use of official
government equipment should take place during the employee's non-
work time.[12]

There is no consistent policy on this issue across all of the state and
local governments, but I would recommend that regardless of the level of
government where you work, you adopt the following approach.

Keep your personal calls to a minimum, and make them during non-
work time whenever possible, because the more you are engaged in your
own affairs during work time, the less you will be contributing to your
job. While the federal government allows you some discretion in using
its equipment, be careful, as it will have a record of all of your personal
calls. That's not to say that someone will actually be tracking your calls,
because in most cases, no one will have the time or inclination to worry
about them. However, if a complaint is ever made about your calling
habits and an investigation ensues, the government will have immediate
access to your calls through its own system.

The better approach is to make your calls, if you need to, on your
own cell phone during lunch or on breaks, in a private area. Remember,
you never know who may be eavesdropping on your calls, so the more
disconnected they are from the job, the better the position you will be in.
The last thing you need is to have someone overhear a call you make
when you are angry or frustrated and then pass the gossip on to others.
Keep your private calls as private as possible.

Using the Government's Computer Systems

Employees "do not have the right to privacy while using Government
equipment, including internet or e-mail service."[13] Moreover, the "use of
Government computer equipment, for whatever purpose, is not secure,
private or anonymous. While using Government office equipment . . .
use may be monitored or recorded."[14]

This means that the government's computer systems belong to the government, not to you. Never forget this. While you do have limited access to this equipment during nonwork time, as described earlier, that access is often restricted by policy. For example,

> [Internal Revenue Service (IRS)] policy cautions employees to conduct themselves professionally in the workplace and to refrain from using Federal Government information technology equipment and resources for activities that are inappropriate based on established standards of conduct. The IRS considers email as inappropriate if it contains large, nonbusiness file attachments; chain letters; jokes; material that is offensive to other employees; or sexually oriented material. Email pertaining to illegal activities and other prohibited outside activities, such as running a business, fundraising, or restricted political activity, is also considered inappropriate.[15]

Because of the potential adverse impact of employees misusing the government's computer systems,[16] offices now have sophisticated monitoring programs that can track your computer usage and determine when you are engaged in inappropriate activities. For example, on December 5, 2007,

> Montana's Department of Corrections . . . announced it was disciplining 74 Montana State Prison employees for misusing e-mail.
> Some of the e-mail messages contained inappropriate jokes, but the more prevalent problem was an overuse of the system for personal messages. . . . One employee sent 150 personal messages during one 8-hour work shift.[17]

The point here is that while you may be allowed to use the government's computer systems for personal business, do not get cocky, as many people do, and abuse the policy. Stay away from inappropriate Internet sites and restrict your personal e-mails. If you don't, you may not get caught for a while, but at some point you probably will. It's simply not worth the risk.

Along these lines, recognize that as a government employee, you may have access to the personal information (names, social security numbers, dates of birth, addresses, and other such information) of thousands, if not millions, of Americans. A security breach could seriously affect the privacy of these individuals. Accordingly, it is essential that you both learn and follow the security policies of your organization so that you are not responsible for a breach.

Such a breach happened in 2006 when "personal data, including Social Security numbers of 26.5 million U.S. veterans, was stolen from a Veterans Affairs employee . . . after he took the information home without authorization."[18] While the disk was eventually recovered without the disclosure of the data, countless amounts of time, money, and energy were devoted to resolving this issue, and several VA employees wound up losing their jobs.

Other Personal Issues

It's been my experience that a surprising number of people will wait until they get to work to pay their bills. Perhaps they do this because they have more quiet time at work than at home. In many cases, people do this before work starts, during lunch, on their break, or after the workday has ended. Technically, there is nothing wrong with doing this. In some cases, I've even seen people pay their bills while on duty time, which is obviously wrong and could subject them to a disciplinary or adverse action.

My advice, however, is to pay your bills at home and not at work, even if you are doing it in an appropriate manner. After all, if one or more people see you writing checks at your desk, they may not be aware that you are in a nonduty status and may conclude that you are simply wasting the government's time. As we all know, people talk to one another, and before you know it, you may develop the undeserved reputation of being a slacker, which will not help your career, especially at its inception. It's better to segregate your personal affairs from your government job, so that no one will get involved in your business.

Another way to achieve this goal is to avoid disclosing too much of your personal life to your coworkers. People don't need to know if you've gotten into a fight with your girlfriend, which one of your children is doing badly at school, and other such information. I strongly suggest that at the beginning of your career, if not for your entire career, you keep all of this information close to your vest, at least until you get to understand the culture of your organization and get to know the individual employees. Otherwise, a piece of personal information may be used against you for who knows how long.

For example, if you are working in an organization that is overtly religious and is dominated by one particular group, your disclosure that you are part of another faith may hurt you. Sure, there are laws to protect employees from religious discrimination, but the discrimination may be covert, and you may not even be aware that people are holding your faith against you. The point here is that until you know what you are dealing with, sometimes less is more.

Also, do not let people know about your financial status. If people learn that you are in excellent financial shape, they may seek to borrow money from you, which you should try to avoid at all costs. Several times I have seen employees lend money to other employees, not be repaid, and then have this become a source of tension on the job. Once a situation rises to the level where other employees and management are involved in your financial affairs, you know you are in trouble.

Conversely, if other employees know that you are experiencing financial difficulty, they may seek to lend you money at a high interest rate and/or with the objective of having you beholden to them. Naturally, this will place you in a very uncomfortable situation. The better approach is to simply try to get a personal loan through your bank or credit union. This is a much cleaner approach that will enable you to keep an employee who may be trying to take advantage of you at arm's length.

Should You Join the Union?

Title VII of the Civil Service Reform Act of 1978 (CSRA), established into law a system for federal employees to form, join, or assist any labor organization, *or to refrain from any such activity, freely and without fear of penalty or reprisal.* Once formed, these labor organizations exclusively represent the bargaining unit employees in all matters affecting their working conditions . . .

On an exclusive-recognition basis, labor organizations represent more than half of the non-postal federal work force. Negotiated agreements, which cover nine-tenths percent of the employees represented, increasingly determine personnel policies and practices.

Although most local unions are nationally affiliated, local officers and stewards are members of the installation's workforce and have been elected or appointed to office by the local union membership.[19]

At the state and local levels,

A number of states have passed laws which either require, or authorize public employers and labor unions to negotiate agreements which require, all employees to either join the union or pay the equivalent of union dues as a condition of employment.

However, as a result of *Abood v. Detroit Board of Education, 431 U.S. 209 (1977)*, a First Amendment lawsuit . . . public employees cannot be required to do more than pay a union fee (typically called an "agency fee") that equals their share of what the union can prove is its costs of collective bargaining, contract administration, and grievance adjustment.[20]

. . . If you work for a state or local government agency . . . in a Right to Work state, you have a right to resign from union membership and not pay union dues or fees.[21]

Thus, to a large extent, the decision you make with respect to joining the union is situational. At the federal level, when unions represent employees, many of those employees see the union as serving an important role, particularly when representing them before management at the local level and when advocating their rights before Congress at the national level. If you anticipate having some problems with management or simply want to ensure that your voice is being heard, at least at the collective level, then joining the union might be the right thing for you.

Another reason why some people join the union is to get more actively and aggressively involved in the discussion of employee issues. These folks may want to represent their fellow employees on individual cases, sit down with management and help to negotiate key labor issues, or simply be closer to the action. If that is what you are interested in, by all means join the union. Recognize, however, that despite laws preventing discrimination based on union membership, some people in management (fortunately, not too many) do look with suspicion at people who immediately seek to become union officials.[22]

Conversely, if you join the union and quickly become a union official, you will have more interactions with management than most employees and will therefore develop a higher profile. This is a good thing because if you act professionally and demonstrate that you are a serious, thoughtful, and trustworthy individual, this will give you the opportunity to shine and, in the long term, get ahead more quickly. On the other hand, if you conduct yourself in a less than optimal manner, this may hurt you, even though that is not supposed to happen under federal labor law. Always remember that people are constantly judging you, so you need to at least be aware of this.

The labor situation at the state and local levels is generally different from that at the federal level. A variety of state laws address collective bargaining for these employees, and they vary by state. There are 26 states that grant their employees comprehensive collective bargaining rights, while 2 others grant their employees the right to negotiate over working conditions.[23] In many cases, unlike in the federal government, the unions are able to negotiate over pay and benefits, which makes them highly relevant to the interests of government employees at this level.

Moreover, unlike in the federal government, certain states have statutorily granted their government employees the right to strike.[24] Interestingly, the vast majority of the government work stoppages have occurred at the local level, which makes sense because this level has the largest number of agreements and covered employees.[25] In addition, as many of us have witnessed, even where government employees at the state and/or local levels are legally precluded from striking, they have sometimes gone on strike anyway.[26]

If you have just started working for the government at the state or local level, research your particular situation carefully and determine the union's impact on you. A good rule of thumb is that the more rights a union has to negotiate on behalf of its members and the more money it has in its coffers, the greater the number of people that join it.[27] In deciding whether to join a union and, if so, the level at which you want to participate in it, consider all of these issues carefully and then make a decision that is right for you.

CHAPTER 4

Your Relationship with Your Superiors

THE RELATIONSHIP that you build with your superiors, especially your first-line supervisor, will go a long way in determining the success of your career, as well as your overall satisfaction with the job. If you have a good relationship with your boss, you are going to feel valued and respected and will act accordingly. You are likely to take the extra step, bust your gut, stay late, and/or do whatever it takes to get the job done and make the boss happy. This is the type of relationship that everyone wants at work, but too few people seem to have.

On the other hand, if you have a boss that you don't like and/or respect, or one who doesn't seem to respect you or treat you well, you will tend to feel lethargic and demoralized and will not look forward to going to work. Work will feel like an ordeal, and that feeling will intrude into other parts of your life. In short, when we do not have a good relationship with our supervisor, we feel devalued and believe that we are not appreciated, which is never a good feeling.

Clearly, there may be times when we work for the boss from hell, and it seems as if there is almost nothing we can do that will make that person happy. However, in the overwhelming majority of cases, the person you work for is not a bad person. He may be very demanding or difficult, which could be a function of his personality or, in many cases, the situation that he finds himself in. That having been said, there is a wide variety of strategies that you can apply that will help facilitate a good working relationship with your supervisor. In fact, most of the time, your relationship with your supervisor is a self-fulfilling prophecy, based as much, if not more, on your approach as on his. *The single most important thing you have to control is your attitude,* since that will in large part determine how you act toward your supervisor and how he will perceive you. Let's take a look at what you can do to build this relationship from the get-go.

Understanding Your Supervisor

It may seem hard to believe, but your supervisor is a real person just like you. He probably started out as a trainee with the government and has gone through many of the same things that you are currently experiencing. He most likely has a family to support; has fears, prejudices, and weaknesses like everyone else; and is trying to do as good a job as he can under the circumstances. On most occasions, the big differences between the two of you are that (1) he has been in the government a lot longer, has seen a variety of approaches and many management styles come and go, and by necessity has developed a thicker skin, and (2) he is in management and you are not, so by definition, he sees the world differently and has stresses and pressures that you do not have and cannot easily understand.

Demands from Upper Management

In my view, first-line supervisors have the toughest jobs in government, because they get pressure and receive flak from virtually every element of the organization as well as from its customers and stakeholders. Upper management always wants immediate results, so it invariably turns to the supervisors and wants to know what is going on, implying that the supervisors must be doing something wrong. If productivity is slipping, if cycle time is poor, if accuracy declines, or if something similar occurs, upper management wants instantaneous answers, and it assumes and expects that the supervisors have them. Often it may request written reports and/or formal briefings that explain what is happening in greater detail.

I have seen first-line supervisors literally cower at having to explain performance problems to upper management. This is because some supervisors are simply not comfortable making presentations, while others have a hard time articulating why changes have occurred. Quite a few are frightened of simply talking to stern upper-level managers, while others are afraid to tell their superiors what they don't want to hear—that sometimes the current problems are a result of the decisions that their superiors have made (e.g., resource distribution or the priorities they've set).

At other times, the supervisors are uncomfortable in these situations because they know that they are doing a poor job and do not want to admit that supervision is a bad fit for them. In such cases, upper management probably promoted an excellent technician into a job that she was ill suited for, a classic mistake that is repeated in many organizations.

Regardless of the reasons for their discomfort, supervisors often find themselves in awkward and difficult situations that can easily affect the way they relate to others. The point here is that supervisors are human just like everyone else, and they all have their individual strengths and weaknesses. These weaknesses tend to be highlighted in high-pressure situations, and for many people, having to explain performance problems to their superiors is, at best, a very uncomfortable thing to do.

The performance expectations placed on the supervisors are perhaps the toughest challenges to meet because they never end. The business of government goes on day after day, and the demands always seem to increase, for many different reasons. It may be that a politician is elevating a specific issue because of complaints from her constituents. It may happen because the media have highlighted an issue (e.g., the response to Hurricane Katrina, the reaction to the treatment of returning soldiers at Walter Reed Hospital, or waiting times at the Department of Motor Vehicles). It may simply be a function of a more informed public (because of higher education rates, the Internet, and other such factors) driving the demands for improvements in government.

What's important to realize is that government supervisors are under constant pressure to improve performance and achieve their performance targets. While that is also true in the private sector, government supervisors are generally working within a system that reacts slowly to change, meaning that they tend to take a lot of heat before the requisite changes occur, even if the problem is not their fault.

For instance, when a priority changes, government managers can't simply go out and hire more people in order to address the new priority. That is because the political process requires the government to operate on an extended budget cycle,[1] which means that unless a government organization has human resources that it can immediately redirect to the new priority, it may be several years before it gets to hire the people that are needed and then one or more years before they are trained enough to begin to contribute. Moreover, in order to train the new people, many of the organization's best employees have to be redirected from their regular jobs. That creates even more resource problems in the short term. Of course, while all of this is going on, the organization, including its supervisors, will continue to receive more criticism for not achieving an objective it was never given the resources for.

A good example of this is the Veterans Benefits Administration (VBA). VBA is responsible for adjudicating claims for veterans' benefits. Even though our country invaded Afghanistan in 2001 and Iraq in 2003, resulting in the deaths, injuries, and illnesses of thousands of soldiers, VBA did not receive additional people to address the wave of claims resulting from these wars until 2007. This means that most of these new hires will not be productive until the 2008–2009 time frame, which is many years after the two invasions occurred. In the meantime, VBA's claims backlog increased from about 253,000 claims pending to over 400,000. This increase received an enormous amount of attention and criticism from Congress, veterans' organizations, and the media and placed VBA supervisors under a great deal of pressure—even though the primary root cause of the rising backlog was a lack of human resources.[2]

Upper management will continue to expect improved performance from its subordinate units; that will never go away and is simply a part of life—both inside government and in the private sector. I remember one year where our organization met virtually every end-of-the-year performance goal. We then started the New Year by concentrating on other areas that we had not focused on. Within a few days, we started receiving calls asking why certain performance indicators were slipping. The lesson here is that for management officials, it is always what have you done for me lately? They can never really take a deep breath and sit back and relax. Moreover, you need to recognize that this is only one of many demands that are placed on the person who is currently supervising you.

Upper management also turns to its supervisors for those special projects and/or urgent action items that always seem to come up. In short, the supervisors are the people who have to constantly drop everything at a moment's notice and go to work to solve the crisis or crises of the day. They are the designated "go-to" people, in part because of their past successes and in part because they directly supervise part of the organization's operation.

I recall one supervisor who used to constantly complain that she was never allowed to do her job. Every time something came up, she would be pulled away from her regular job to take care of the issue in question. On the one hand, this was definitely a compliment because it was a clear demonstration that management had a high degree of confidence in her. On the other hand, many people resented the fact that she was the one who was always chosen for these special projects, since rewards were often given for successful completion of these projects. Moreover, her team suffered from her frequent absences, since she wasn't there on a consistent basis to guide it in its day-to-day activities, and she was well aware of this. Ultimately, she became more and more stressed and distraught, simply because she was pulled in too many different directions and was not allowed to focus on her primary job.

Dealing with Employees

Senior managers also want to know what the supervisors are doing to hold their employees accountable, since poor employee performance harms the unit's ability to achieve its goals. This, of course, then places pressure on the supervisors to deal with problem employees in a manner that is less than pleasant.

Since for every action there is a reaction, if and when the supervisors deal with problem employees, those employees are usually going to react in a negative manner, which places even more stress on the supervisor. For instance, if the employee chooses to be represented by the union, which is usually his right, he may file a grievance and/or an equal employment opportunity (EEO) complaint against the supervisor, requiring the supervisor to defend herself for doing exactly what upper management had requested. Now imagine if the supervisor has to deal with several problem employees concurrently; she may be addressing multiple complaints, a variety of union officials, and even third parties such as the Merit Systems Protection Board (MSPB), EEO administrative law judges, and/or government attorneys. As you can see, such a situation, which is not uncommon for government supervisors, can be very stressful and can redirect an enormous amount of the supervisor's time away from her regular day-to-day job.

Let me give you a real-life example. A nurse who was a relatively poor performer started filing complaints left and right against her supervisor and her supervisor's boss. She knew deep down that she was not going to make it in our organization, so she decided that the best defense was a good offense. Within a relatively brief period of time, she filed well over 40 complaints, based on the fact that she was an African American female.

The sheer number of complaints overwhelmed her supervisors and placed them on the defensive, which was the nurse's goal. They had to respond to EEO counselors and investigators and confer with upper management, human resources management specialists, and government attorneys, all because of this one employee. Moreover, they also had to gather and review an enormous amount of written material and ultimately participate in what proved to be a highly tense four-day EEO hearing. Lastly, and perhaps most sadly, they had to watch every word that they said and wrote to this nurse because they knew that she would use their words against them.

As you can imagine, this was a very difficult situation for these supervisory nurses to work in, especially because at the same time, they were responsible for overseeing the health-care needs of a wide variety of patients. While all of the EEO complaints were eventually dismissed and the nurse later agreed to resign, her supervisors paid a very steep emotional price in having to deal with the pressure of the complaints brought by this one individual.

Before I go forward and discuss other problems that your supervisor may be grappling with, it is important to emphasize that while your supervisor may have many employee problems to deal with; there are tried-and-true strategies that, if applied properly, will at a minimum make that supervisor's job a lot easier. *Managing Government Employees: How to Motivate Them, Deal With Difficult Issues and Produce Tangible Results*, by Stewart Liff (AMACOM, February 2007), contains a variety of tools, tactics, and techniques that will assist every government supervisor who is trying to cope with a myriad of employee problems. That book is a perfect companion piece to this book, as it will provide the reader with multiple perspectives on how to manage a wide range of government employees successfully.

Supervisors have to deal with more than just problem employees; they have to deal with all employees on a variety of issues that require time, planning, and paperwork. For example, they have to plan and adjust vacation schedules for their unit, ensure that employees use all of their allotted vacation time by the end of the leave year (so that the employees don't lose the leave[3]), react to requests for sick leave, ensure that time cards are properly completed, and so on. They also have to conduct periodic individual performance appraisal conferences, prepare written employee performance appraisals, make decisions on incentive awards, set up and sometimes give employee training, and possibly even develop individual employee development plans. Lastly, in order to ensure that jobs under their jurisdiction are filled promptly and by the right person, supervisors have to write up position descriptions, may have to attend job fairs in order to recruit potential candidates, and have to conduct job interviews and recommend selections. Of course, once the new hires come on board, the supervisors will then have to ensure that they have desks, the appropriate equipment, and other needed resources.

Many of these issues can be more complex than you might think. Let's look at a couple of examples. Our union contract required that when conflicts arose over requests for leave, preference would be given to the employees with the longest amount of government service. That sounds reasonable and easy enough to administer; however, it resulted in our newer employees always being denied leave for the most desirable holidays, such as Christmas and Thanksgiving. Over time, they became angry and frustrated with this situation and complained vehemently to their supervisors, who were placed in the unpleasant position of trying to resolve the competing interests of two different groups of employees. While management eventually reached an accommodation with the union to resolve this issue (longer-term employees were given first preference for their highest-priority holiday, instead of all holidays), an enormous amount of supervisory time, energy, and effort was invested to solve what initially seemed to be a relatively simple concern.

On another occasion, several employees complained that they should have received end-of-the-year incentive awards, since their performance was similar to that of other employees who did receive awards. When their supervisors looked into the matter, they pointed out that the other employees' performance was indeed better, but the complaining employees insisted that the data were wrong. This prompted the supervisors to go back and review the way in which employee output was being captured, and sure enough, they discovered that some mistakes had been made. After recalculating the numbers, they realized that some of the employees were correct, which meant that they had to prepare incentive awards for these employees. To complicate matters, the new fiscal year had already begun and their organization was operating under a continuing resolution,[4] so they had to find money in the budget to pay for these unanticipated awards.

Demands on Your Supervisor's Time

In addition to dealing with employee issues, your supervisor has many other issues to contend with. For example, he not only attends the team/unit meetings that you attend, but also attends a variety of management meetings on multiple topics, which can last for hours. Prior to these meetings and/or after they have concluded, your supervisor may have to address the inevitable questions related to the topics being discussed.

As a management official, I remember how frustrated I was at having to attend so many meetings. I was serving as a personnel officer (the chief of a small personnel office) when a new director arrived who was very "hands on." It seemed to me that I was spending at least four hours a day with him in meetings revolving around a variety of personnel issues. From my perspective, these constant meetings prevented me from focusing on the day-to-day needs of our personnel office (filling vacant positions, classifying jobs, advising other management and supervisory officials, processing personnel actions, and so on). Finally, I complained to him that he was monopolizing so much of my time that I was unable to do my job. He replied, "Your job is to advise me on personnel issues, and right now I need your advice." Instantly, I realized that he was right, and I never again made that complaint to anyone I was working for. At the same time, it made me appreciate the many competing demands that are placed upon a management official's time, and why he can often seem to be stressed out or unfocused.

As well as attending meetings, your supervisor may also have to attend training sessions that you do not have to go to, which can place additional demands on his time. These sessions can range from workload management to a wide variety of HRM topics (performance management, leave administration, EEO, labor relations, and so on) to something as simple as how to complete your time card electronically using a new time and attendance system. Moreover, he may even have to attend training classes and/or conferences in other locations in order to learn about national issues and to meet fellow supervisors from other offices.

One supervisor that I know attended several out-of-state training sessions each year, and was also asked to give training to employees from other offices. From the big-picture perspective, all this training was a good thing because it provided him with valuable information, the chance to network with people in similar situations, and the opportunity to grow as a government employee. Moreover, being given the opportunity to train others was a sign that he was highly respected throughout the organization. However, from the supervisor's perspective, it sometimes felt as if he was on call 24/7 and there was never enough time in the day to do his job.

Along these lines, I often conduct training for government officials on a multitude of subjects ranging from visual management to human capital management. As I interact with these individuals, I'm often struck by their body language. Many of them initially don't want to be in the class, and they appear anxious to get back to work and do their "real jobs." Fortunately, once I get their attention and make them realize that the subject matter I am teaching can help them do their job better, they usually come around, focus on the class, and learn new skills that do make a difference. However, if they perceive the subject matter as being redundant or irrelevant to their jobs, they will quickly be turned off and mentally check out of the class.

Many of us receive dozens of e-mails each day at work, and this, in and of itself, can be overwhelming. However, I can virtually guarantee you that your supervisor is receiving far more e-mails than you or anyone else on your team. We all receive daily announcements, policy statements, training material, and so on. Many of us also receive an occasional e-mail from a friend or colleague asking for assistance or just saying hello. Your supervisor receives all of those e-mails and many, many more. He receives e-mails from management that are intended only for other management officials. He also receives e-mails from other activities within or outside of the immediate organization requesting information, correspondence, or other documentation. He receives e-mails from his subordinates requesting time off, work assistance, policy guidance, or help in many different areas, and he gets copies of messages that are sent to him just to keep him informed. He may even receive e-mails from the union asking him why he gave certain instructions to the bargaining unit or questioning his interpretation of a specific practice or labor clause. Lastly, depending on his job, he may have to respond to a variety of e-mails from members of the public, many of whom are quite angry, asking why things are not proceeding as smoothly as they would like.

Sometimes, when I returned to work after being absent for several weeks, I would find several hundred unread e-mail messages, not counting the hard-copy mail that I would also receive. Sorting through this information was always a daunting and unwelcome task.

On top of this are the phone calls from people with whom the supervisor interacts on a daily basis. Depending on your perspective, voice mail is one of the best or one of the worst inventions ever introduced into the workplace. It's been my experience that more and more supervisors seem to use voice mail as a shield to avoid answering all the calls that are made to them. Along those lines, whenever I walked around my office or other offices, I was often struck by how many supervisors' voice mail systems were completely full, meaning that they were unable to record any more messages. To me, this was another clear indication that these people were overwhelmed by all of the demands on their time.

Dealing with Constant Scrutiny and Requests for Information

Supervisors also have to respond to many issues that their subordinates are frequently unaware of. That is because government employees, particularly supervisors who are responsible for the bottom line, work in a world that is constantly scrutinized. In any organization, you can expect to be reviewed by people who are above you in the chain of command, for example, your headquarters, an area director, or another such person. This may entail periodic evaluations, visits, analyses, and so on.

However, in the government, you can also expect to be scrutinized by organizations that are outside your immediate chain of command, but that have a strong interest in and influence on your organization and its mission. For example, your supervisors will probably have to respond to the Office of the Inspector General (OIG), which conducts audits and investigations. The OIG periodically audits different aspects of the government's operation, and preparing for and responding to these audits requires a lot of time. Naturally, much of the burden of assisting the auditors prior to, during, and after an OIG audit falls on the shoulders of the supervisors, who are normally technical experts in the matters being audited.

OIG investigations generally involve inquiries into complaints about a wide variety of matters (poor management, improper actions, criminal activity, and so on), and once they get underway, they can take on a life of their own. They can be very time-consuming, and responding to requests for information can pull the supervisor away from her job. Moreover, they can be very nerve-racking, as you sometimes do not know who the target(s) of the audit/investigation are, where it will lead, and what the fallout will be.

I have had to respond to multiple OIG audits in the course of my career. Some of them have been relatively tame, while others were quite tense. All of them required us to gather and sift through a significant amount of information and to then explain to the auditors what the material actually meant. Once the auditors were on station to conduct their audits, we had to cater to their needs and interests, such as supplying them with office equipment, reviewing files, and responding to their initial findings. We would then have an exit briefing, which normally took several hours, followed by a final report that we were required to respond to in writing. We then had to follow this with periodic reports describing how we were implementing the auditors' suggestions until, mercifully, the audit was finalized and closed out.

OIG investigations can be even more difficult to deal with because they are based on a specific complaint or referral. I have seen people's careers seriously damaged or destroyed by these investigations, since it is very difficult to survive a high degree of scrutiny. In fact, employees have sometimes complained to the OIG about their supervisor as a tactic to hurt that individual and insulate them from their own problems. While it is important to emphasize that in our country, government employees have a legal right to complain about fraud, waste, and/or abuse, it is also important to understand the profound effect that the abuse of such a right can have on a management official.

Every government organization seems to have a large number of attorneys who also interact with the supervisors. While their role is to protect the government, not the supervisor, they sometimes work with supervisors on matters that involve outside scrutiny or complaints. This may be a personnel case that is going to a third party, a tort claim, or some other legal matter. It may also involve the implementation of a court order or an internal or external investigation. The point here is that this is one more way in which your supervisor can be pulled apart.

Outside the organization, supervisors also may have to deal with such diverse groups as the federal, state, or local Office of Management and Budget and Congress or the appropriate legislature. This may involve periodic meetings, briefings, reports, and other such interactions. They may also have to deal with organizations that they partner with. For example, on occasion, the local police may have to coordinate their activities with the FBI, and the VA frequently works with the Department of Defense to assist returning veterans. This may involve the same types of interactions as described earlier along with a high degree of information sharing through data mining, computer interfaces, and other such methods, all of which often require supervisory participation.

In my last organization, our supervisors were responsible for paying benefits to clients who were in financial need and who met certain legal criteria. In order to administer that program as intended, they had to ensure that the income being reported by our clients was consistent with what they reported to the IRS and what they received from the Social Security Administration. To do this correctly, they had to spend a fair amount of time coordinating this information with those organizations.

Government organizations are always subject to the lens of the media, particularly when they screw up. The first- and second-line supervisors rarely interact directly with the media, since that is the job of higher-level management officials and the organization's Office of Public Affairs. However, when a problem comes to the attention of the media, these same supervisors will be responsible for gathering all the information necessary to enable those other individuals to respond appropriately.

For instance, I was once called upon to serve as acting director of a government organization where the director had been charged with sexually harassing one of his employees. This charge made the front page of the local newspaper. While I was the spokesperson for that organization and conducted several interviews with the media, I had to rely on lower-level supervisors to provide me with accurate information that would enable me to respond appropriately.

And Still More Issues

On top of everything else I have just described, government supervisors also get involved in issues that they have absolutely no expertise in. This is because they are the "go-to" people on virtually any problem that pops up in their team or unit. For example, if the employees complain that the work area is too hot or too cold (sometimes supervisors will receive both complaints at the same time), the supervisor is generally expected to address this situation. This may be as simple as calling the liaison to the building manager, if such a person exists in the organization, or it may involve a lot more effort and work on the part of the supervisor if there is no such liaison and the building manager (whether she works for your government organization, works for another branch of government, or is part of the private sector) is unresponsive.

When I served as a first-line supervisor and received such complaints from my subordinates, I had to work through the bureaucracy in order to resolve these issues. On occasion, these situations took on a degree of complexity that I had never imagined. For example, one day the union complained to me that several of my employees were becoming sick because of the building's poor air quality. Having no expertise whatsoever in this area, I conferred with the chief of the Administrative Division. He then spoke with the building manager, who assured him that the air was safe. However, this did not satisfy anybody, and our employees continued to get sick.

Finally, I asked our Administrative Division chief to contact the Occupational Safety and Health Administration (OSHA) and request that it conduct an inspection of our facility, which it did. The inspectors eventually determined that the air was unsafe and ordered the building manager to make a series of improvements in the infrastructure. Of course, while the improvements were being made, I and other supervisors were intimately involved in the planning and execution required to make these changes a reality (moving employees around to accommodate the contractors, ensuring that the employees would not be distracted by the construction, making certain that the computer system would still be operational during the alterations, and so on).

Another time, when I had just become a supervisor for the first time, one of our employees complained that our photocopier was broken and that she needed to make copies of a large personnel case file immediately. I looked into this and learned that a repairman would not be able to fix the problem until the following day. I then told this employee to go next door to our Supply Division and use its photocopier. Five minutes later, she came back and angrily told me that the chief of Supply had refused to let her use the division's machine.

I immediately went over to Supply and noticed that no one was using its photocopier. I started making the requisite copies, and the chief of Supply came over to me and told me to stop. I advised her that we worked for the same government and that I needed the copies immediately. She again told me to cease making any more copies, but I firmly replied, "No; try and stop me," and copied all the documents I needed. The net resul' of my actions was that (1) I got the job done, (2) the employee reali' that I would stand by her, even in difficult situations, and (3) I ma enemy of the chief of Supply.

In retrospect, I could and should have handled the situ'

more skill and finesse, but I was a young, bullheaded supervisor at the time. The real point of this story, however, is the number of weird, screwball situations that supervisors often find themselves in that can easily cause them to become both distracted and frustrated.

Another situation that periodically requires the attention of your supervisor is security. Security issues range from unauthorized people having access to the work area to the mailing of suspicious objects to threats made by distraught employees and/or members of the public. Obviously, all of these situations need to be taken seriously, and while most government organizations have some form of security staff, either on their rolls or through contract, the supervisors still need to work closely with these individuals to guard against such threats.

For example, one day our employees complained vehemently that members of the public were walking into their work areas uncontrolled, asking questions, and in some situations even arguing with them. A number of the employees emphasized that they felt at risk and demanded that we do something about the situation. Several of the supervisors approached me on this issue (I was the director at the time), and we all went to the landlord (which in this particular case was the U.S. General Services Administration) and asked it to install security locks on all the doors, other than in our customer contact areas. This was the right thing to do; it worked well, and our employees appreciated our efforts. The only downside was that it was one more issue that took management's attention away from the day-to-day work.

On the flip side, I once had several customers complain that getting in to see one of our higher-level supervisors was like getting into Fort Knox. The problem had arisen because a security lock had been installed at an entrance that had traditionally been open to members of the public. Above the lock was a video camera along with a microphone into which the visitor talked. Under this system, each visitor had to be identified both orally and visually before being buzzed in. Such a system is not unusual in many organizations, and, where it is appropriate, it works well. However, in this particular location, it sent the message that we did not want to see our customers, which was the wrong message. Before removing the system, I had to research why the system had been installed, whether there were any security problems that had led to its installation, and so on. The point here is that supervisory time was taken up by several different security concerns, all of which in essence involved the same issue.

Along these lines, when a large-scale disaster occurs, it invariably has a major impact on supervisors' time. The Oklahoma City bombings and the 9/11 disaster caused revisions of security procedures (disaster planning, screening of mail, identification procedures, access to government buildings, and so on) that in many cases were implemented and monitored to varying degrees by the supervisors.

For example, after 9/11, all of our employees were required to have new ID badges and to go through a special employee entrance. If someone forgot his badge, he had to go through the metal detectors like every other member of the public. One day, an employee forgot her badge but refused to go through the metal detector, insisting that she was a government employee. She became very agitated, which prompted the guards to first detain her and then notify her supervisor of her inappropriate behavior. The supervisor had to drop everything, come down to the lobby, and prove to the guard that she was a government employee. He then had to brief his supervisor regarding the incident, take disciplinary action against her for improper conduct, and arrange for her to get a new ID badge.

By this time, you are probably beginning to realize how difficult it is to be a first-line supervisor in the government. The intent of this section is to give you an idea of the pressures that your supervisor is under and, as a result, to give you a better understanding of how to deal with him. It is not intended to give you a full picture of the pluses and minuses of being a supervisor, since, as a new employee, you are unlikely to become one for at least a few years. I will address that subject later in the book.

The key point here is that people often blame a poor relationship with their supervisor on their supervisor. You may indeed have a supervisor who does not have good people skills and who is a poor manager. That is sometimes the hand you are dealt.

That having been said,

43% of workers in a recent survey said a dislike of their boss' performance would be a main reason for taking a new job in 2008.

According to the Yahoo! HotJobs annual job satisfaction survey, more than 7 in 10 workers are open to landing a new job in 2008. . . .

"It's clear from the survey that employers need to pay attention to the boss-employee dynamic if they want to retain talented workers," said Susan Vobejda, vice president of marketing for Yahoo! HotJobs. "In addition to factors like salary, competitive benefits, and good work-life balance, employees equate job satisfaction with knowing that their contributions are recognized and valued by their managers."

In fact, 55% of the survey respondents agreed with the statement, "People don't leave companies; they leave managers."[5]

To me, this survey is an accurate reflection of the importance of having a strong supervisor-employee relationship. That is why organizations spend billions of dollars on improving the skills of their supervisors and why there are hundreds, if not thousands, of books, videos, and other training materials available on supervisory training and development.

I also believe that the supervisor-employee relationship is a two-way street that is influenced as much by the employee's approach as it is by the supervisor's. Experience has taught me that if employees had a better understanding of what their supervisors are up against and what they are looking for in an employee, they would act in a more positive and professional manner and help cultivate a better relationship. In short, if you control your attitude, conduct yourself appropriately, and employ the strategies laid out in the next section of this chapter, you are likely to establish a positive relationship with your supervisor and, to a large extent, make it a self-fulfilling prophecy.

Building a Good Relationship

Ask yourself this question: If you were a supervisor, how would you like your employees to act? I think most people would say that they wanted their employees to come to work on time and be reliable, have a positive attitude, and do a good job. On some levels, it's as simple as that. The overwhelming majority of people that I've seen begin their careers with the government have tried to do just that; but as time went by, too many of them lost their way; their relationship with their supervisor soured, and they became cynical and, in some cases, even bitter. Many of these people wound up changing jobs, only to see the same problems develop again and again. That is because most of the time, the solution to your problems lies within you; they are not caused exclusively by outside forces, namely, your supervisor.

The last chapter discussed how to get off to a good start and make a positive first impression (have a professional appearance, come to work on time, display a positive attitude, avoid personal business, and so on). If you follow those guidelines, you will almost certainly get off to a good start with your boss. The next step is to leverage that successful first impression by having the personal discipline to stick with the plan even if things go awry, which they usually do. Let's look at some things you can do to continue to build a successful relationship with management.

Do Your Best

This one is rather obvious, and is something that I emphasized in the last chapter. I am stressing this point again because many people get off to a good start, learn the basic elements of the job, develop a good first impression, and then seem to go on cruise control. It may be because they have learned to do this from their peers, i.e., slow down, take it easy, and don't make anyone else look bad by working too hard. It may be that they are not hard workers by nature and they buy into the view that government workers have a job for life. Or it may be that they feel that they have been treated poorly by their supervisor, and they have decided to passively resist management. There are many reasons why some people tend to slow down after getting off to a good start. The point is that while there are many reasons for slowing down, virtually all of them are bad reasons.[6]

I'm not saying that you can't have a bad day at work or that your energy level shouldn't wane a bit from time to time. That happens to everyone. What I am saying is that you need to get into the habit of coming to work every day and giving it your best, even if some days you are not at your best. That is what management and the taxpayers expect from you, and it is what you should expect from yourself. Don't be the type of employee who says, "All I am required to do is meet the minimum performance standards of my job, so that is all I will do." That type of person is a cynic and will ultimately be a loser, at least from a career perspective. After all, who would promote a person who has that kind of attitude? The type of person you want to be is one who does her best, one who can be counted upon even if she has a cold or a myriad of personal problems.

Moreover, if you do slow down, the change in your performance will undoubtedly be noticed, both by management and by your peers. Remember, nobody is stupid and everybody watches everybody else at work, so there are serious consequences for slowing down. If you take this approach, the positive first impression that you have created will slowly but surely vanish. You will also be viewed as insincere, since people will conclude that you work hard only when it is to your benefit, which means that you are somebody who can't be counted on in a crunch.

If you are slowing down because you think your supervisor is ignoring you or has been gruff or unfriendly to you, remember what your supervisor is dealing with on a daily basis. The odds are that if you have been doing your best, but your relationship with your supervisor has suffered a bit, it is probably because of the problems and issues that your supervisor has been trying to address and not because of you. However, if you respond to his behavior by slowing down, he will eventually notice this, either by observing your actions or by reviewing your performance metrics, or both, and that will only lead him to conclude that you are one more problem that he now has to deal with. In short, you will have turned what was most likely a short-term bump in your relationship into a more serious, long-term, self-fulfilling prophecy.

The better approach is to simply keep your nose to the grindstone and do the best possible job you can, regardless of the circumstances. This may not get noticed in the short term, but eventually your supervisor will recognize that you are someone that she can count on. When she has a little bit of free time, she is likely to thank you for your hard work and/ or tell you that she appreciates what you have accomplished.

I remember a period when I was a first-line supervisor and I was completely swamped with work, much of which only I could do (a series of complex cases that required my personal attention and interaction with upper management). I had very little time to spend with my employees; all I could do was delegate work to them and focus on the tasks at hand. It was a highly pressurized time for me, and I was probably short and curt with my subordinates during our limited interactions. However, when things settled down a bit and I started reviewing their completed work, it became quite clear to me who had stepped up to the plate and who had merely coasted. I made a point of thanking those employees who had produced work of high quality and apologized to them for my lack of attention. As for the other employees, I returned their work with a series of corrections and explained to each one of them that he needed to give it his best, whether I was accessible to him or not.

That is not to say that all supervisors will take the same approach that I did. Some do not have the people skills, while others may feel that the employees are merely doing their job, so why do I have thank them for doing what they are getting paid to do?

The point here is that supervisors vary in personality, skill, and talent, so the reaction that you will get for the same performance can easily vary depending on the person you are working for. However, even if your supervisor does not say anything to you, she is certainly aware of who are the hard workers and who are not, and in the long run, that is going to either pay off or hurt you. It will certainly pay off in terms of earning your supervisor's respect and appreciation, and it will probably pay off in terms of rewards, training opportunities, and future promotions. On the other hand, if you don't pull your weight, that will also get noticed, and it is likely that your career will quickly stagnate.

Take the Extra Step

Doing your job as well as you can is always the right thing to do, but you will often find that there are opportunities for you to go above and beyond what your job description calls for. By all means, take advantage of these opportunities, as they will establish you as someone who is highly motivated, cares about his job, and is willing to do whatever it takes to help the organization.

For example, after you have been on the job for a while and have established your credentials as a knowledgeable journeyman, your supervisor may ask you to train and/or mentor new employees. I strongly encourage you to agree to such a request, as this will give you the chance to show your stuff in a different capacity and to perform well in a role that has a higher profile. People who are willing to train others and can do so successfully are always valued by management. Moreover, they also earn the respect of their peers, who know that it is not easy to be pulled away from your job in order to train others.

Throughout my career, I was asked to give training classes, and I always embraced this type of request with enthusiasm. First of all, it was an acknowledgment that I was an expert on the subject that I was being asked to teach, and I appreciated the recognition. Second, it gave me a chance to put my imprint on the organization by shaping the minds of other people who I knew would be serving our country's citizens. Third, it gave me the chance to express my creativity, since I always had a fairly wide degree of latitude in designing the training, as long as I stuck to the basic framework of the curriculum. This meant that I could incorporate videos, drawing lessons, novel exercises, and other such measures, as long as I was able to train the class successfully. To me, this wasn't work; it was fun, so why would I ever want to pass up such an opportunity?

Another area where you can show your stuff is on special projects. As I described earlier, higher-level management often gives these assignments to the first-line supervisors. However, because of other pressures on them, the supervisors sometimes have to delegate these projects to a trusted subordinate. To me, when you have an opportunity to work on such a project, you should immediately volunteer and give it your best. This provides you with another chance to shine and, at the same time, earn the gratitude of your supervisor, who, as I hope you now understand, is often beleaguered.

For example, early in my career, my division chief called me into his office and explained to me that he had a bit of a crisis on his hands. An important report, which was supposed to be very lengthy and detailed, had not been completed (in fact, virtually no work had been done on it), and he was now receiving a lot of pressure to submit the report to our headquarters in Washington, D.C. Since he had lost faith in the person who was responsible for preparing the report, he turned to me because I had a reputation for being a hard worker and being someone who would do whatever it took to get the job done. He asked me to complete the report by the end of the week, even though he knew it should take a lot longer than that.

I immediately agreed and got to work on the report. I quickly realized that the basic information that I needed to complete the report wasn't easily accessible, as the person responsible for collecting the data was extremely disorganized. Rather than complain about it, I examined every nook and cranny in his work area until I found the information I needed in order to begin compiling the report. For the remainder of the week, I worked late into the night, doing everything I possibly could to complete the report on time, which I did. When it was over, I felt a great degree of personal satisfaction at having pulled off something that seemed to be nearly impossible. Moreover, I earned the respect and appreciation of my division chief, who, when the time came, enthusiastically recommended me for a higher-level position in another agency, which I received.

On another occasion, an office that I was working in had a severe problem with tracking its cases that were pending appeal. Each case was supposed to be updated in our computer system with a series of diary dates (indicating when a specific action was due), but many of the cases had either no diaries or outdated diaries; this meant that it was extremely difficult to know when an action had to be taken on a specific case. The acting supervisor at the time took it upon herself to review each case and ensure that the diaries were added or updated as required. This enabled us to keep much better track of these cases and to process them more expeditiously. Shortly thereafter, she was made a permanent supervisor.

I also recall a time when our organization was under tremendous pressure to comply with a court order. The order required us to review every case that fit within a specific category and report back to the court through our headquarters by a firm date. This was a very high-profile situation, since a lot of time, money, and energy was at stake, and every office in the nation was facing the same requirement. As the due date approached, we simply could not locate one of the claims folders covered by the order. We searched everywhere in our office and contacted other offices, but we simply could not find the folder, and we started receiving more and more phone calls and e-mails asking where it was. Fortunately, one of our file clerks took it upon himself to contact another office, because he suspected that the folder might be located in that organization's file banks. Sure enough, that was where it was, and we were able to meet our deadline date.

This individual, who had been a GS-4 for many years, decided to take the extra step and ultimately saved the day for us. By thinking outside the box and finding a way to help the organization when the chips were down, he earned management's respect and gratitude and helped himself in the process. His supervisors began to see him in a new and improved light, and he was ultimately promoted.

Be a Leader

In its most basic form, your supervisor's job is to guide her group, team, or unit toward achieving its goals, see that all members of the team are performing properly, and resolve problems as they arise. As we've discussed before, that is a very difficult and sometimes thankless job. A great way to build an excellent relationship with your supervisor is to become an informal leader within the group. By this I mean serving as an example for other group members on how to work, how to behave, and so on. This also means working behind the scenes and sometimes talking to your peers when they get out of line.

I do not mean that you should usurp the supervisor's role; that would be inappropriate. Rather, what I am suggesting is that sometimes you can help to resolve issues before they require your supervisor's attention. For example, if someone is unhappy with a portion of the training he has received, perhaps you can assist him in clarifying issues that are unclear or confusing. If there is a dispute between two members of the group, try mediating it before it morphs into a more significant problem. Should someone behave inappropriately, why not talk to her, explain that what she is doing is wrong, and advise her on how she can correct her behavior? If the team is afraid to address a controversial issue, why not stand up and tell it like it is? These actions require you to be more than just another member of the team; they require you to lead, which will ultimately help the team, come to the attention of your supervisor, and assist both you and the organization in achieving your goals.

For example, I recall a situation where an employee was very cynical and was constantly complaining. She felt that she was being poorly trained and mistreated, and this clearly affected both her behavior and her relationship with her team. One of her coworkers, a respected employee who had a lot of credibility because of the way he performed and the manner in which he comported himself, decided to informally confront her. He told her that her actions were hurting the team, that she needed to do better, and what she could do to improve. He also offered to help her in any way he could. Because the other employee had so much credibility, the employee took the discussion to heart and did indeed improve. In this instance, the employee stepped up and led, and his supervisor was very appreciative of his actions. In fact, he was subsequently promoted to a supervisory position.

On a different occasion, a work unit was very unhappy with the actions of its supervisor. In response to this, several employees chaired an employees-only meeting to air all of their grievances. Eventually, these employees put together a document that clearly laid out the employees' concerns, presented it to the supervisor, and personally met with him to discuss the issues. These employees clearly took a risk, because if the supervisor had reacted to this document in an adverse manner, they would have been the ones who bore the brunt of his anger, not the other people who were hiding behind them. However, the supervisor recognized that many of the concerns were right on the mark and pledged to do better. Moreover, he acknowledged the employees who came to him and thanked them for their leadership.

In another instance, a group of employees was meeting with senior management officials regarding a wide range of topics. During the meeting, one of the members complained about some of the people in the organization, and before you knew it, the group went into an attack mode, with one individual after another mocking those same people. The senior management officials were distressed at this unusually harsh reaction from the group and were at a loss as to how to respond. Finally, a lone member of the group spoke up and indicated that he had a different perception of the people in question. He stated that they were good people working in a bad system, explained why the system was causing these problems, and indicated that the solution was to change the system, not castigate the people. Instantly, the room went silent, as the others realized he was right.

When the meeting ended, several team members came up to him and complimented him for standing up and being a voice of reason. One of the senior officials who had been present also came up to him and asked him to be an organizational spokesperson on the systemic issues that he had raised in the meeting. Again, by demonstrating positive leadership, this individual helped himself, his supervisors, and his organization.

Working for a Difficult Boss

I've worked for all sorts of supervisors in my career. Some were outgoing and personable, while others were quiet and introverted; some I liked and became friends with, while others I didn't particularly care for; some I admired and respected, while others I wondered about; and some treated me very well, helped me whenever they could, and became lifelong mentors, while others treated me poorly, did very little to help me, and, in fact, often undermined me.

My personal experience with a wide range of supervisors is probably no different from that of most people who have had a long career. Sometimes you have a good supervisor, at times you have a bad one, and at other times you have a boss who falls somewhere in between. If you follow the approach I've described in this chapter, I am confident that in the overwhelming majority of situations, you will get along just fine with your boss. However, it is also possible that at some point in your career, you may wind up with the boss from hell, that is, the boss who treats you so poorly and makes you feel so miserable that she literally has an adverse impact on your personal life (e.g., you are under so much stress that you can't sleep well, your personal relationships are affected, and so on). In the event that this happens to you, it is important to examine how to handle this type of situation.

Is It Him or Is It You?

If you find yourself in a situation where you think your boss is unreasonable, is harassing you, and/or is placing you under a great deal of stress, the first thing you need to do is take a good, hard look at your situation and determine what the root cause is. You may eventually find that your boss is giving you a hard time because you are underperforming, because your attendance has been poor, or because your behavior has been less than optimal. You may even find that, although you have been doing your job and following all the rules, you have become very cynical and are polluting the office atmosphere. Under these circumstances, the problem is not your boss; the problem is you, and your supervisor is merely doing his job.

If you are not sure what the root cause is, try speaking to your supervisor about your perceptions and see if you can develop a meeting of the minds. Alternatively, discuss your situation with a trusted yet dispassionate third party (for example, a friend or a mentor) to get a second opinion. Again, you may discover that your boss is not nearly as unreasonable as you might think.

Obviously, I did change jobs from time to time, but that was because I was seeking a promotion, a career change, or an opportunity to work in an organization that was a better fit for my skills, abilities, and core values. However, that was never a function of my immediate supervisor; it was a function of what I deemed to be best for my career.

If, after taking a good, hard, honest look at the situation, you conclude that you do have a boss who is making your life miserable through no fault of your own, then you really have only three options: (1) manage your boss, (2) adjust your attitude, or (3) get another job. Let's examine these options in greater detail.

MANAGING YOUR BOSS

The first thing you need to do is recognize that you are not going to change your boss. That may be painful to accept, given the fact that you are dealing with someone who is difficult. However, it can also be liberating, since it is exhausting to try to change anyone's behavior, particularly that of someone who is your supervisor. The better approach is to try to get to know her, learn how she thinks, understand what her goals are, and recognize what her buttons are so that you do not push them. Moreover, when you present a problem to her, make sure that you also offer a solution. Let's look at each one of these strategies.

I have found that people are much more likely to treat you with respect and dignity if you know each other on a personal level. If you get to know her, your boss is less likely to see you as a disposable resource and more likely to see you as a person who has feelings just like she does. You will also find out, at least to some extent, what drives her, what motivates her, and, hopefully, what it takes to please her.

I recall the time that a tough new manager, whose job it was to clean the place up, arrived in our organization. Everyone was initially afraid of him and didn't know how to act. One day, I started a personal conversation with him and learned that we shared some similar problems in our private lives. This helped to form a common bond between us and opened the door for me to begin to understand what made him tick. From his perspective, he got to see me as more than just another employee, and he started asking me for my opinion on a variety of issues. Eventually, we built a strong and close relationship that lasted well beyond his tenure at my office.

Knowing what your supervisor's goals are is extremely important because you do not want to be working at odds with those goals. Any supervisor will be frustrated if his employees are focusing their energy on areas that are not important to him. Make sure you know what your supervisor is trying to accomplish, and then be certain that you are keeping your eye on the prize.

For example, I once gave one of my employees an assignment to work on an important study of the use of sick leave in our organization. Instead, she decided to first focus all of her attention on trying to transfer one of our employees to another office. When she proudly told me that she had effected the transfer, I asked her where the sick leave study was, and she admitted that she had not yet begun work on it. I then replied, "If I asked you to wash the dishes in the kitchen and you scrubbed the floor instead, I wouldn't care how great the floor looked, since you still didn't wash the dishes."

This employee repeated this story to me on several occasions over the years, as it obviously had a great impact on her. She never made that mistake again, became my most valued employee, and today is the chief of HRM for a large federal administration.

It is absolutely essential that you get to know your supervisor's "hot buttons." By this I mean the things that will make her angry if they are said or done in a certain way. We all have our own hot buttons, and we generally know how to push the hot buttons of those people who are close to us, but in the case of your supervisor, that's the last thing you want to do. After all, who wants to have a boss who is constantly angry with him?

I once worked for a supervisor who absolutely hated to be blindsided (in my experience, that is a hot button for most supervisors). I found that if I kept her in the loop, she would be able to respond successfully if and when an issue that I was responsible for finally reared its ugly head. I therefore decided that, if anything, I would overbrief her on key issues; at one point, I even gave her weekly written reports on what was going on in my neck of the woods. This approach ensured that her blood pressure never rose too high, at least with respect to the areas that were under my jurisdiction.

We all seem to live in a world of never-ending problems, and many of those problems have to be brought to the attention of our supervisor. From the supervisor's perspective, it often feels as if problems are constantly being dumped into his lap, which is an exhausting and debilitating feeling, especially if his employees are expecting him to solve the problems. On the other hand, if you bring a problem to the supervisor's attention and say, "This is what I'm doing about it," or "Here are several options for resolving this problem," your supervisor will see you as someone who is part of the solution, not part of the problem. If you can draw that distinction in your supervisor's mind, the odds are that he will eventually come around and treat you in the manner that you desire.

For example, an employee once told me that he was unable to complete a report because he couldn't get access to some of the required information. However, he also told me that he had contacted our headquarters, received an extension on the due date for the submission of the report, and arranged to get a special computer run to access this information. He was clearly someone who was part of the solution.

Many problems with our bosses seem to develop over communication. If you communicate only in the style that you are comfortable with, you can easily frustrate your supervisor if she prefers a different method of communication. In my view, as subordinates, it is incumbent upon us to learn our supervisor's preferred communication style and then express ourselves in that manner. After all, some supervisors prefer brief, oral explanations, some want long, detailed explanations, others want things in writing, and still others want to see charts and tables full of data. Many want some combination of all of these methods. Again, it is up to us to figure out what works best when communicating with our supervisor.

Early in my career, a new leader came to our organization and requested briefings from his key subordinates. The people who went ahead of me gave long-winded oral explanations that seemed to turn off this new leader, who was obviously a bottom-line, no-nonsense type. Fortunately, I had contacted his previous place of employment and learned that he liked to see plenty of charts containing a multitude of data. Even though I didn't have a lot of experience in this area at the time, I put together a series of rudimentary charts that he seemed to really appreciate. In fact, he then instructed my coworkers that whenever they came to brief him on a particular topic, they should bring charts and data in the same way that I did.

The same approach did not work as well with a different supervisor. He was a very charismatic and social individual. He was the type who always joked with you, had a sharp wit, and was likely to slap you on the back good-naturedly. He also had a relatively short attention span, so you rarely had much time to get your point across.

I tried communicating with him through charts and tables, in the same way that I had done with the supervisor described earlier. However, it became obvious that he was not interested in a lot of detail and did not particularly care for all the data that I presented to him. In retrospect, this approach soured our relationship until I finally adjusted the way I communicated with him, i.e., with some humor followed by a quick and concise explanation.

ADJUSTING YOUR ATTITUDE

If you are doing everything that is expected of you, but you are still taking grief and are unable to successfully manage your boss, then the next person you have to look at is yourself. Under this scenario, you may reluctantly conclude that you are in a bad situation, and that despite your best efforts, you cannot change things to a significant degree. In that case, one alternative is to change yourself.

Throughout my career, I was very successful at getting along with my supervisors, and I rarely had any trouble with them. That all changed toward the end when a new leadership team took over. These people applied a rigid, top-down management approach that involved a high degree of micromanagement and was uncomfortable to work under. Moreover, they intentionally withheld resources from several offices (including mine), gave us performance goals that were at odds with the resources they had given us, and then held us accountable for not achieving some of the goals, even though our failure to do so was the result of their decision to withhold resources. The worst thing for me, however, was that their core values were completely at odds with mine (e.g., they did not seem to value people, output was far more important than satisfying our customers, and creativity was discouraged). Quite frankly, for the first time and only time in my career, I found myself in a situation where I was pretty miserable.

I commiserated with many of my friends in the organization, because they felt the same way. I also did an enormous amount of self-reflection. I finally concluded that the only thing I could control was my attitude, and that it needed some adjusting. First of all, I decided to embrace and lead the change that was being imposed upon us. While I didn't agree with it, I was still a member of that organization and owed it my full loyalty, so I made sure I did the best I could in a bad situation. Second, I reconciled myself to the fact that I would not receive any more resources, probably for the rest of my career. In a way, this was liberating, since I was no longer hoping for something that deep down I knew I would never get. I stopped whining and simply played the cards I was dealt.

I also reinvented myself, which proved to be enormously helpful and ultimately gratifying. I decided to rebalance my life and ensure that it was not as centered on my job as it had been in the past. I spent more time with my family, started writing my first book, began to play tennis on a more serious level, became more involved with my synagogue, and made sure that I smelled the roses.

While this approach did not solve all my work problems, it certainly gave me a greater sense of inner peace. Things that had previously bothered me did not bother me as much, because my perspective had changed. In essence, this experience thickened my skin and made me a better and stronger person.

Interestingly, many of my peers took the same approach. While some of them decided to retire or change agencies because they no longer wanted to be a part of this organization, others decided not to do so for a variety of reasons (they didn't want to quit when the chips were down; they were too young to retire, and from a career standpoint, it would have been extremely difficult to change jobs without taking a cut in pay; and other such reasons). Many of these folks started to travel more, joined a health club, quit smoking, or did a variety of other things that enriched their lives and made them less job-centered.

Most of us concluded that we had to adjust our attitudes, and by doing this, we were all better off.

GETTING ANOTHER JOB

Of course, another option is to simply change jobs. However, before you take this option, I suggest that you at least consider the following: (1) How committed are you to your current position or career, and how will changing jobs affect your long-term prospects? (2) Has the same thing happened before, and if so, is it likely to happen again? (3) How much longer do you expect your supervisor to remain in her current position? (4) Are you likely to change jobs anyway as part of your normal career progression? Let's look at these issues in more detail.

I've seen people who were so unhappy with their bosses that they left a satisfying, high-paying job that they loved for a lower-paying and less satisfying position. They did this out of desperation, and in most cases, they ultimately regretted the move. If you know what you want to do and where you want to be in your career, do not make an emotional career decision and take the first job that is available. Take your time, find a job that gives you what you need, and then make your move. Do what is right for you, on your own terms, and you will be better off for it.

If you are the type of individual who leaves a job every time you feel slighted or disrespected, you might want to take a good, hard look at yourself. Are you constantly searching for the ideal situation, which we know doesn't exist? You may learn what Dorothy found out in *The Wiz-*

ard of Oz—that is, there is no place like home. My only point here is that if you keep changing jobs because you are unhappy with your supervisor or your situation, you may find that the real problem lies within you. In that case, you should ask yourself why you keep moving from job to job and what would truly make you happy.

If the problem is your supervisor and nothing else works, sometimes the best approach is to simply wait him out (government employees have used this strategy for years). If you believe that he is likely to leave within a reasonable time (as defined by you), for reasons that may range from retirement to promotion or reassignment to rotation of supervisors, you should at least weigh the probability of this happening against the difficulties you are currently experiencing on the job.

Lastly, you should also weigh your own situation before looking elsewhere. Are you due to be reassigned to a different team? Do you expect to go on a long-term special project? Are you likely to be rotated to a new unit? If so, consider these possible scenarios before making a change.

As I said earlier, there is nothing wrong with changing jobs. People do it all the time for a variety of reasons. Just make sure that if you decide to make a change, you are doing it for the right reasons.

CHAPTER 5

Developing Perspective

HOPEFULLY, BY NOW you have acclimated yourself to working for the government, have made a good first impression, are continuing to improve your skills and expertise, and have built a good relationship with your supervisor. At this point, you want to begin to develop a larger view of things so that you can understand where you fit into the big picture, comprehend how things really work on a broader scale, and figure out where you can go from here. To do this successfully, you need to understand the forces that are at play in the government.

Understanding What Is Really Going On

Be Aware of the Key Broad-Based Political Forces at Play

Early in my career, I focused almost exclusively on simply doing a good job. That was all I really paid attention to at work, although of course I read the newspapers, watched the evening news, and read many books. However, perhaps because I was too young and unsophisticated at the time, I didn't really pay attention to national politics and how they affected my job. Sure, I heard all sorts of rumors that were flying around regarding cutbacks, consolidations, changes in direction, and other such issues, but I didn't pay much attention to them; after all, I had a government job, so I figured I was safe. However, I was soon in for a rude awakening.

Near the end of my first year of government service, I learned that my office was about to be consolidated and that my job as a personnel management specialist with the Department of the Army was probably going to be eliminated. While I took a mild degree of comfort in knowing that the Army would eventually offer me a job in another location, I knew that it would probably be out of state. This meant that I was going to have to move, which was something that I did not want to do at the time.

Since there were plenty of other federal agencies in New York, where I was living at the time, and since personnel specialists with some training always seemed to be in demand, I was not overly concerned about finding another job. As a result, I mailed out a bunch of résumés and waited for the job offers to roll in. However, as time went by and I had not yet secured another job, I began to worry and intensified my job search. Finally, I received a call from the General Services Administration (GSA), asking me to come in on Saturday for a job interview. I agreed, but I asked why the interview would not be held the following week, during normal business hours. The caller responded, "There is going to be a government-wide hiring freeze starting on Monday, so if we are going to hire you, we will have to make an official job commitment before then."

Instantly, I understood why nobody had contacted me regarding all the résumés I had mailed out earlier. Most agencies had already had a hiring freeze in place, but I had been too absorbed in my own personal situation to realize that. The lesson here was simple: (1) The world did not revolve around me, and (2) the more I knew about what was going on around me, the better position I would be in to make wise choices.

Fortunately for me, GSA hired me on the spot. Later on, I was detailed to the Federal Energy Administration (FEA), which was a relatively small federal agency. Because of the nature of my detail, I got to work pretty closely with the FEA's regional administrator, and I had the opportunity to see some of the political pressures that he had to deal with, especially from his headquarters. These ranged from purely political issues, to people second-guessing some of his management practices, to special interest groups making demands on his time. This was another eye-opener for me and made me realize that there was a much bigger world out there than my little niche.

Once I returned to GSA, I started paying more attention to outside events, both national and international. I began to wonder how the Iran oil embargo would affect GSA,[1] how Jimmy Carter's policies would affect me, and so on. I also began to notice that GSA, whose mission is "to help manage and support the basic functioning of federal agencies,"[2] was undergoing change. For example, GSA's emergency management functions were transferred to the Federal Emergency Management Agency (FEMA) in 1979.[3] Moreover, I also noticed a trend toward privatizing some of GSA's activities. I questioned whether GSA was the right organization for me from a career standpoint, and I eventually transferred to the Department of Veterans Affairs (VA), which I thought was more stable and which had a mission that I found to be more compelling. Initially, I worked on the hospital side, then I moved to the benefits side, where I remained for the rest of my career.

One of the things that I quickly learned about the VA was that it had an enormous amount of political support in Congress. After all, who was going to be opposed to programs that supported veterans? Moreover, I learned about the power of the veterans' services organizations such as the American Legion, the Disabled American Veterans, the Military Order of the Purple Heart and the Vietnam Veterans of America, and how they would do everything that they could to help veterans by serving as advocates for the VA.[4]

I learned even more about the political forces at play after Ronald Reagan came into office. I was very concerned about his impact on my career because I knew that he felt that government was part of the problem and had vowed to shrink it precipitously. He proved me right; shortly after I moved over to the benefits side of the VA, he proposed consolidating the 58 benefits offices that were in existence at the time into 3. I began to wonder if I had made a mistake in transferring from the hospital side of the VA, which seemed to be much more secure, to the benefits side, which suddenly didn't seem that way.

Fortunately, I was able to speak to other higher-ranking people in the VA, who already understood the national political picture much better than I did. They all insisted that this would not happen because Congress, in part because it was bowing to the wishes of the services organizations and in part because at that time a high percentage of its members were veterans, would not approve it, and they were right. Again, the lesson that was reinforced to me was to learn the big picture so that I could plan my career accordingly.

The same principle holds true even if you are working in state or local government. An incoming governor, a new mayor, or a crisis du jour can cause a sudden change in direction, and you need to be prepared to adjust your course accordingly. For example, when the economy goes south, that tends to have a big impact on the ability of governments at all levels to collect taxes. However, because of their size relative to the federal government, state and local governments normally take much bigger hits. If you become sophisticated enough, you can identify these trends as they develop and not get caught off guard. The key is to keep your eyes open, constantly follow and understand the relationship of the key forces at play, learn from history, and then be prepared to act or not act in a manner that is appropriate for you.

Another reason why you want to be in tune with the political forces is simply to maintain your own sanity. In my experience, people who are disconnected from the political realities of government and do not understand what is truly going on tend to come up with all sorts of absurd reasons why decisions are being made. Since they don't understand the forces that are actually at play, they tend to see more sinister forces at work in the decision-making process, which inevitably causes fear. As Yoda, the Jedi Master from the *Star Wars* series, once said, "Fear leads to anger. Anger leads to hate. Hate leads to suffering."[5]

While that is of course a bit of an exaggeration with regard to the types of situations I am talking about, it is analogous. Far too often, people have no idea how and why decisions are made, so their fears start to take over. They assume that a small group of people, hidden behind closed doors in smoke-filled rooms, is making decisions that are designed to hurt them. They see plots everywhere and repeat their concerns to others, and before you know it, the rumors start to fly, making everyone even crazier.

That's certainly the way I saw things for a number of years because people who were not politically savvy were constantly passing on information about something nefarious that was always about to happen (e.g., workload consolidations were about to take place, this individual was in trouble, and so on). I would then anxiously discuss these rumors with my mentors, who would invariably tell me to ignore them because they generally didn't make any sense (there was no political will to pull off the alleged consolidation, or the employee who was in trouble was acknowledged to be a good employee).

At first blush, to a relatively unseasoned employee, these rumors had a ring of truth to them, since they were always passed on with a sense of urgency by someone who sounded as though he knew what he was talking about. However, once my mentors explained to me the real political forces that were at play, and I slowly started to see that these rumors rarely panned out, I began to understand things more clearly, and I paid less and less attention to what other people were telling me. I made a point of trying to grasp the large-scale political forces, tried to periodically confer with other people who were in the know, and became more confident in my ability to separate truth from fiction. Quite frankly, this allowed to me to worry less, sleep better at night, and concentrate more on doing my job.

Familiarize Yourself with the Local Politics and Strategy

To have the best possible picture of what is going on, you also have to understand what is going on at the local level. By this I mean that you need to learn what is happening in your own individual organization. This may sound simple enough, but you would be surprised at how many people don't pay attention to what's going on in the office where they work.

It's been my experience that many people simply adopt the mind-set, "I will come to work each day, put in my eight hours, and then go home." To them, anything that develops that is outside their immediate job is something for management to deal with. When management schedules town hall meetings to brief the employees on what is going on, these people rarely attend unless the topic that is being discussed is one that is near and dear to their hearts. Naturally, these are often the same people who pass on the most far-fetched rumors because they don't really understand what is happening and why.

If you don't understand what's driving your local managers, you will eventually become confused by and frustrated with them, and you may easily fall into the trap of concluding that they are either incompetent or acting against the best interests of the employees. For instance, I have often heard my fellow employees complain that management is constantly changing its priorities—which, unfortunately, is usually true. However, these priorities are not changed in a vacuum; they are invariably changed in response to one or more of the forces we have already discussed. They may change in response to a newspaper article, after a complaint was made by a local politician, or because of a national, statewide, or citywide push to improve performance in a certain area. The point here is that these types of pressures come from all angles, and they never really stop.

You also need to understand the local strategies that are being implemented to try to attain the performance objectives that have been set for your organization. These may involve a shift in resources, a short-term focus on a specific area, or some other action. The key is understanding what is behind these decisions so that you won't constantly feel as though the ground is shifting underneath you.

One of my personal rules of thumb as a government leader was that if most people sat in my chair and had access to the same information that I had, they would probably make the same decisions that I made. Not all the time, but most of the time. I found this to be the case with government unions, because whenever they questioned one of my decisions and I explained to them both the rationale behind the decision and the forces that were at play, they were generally supportive.

The problem is that employees, particularly those who are not in management, do not have access to this information, so they base their evaluations of management's actions on the limited information that they do have. This is one reason why managers hold employee meetings, manage by walking around, issue policy memos, and take other such actions. It's to let people know what's going on and why. However, those employees who choose to stay on the sidelines and do not take advantage of these opportunities to gain information will become angry and frustrated when they suddenly learn about decisions that are being made that do not please them; even though they have made no effort to learn about the key issues that were involved.

The better approach is simply to get involved. Attend every town hall meeting that is offered; take advantage of opportunities to meet with higher-level officials and ask them as many questions as you can; talk to your supervisor as often as possible and pick her brain regarding why things are happening. Talk to the union as well, since union officials frequently interact with management and usually have a pretty good feel as to what is going on. Moreover, union officials will provide you with an important perspective that you will need to be aware of, especially if you decide to go into management. Again, you will find that the more you know about what's going on and why, the better you will be able to understand how things work and ultimately use this knowledge to your advantage.

Another good way to follow management's thinking is to pay close attention to the performance trends in your office. In some cases, these trends are posted for all to see; in other situations, you may have to search for this information on your internal computer system. If you track these trends and follow management's actions in response to them, you will develop a good perspective on why local management is operating the way it does. Eventually, you should be able to anticipate many of the actions that it will take.

None of these steps involves rocket science. They are simple, commonsense approaches that will keep you in the information chain and prevent you from adopting an "us versus them" mentality. This is something you want to avoid at all costs, since once you see work as a contest between management and the employees, you are headed down the path toward the dark side of the force.

Develop a Cadre of Mentors

Another great way to develop perspective is to find a diverse group of people to mentor you. Learning from the successful and experienced employees in your work unit (as recommended in Chapter 3) is a good start, and you should continue to learn from them and pick their brains. However, as you begin to learn the ropes, become more comfortable with your career, and start to look down the road, you will need to expand your brain trust.

By this, I mean that you will need to find individuals to learn from who have a broader and more complex point of view than the people who work in your immediate work unit: people who have had such diverse experiences that they can see the big picture more clearly than most, and can help you to see it as well; people who have worked in a number of different areas and locations around the country, state, or locality, as appropriate, and understand how decisions are made and the way in which power is often wielded. These people have much to offer in the way of information, guidance, and influence, so whenever and wherever you can find a good mentor, by all means do so.

As you can imagine, mentors play a major role in shaping people's careers. In fact, if you take the long view, I have found that you can almost predict the arc of a person's career, the way she will ultimately comport herself, her reputation, and so on based on the mentors she ultimately chooses. That's because most people try to align themselves with mentors whom they admire, while most mentors try to assist people who have the character, abilities, and potential that they feel are worth developing. Thus, someone who is creative will often try to find a mentor who has a reputation for innovation and creativity, while someone who is a more hard-nosed, bottom-line type of individual will try to find a mentor who has a similar predisposition.

As your career progresses, you should begin to have opportunities to meet people from outside your immediate work environment. These opportunities may come from attending training sessions, where you can network with people from other offices and listen to influential trainers and speakers; they may come from attending conferences, where you can get the chance to see who the movers and shakers are; they may come from an internal organizational development program, in which interested employees are paired with mentors so that they can learn from more senior employees; or they may come simply from interacting with someone you grow to respect in the normal course of doing business.

The point here is that there are plenty of opportunities to find good mentors. What you need to do is find mentors who are right for you and then seize the moment. You don't have to immediately ask someone to become your mentor. Simply start a discussion and begin to build a relationship. If the chemistry is right, you will know it soon enough, at which point you can ask that individual to take your relationship to a higher level.

As you look for mentors, try to find individuals who have varied backgrounds and different experiences and perspectives. This will ensure that you get as well-rounded a picture as possible and will not become too narrow in your thinking. Try to find mentors who are in your area of expertise and mentors who are experts in other areas; try to find mentors who work in your location and mentors who work elsewhere, particularly folks who work in or have a lot of experience working in your headquarters; and try to find mentors who work both inside and outside of government. You'll find that the more diverse your mentors are, the more your intellect will be challenged, and the more you will grow as an employee and as an individual.

In my case, I started out as most people do: with mentors in my immediate office. Since I switched jobs several times during my early years with the government, I was able to build a small but helpful group of mentors, although their expertise was limited primarily to the personnel community.

As I began to establish myself, I started meeting more accomplished individuals who made me question some of my initial premises and beliefs. These individuals showed me that there was "more than one way to skin a cat," and that while I was pretty good, I had a long way to go before I could play in their league. Fortunately, most of these folks were open to working with me, and I built solid, long-term relationships with several of them.

Eventually, I built similar relationships with dozens, if not hundreds, of people. Some of them became informal mentors; many of them became my confidants; others I bounced ideas off of or shared information with; and almost all of them became my friends. Every one of these people had an important impact on my professional and personal growth, and I treasured each one of those relationships.

Of all of the people who influenced my career, four stand out in particular: Tom Lastowka, Joe Thompson, Bill Snyder, and Paul Gustavson. Each one of these individuals has been both a friend and a mentor, and has had a profound impact on my life. Not surprisingly, when I retired from the government after 32 years of service, they all flew to Los Angeles to attend my retirement party. Let me tell you a little bit about each one of them and how he affected me.

I met Tom Lastowka when he was appointed director of the VA's New York regional office. I was the personnel officer at the time. Tom was sent to that office to "clean it up" because it was performing poorly and had a supervisory staff that generally believed that the people in Washington, D.C., simply didn't appreciate how difficult it was to run that office. Tom worked hard to change the mind-set of the people in that office by showing that things could be accomplished, even under difficult circumstances. He dealt with difficult issues, reallocated resources to where they were truly needed, and brought a degree of professionalism to the office that it previously had not had.

On a personal level, he saw something in me that was worth developing, and he took me under his wing. He taught me how to think more analytically and to look at things from a broader perspective. Over time, he patiently answered thousands of my questions on topics ranging from productivity and effectiveness to statistical quality control. Eventually, I was appointed as Tom's assistant director, and we started going to lunch every day. These lunches provided me with new opportunities to learn from him, since the topics we discussed ranged from government and business to finance and investments to religion and the meaning of life.

Joe Thompson replaced Tom. The day he arrived, I gave him a briefing on how our office was doing. I proudly told him that we were meeting 13 out of 13 timeliness standards. Joe simply looked at me and said, "Stew, I don't want my tombstone to read that I met 13 out of 13 timeliness standards." I never forgot this comment because I realized that this was a different way of viewing things, and I had not worked with anyone who had thought that way before.

Joe was a more creative, but less structured individual than Tom, and he challenged some of the premises that I had been operating under. He encouraged me to "think outside of the box" and to read a wider variety of books, both on management and on other topics. Unlike most directors, Joe was not as interested in improving performance as he was in changing the basic systems under which we operated. He brought in a wide variety of consultants who worked with us to analyze our business processes and eventually to change the way our entire organization operated. As I mentioned earlier, under Joe, our office received the first Hammer Award from Vice President Gore for reinventing government.

Both Tom and Joe were outstanding mentors to me because they were smart, broad-minded, caring, and patient individuals. While they had contrasting personalities, styles, and approaches, their differences proved to be a good thing for me because I was exposed to much more than I would have been had I worked with two people who were simply clones of each other.

One of the consultants that I met while I was working for Joe was Bill Snyder. Bill is an expert in the field of knowledge management; specializing in building communities of practice that enable members of large organizations to extend learning across organizational boundaries.

Bill is a Harvard graduate who was interested in working with us because he believed in the VA's mission, wanted to support our efforts to reinvent government, and saw this as an opportunity to make a difference. Bill was unlike anyone I had met before; he was very quirky, looked at things from many different perspectives, and was always willing to challenge the conventional wisdom. He often surprised us with his insights, and he frequently tried to explain things by saying, "Well, one way to think of this is by . . ."

Bill introduced me to some of the best business minds outside government, as he had studied with or knew many of the top people in the field. He would suggest books and articles to read or tell stories of how other organizations had dealt with their particular challenges. He also loved to sketch out complex organizational theories and models on a bulletin board (not that I was always able to follow his abstract-expressionist illustrations).

He was also able to give us some context for some of the challenges we were dealing with in government. Having someone with his intellect give you perspective, assure you that things would be okay and that you were simply ahead of the curve, or suggest new approaches was both comforting and stimulating. I learned from him that there is a bigger world out there and that it is up to me to decide whether I am going to think big or think small.

Paul Gustavson was one of Bill's mentors, and I met him several years after Bill had first gotten involved with our organization. He is a leading organizational design architect specializing in strategy making, the design of high-performance work systems, change management, and knowledge management. One of the first things that I learned from Paul was, "Organizations are perfectly designed to get the results that they get," a lesson that was later reinforced time and again throughout my career.

Paul taught me many things about strategy, communication, and organizational design theory and implementation. However, what has stuck with me the most is his concept that an organization's outcomes are a function of the behaviors, feelings, and attributes (BFAs) of its employees, and that these BFAs are influenced by the design choices that the organization makes (in its technical systems, decision-making and information systems, people systems, and other such areas).

With this concept, Paul provided me with a framework for thinking more systematically. Whereas before this, if a problem arose, my first instinct had been to find some person to blame, I now realized that most problems are caused by the systems that are in place, not by the people; and therefore, if a problem arises, the first place to look is at either the design or the implementation of one of the management systems. This insight and approach guided my thinking throughout the rest of my career and continues to serve me well as a writer, teacher, and consultant.

Paul also invited me to his house, where I had the opportunity to meet a group of his consultant friends (Bill was there, too) that gets together several times a year for learning and to do pro bono work that helps society. This proved to be a wonderful and stimulating experience for me, and I am pleased to report that I have since become a member of that group.

Having first-class mentors is a superb way of broadening your horizons. That is why you should constantly be on the lookout for new ones. If you find the right one, he is sure to be worth his weight in gold.

Build a Network

Another way to improve your understanding of the way things work is to build a strong and reliable network. By this I mean a network of people that you interact with on a periodic basis to learn from, share information, discuss ideas, complain about things that are bothering you, or simply shoot the breeze. While your mentors are part of your network, your network should extend well beyond them. It should include your peers, people in other parts of your organization (including people at your level, above you, and below you), people who interact with your organization, and people who have nothing whatsoever to do with your organization or your job.

Your network should include men and women; blacks, whites, Latinos, and Asians; people your age and people who are both younger and older than you; supervisors and nonsupervisors; and people with all sorts of ideas, points of view, and experiences. The wider your network, the more perspectives you will hear, meaning that you will be able to see things more clearly.

Having a strong network will also keep you more in the loop, meaning that you will have a greater understanding of what is really going on in your organization, and may even give you the chance to influence things. For example, early on, I learned to befriend the secretaries in my organization, i.e., the administrative assistants of those individuals who made the key decisions and controlled the power within my organization. I found that these secretaries had the inside scoop on things, and on many occasions were willing to share information with people whom they trusted (e.g., what the current thinking was on a certain subject or whether the rumor of the day was true).

I also found that if I shared information with them, they would often pass it on to their bosses. For example, on a couple of occasions, I wanted to ensure that some of my coworkers were receiving appropriate credit for their accomplishments. I found that if I truthfully explained to these secretaries what my coworkers had achieved, they would (1) appreciate having this information, (2) pass it on, and (3) in many cases, help these individuals' careers. Doing this also established me as a reliable source of information and boosted my credibility with them, and with their bosses as well. This approach works well as long as you are always honest and up-front and are not passing along any inappropriate information.

Having a large network also ensures that you have people to turn to when things get a bit sticky. For example, midway through my career, I heard from several reliable sources that a senior management official had put together an "enemies list," i.e., a list of people whom he considered to be disloyal. Most troubling to me was that I apparently was on the list, not so much for what I had done, but because of the people that I hung out with.

Worried and concerned, I called one of the people in my network whom I trusted. I called this particular individual because he was more experienced than I was and because he was close to the individual who had compiled the enemies list. He immediately confirmed the existence of the list and that I was on it, and then defiantly proclaimed that he too was on the list. When I asked him if he was worried about being on it, he replied, "Why should I be? Looking at the names of the people who are on that list, I'm proud to be on it."

Hearing this perspective was very comforting to me, and I calmed down immediately. It also didn't hurt when he added, "What are they going to do to us? We haven't done anything wrong."

For the first third of my career, I had a network that was made up almost entirely of people within a very narrow spectrum. That changed as I began to move up and became exposed to people who had large networks. I realized very quickly that they knew far more about the inner workings of my organization and the government than I did. I saw that I was always at the tail end of the rumor mill chain, and that by the time a rumor filtered down to me, it was way past its prime.

Moreover, I realized that while most people in my organization knew who these individuals were, very few people outside of my circle knew who I was or what I had accomplished. I understood that I needed to work at building a network, although not to the extent of neglecting my job—one should never do that. Rather, I needed to build my network because it would make me a more knowledgeable, confident, resourceful, and well-known employee, and this would enable me to do a better job and enhance my career potential.

Even though I've been gone from the government for almost two years, I continue to stay in touch with many of the people in my network. Sometimes it's for social reasons; other times it's simply to lend an ear to a friend in need; on some occasions, it's to partner in a business endeavor. The point here is that your network does not end when your career ends. It simply evolves, as long as you are willing to take the time to ensure that you stay in contact with the members of your network.

Act Appropriately

As your government career progresses and you begin to develop perspective and confidence, it is important that you act in a manner that is consistent with your growing body of knowledge. This means that you continue to strive to do your best and that you don't fall into a midcareer rut, as so many people seem to do.

Fight the Feelings of Entitlement

Many people seem to feel that because they have worked hard and paid their dues, they are somehow entitled to certain benefits and privileges. The fact of the matter is that you are expected to work hard, and while you may have done what has been expected of you to date, so have many other people. This is a very competitive world, and the way to get ahead is to compete hard, day after day. If you develop the mentality that the government owes you a paycheck and periodic promotions, the only person you will be fooling is yourself.

You get a paycheck for doing your job. If you do your job well, you can expect to continue to get paid, subject to the unlikely event of a reduction in force. If a promotion opportunity then opens up and you apply for it, you can expect to be considered for it. If you are the best candidate, hopefully you will be selected, although we all know that things don't always work that way in the real world. If you do not get selected for a job you want, do not go into your shell or feel sorry for yourself. Stuff happens, and no one gets her way all the time. Simply get off the canvas, get back into the game, and create new opportunities for yourself.

Keep in mind that life is not fair, and neither is work. Management tries to set up systems that are fair, and the best organizations succeed at doing this to a large extent, but there are always pressures out there that can influence the process. The pressures may come from politicians, they may come from headquarters or from the union, or they may come from a particular group that feels that its members have been shortchanged. The point here is that competing pressures do influence management's decisions, and that sometimes they will work in your favor and other times they will not. Remember, there is no long-term plot against you, as tempting as it may be to feel that way sometimes. You are simply not that important in the overall scheme of things, and neither am I.

That having been said, I do believe that there is a rough sense of justice within the government. By this I mean that good people eventually get ahead, although not always at the pace they would like. Moreover, I also believe that people who act or perform in a less than optimal manner eventually pay a price for doing so, although perhaps not right away and in some cases not for years down the road. Eventually, poor performance and/or arrogance do catch up with you. It may be when the leadership changes and you are no longer protected by your buddy; it may be when you retire and you suddenly find out that you have no friends after spending 30 years making enemies—it's hard to say. However, it's been my experience that we are all held accountable for our actions, although sometimes the Lord seems to work in mysterious ways.

Behave as if Your Job Is Always on the Line

To me, this is the mentality that you need to retain throughout your career. By this, I mean continuing to maintain "the eye of the tiger"—that is, staying hungry and always looking for new ways to improve and contribute to the organization.

As you start to understand the way things work, learn from your mentors, and build your network, you may find yourself coasting a bit, figuring that your rank and your contacts will help you get ahead. By all means avoid this temptation. If you don't, once you figure that you've got it made, that you are part of the "in crowd," that you are on the fast track, and that your career is set, you will start to go downhill—not right away, but slowly and surely. You will begin to develop bad habits that will eat away at your position and will eventually come back to haunt you. Let's take a look at a few examples.

I recall one individual who accomplished everything that he set out to do. He became a member of the Senior Executive Service, was making good money, and received plenty of recognition for his accomplishments. However, all of this eventually went to his head, and he began to act in an imperial manner. For instance, he started belittling the people under him, apparently because he believed that he was better than everyone else. He even opened up a private business that he managed from his government office on the government's time. When word of his behavior began to leak out and the noose tightened around his neck, he was eventually forced to leave the government before he was ready.

Arrogance can exist at any level of government, not just at the executive level. On another occasion, we noted that one of our senior technicians had been vehemently complaining about the manner in which we conducted our quality control reviews. We looked into his complaints, concluded that our actions were appropriate, and informed him accordingly.

However, that did not seem to satisfy him, and we began to notice that our quality control records kept disappearing from his division chief's office. In order to get to the bottom of this, we placed a hidden video camera in that office. The following day, when we reviewed the videotape, we saw that the technician had a key to the division chief's office and had sat in his chair and rummaged through his files, examining all of the items on top of and inside his desk with great interest. Naturally, we got rid of this employee, which to some extent was a shame because he was very knowledgeable and quite productive. However, he had reached the point where he believed that he was more important than the organization, which left us with no choice but to end his career.

Conversely, I know of another individual who held the exact same job as this person. She was as at least as knowledgeable as the person described in the last two paragraphs. All she wanted was to simply do her job and nothing more. She had no desire to progress any further in her career, and she certainly didn't want to go into management.

Year after year, she continued to be one of our best and most productive employees and never slacked off for a moment. She eventually agreed to share her expertise with others by training groups of new employees, and this also proved to be a success. She has now completed almost 40 years of service with the government and shows no signs of slowing down. Her approach to work is what it's all about—a professional giving it her best day after day.

The best and most successful employees never feel that they have "made it" or that the world owes them a living. They understand that they need to continue to produce, continue to improve, and continue to learn, because they owe that to their customers, the taxpayers, their organization, and themselves. They also recognize that as the world evolves, the bar is constantly being set higher and higher, and they want to be the drivers of change rather than simply going along for the ride.

I remember watching one of my employees, who was responsible for managing 3,000 foreclosed properties. In order to sell these properties, he did the same thing that his peers in other offices did: He placed large and very costly advertisements for these properties in the newspapers. Each week, he then had to use several employees to review the bids for these properties, award them to the winning bidders, and prepare all of the appropriate paperwork.

This employee felt that the process was expensive and inefficient and looked for a new approach. He decided to advertise the properties on the Internet and have prospective buyers submit their bids electronically; this enabled the computer system to review the bids and determine the winner, and freed up the employees who used to perform these tasks to do other work. His actions saved the office over a million dollars a year and resulted in a greater number of properties being sold more quickly and efficiently.

Other offices also adopted this approach, saving the government at least 10 times that amount. Moreover, this employee, who had already risen quickly in his career, but had chosen not to rest on his laurels, was recognized for his actions and was selected for a national Assistant Director Trainee Program and then for an SES Development Program.

Another employee, who was not in management, noticed that our office had not been collecting certain monies that were owed us by local and municipal governments. On his own, he contacted these governments and started quietly recouping this money. By the time he brought this to our attention, he had collected well over one hundred thousand dollars.

It turned out that other offices were not aware of this gap in our system, so we brought his findings to our central office, which exported this approach to the remaining offices and granted him a sizable award for his efforts. Here was another individual who chose not to sit back and coast, but rather found new ways to make the government more effective and efficient.

I also know of another employee who rose through the ranks by attaching himself to people in power. As his career progressed, he slowly began to feel that he was better than the people below him and acted accordingly. Over time, he became arrogant and developed several enemies.

Once he was promoted to a high-level job, he lost the protection of his latest "rabbi," and he was left to fend for himself. Suddenly, he noticed that people who used to bow down to him were no longer supportive and wouldn't give him the time of day. Moreover, the imperial style that he had adopted did not endear him to the new group of employees he was charged with leading. As time went by, this individual realized that his career had stalled because he had acted as though he was entitled to continual promotions.

Never Become Cynical

Throughout your career, you are going to see things that you don't like, that you think are unfair or find distasteful. Unfortunately, in a world populated by people, these things are going to happen, so you had better get used to it. That's not to say that you should not be angered by an injustice or try to right a wrong, because you should. What I am saying is that you can't fight every injustice or right every wrong; that is simply impossible. Moreover, it would simply be too exhausting to even try.

During my time with the government, I felt as though I had seen the whole kit and caboodle. I saw people sell drugs, sexually harass those who were not in a position to resist, steal millions of dollars, and threaten and, in some cases, even physically harm others. I saw people misuse their positions to hurt other people's careers and advance their cronies who were undeserving. I even saw people who I thought were my close friends turn on me when they thought it would make them look good.

On the other hand, I saw people go out of their way to help others, donate large sums of money to those who were less fortunate, comfort people who were suffering, and commit wonderful acts of kindness. I also saw people stand up to those individuals who misused their power and take steps to help others, even if it was to their own detriment. I even saw people whom I hardly knew try to help me during my time of need.

In short, I saw people act in many different ways, both positive and negative and everything in between, which in reality is the history of the world. The point here is that you have to take the bad along with the good, and you can't let the bad things that happen color your view of the world. If you do, you will become cynical, which will hurt you, your career, and your organization.

If the truth be told, early in my career, I became a bit cynical. I was young and impressionable, and I started hanging around with the wrong crowd. These folks kept pointing out things that management was doing wrong, and it made me angry. I began to adopt their point of view, i.e., that management was "out to get" the employees and that every action the managers took had bad intentions, even if I couldn't see how.

Fortunately for me, as I got to know some of the supervisors a bit better, I began to realize that management was not trying to hurt the employees. I saw that the managers were simply doing the best they could under what seemed to be pretty difficult circumstances. I eventually weaned myself away from this group, adjusted my attitude, and found a different group of people who were not cynical and were more interested in doing a good job than in whining and complaining all the time.

Sadly, I've met far too many people who were so cynical that it seemed to color every important decision that they made and ultimately hurt their careers; which of course only made them even more cynical. Let me tell you about one such individual. This person was one of the smartest and most technically capable individuals that I had ever met. He knew the job inside out, and he had a wide range of experience and a pretty broad point of view.

Early in his career, he became a high-level manager, but shortly thereafter he was removed from that position for reasons that to this day are unclear to me. He changed positions several times after that, sometimes becoming a first-line supervisor, and other times returning to technical positions. During the entire time that I knew him, he always came across as antimanagement, very rebellious, and definitely not a team player, although to be fair, he usually helped out on a technical level. He would openly challenge management at town hall meetings, and on occasion he tried to turn other employees against the organization. Deep down, I believe that he truly cared about the organization's mission, but he had become so patently cynical that he couldn't suppress his anger, and that clearly hurt him.

This individual desperately wanted to get back into senior management because he felt that he had the skills to make a good manager, which in fact he did. Many times, he was the best candidate, on paper, for the positions he applied for. However, his cynicism colored everything that he did, and he proved to be his own worst enemy. His reputation had been formed, and no one in the organization was willing to take a chance on moving him back into senior management. In short, his cynicism became a self-fulfilling prophecy.

Let me compare his career with that of another individual. This woman never wanted to go into management, as she viewed herself as the consummate staffer. She was the type who was more than willing to support other leaders but never believed that she had what it takes to be a true leader. She was an incredibly hard worker and a quick learner, she cared deeply for others, and she had an enthusiasm that could best be described as contagious. She was frequently asked to take on special projects, and she always did so with passion and accomplished the tasks assigned to her with both skill and grace.

Despite her protests, on several occasions, she was asked to apply for management positions with increased responsibility, which she reluctantly did. Each time, she was selected for the position, and she rose to become a senior executive before she reached the age of 40.

She wound up managing one of the toughest offices in the country, and for many years, she received little support, other than lip service, from her headquarters. Despite this, she continued to work hard, never lost her enthusiasm, rarely complained to anyone, and simply concentrated on those issues that were within her sphere of influence. She maintained that it was more important to focus on serving her customers and taking care of her employees than to moan and groan about things that were beyond her control.

Meanwhile, other people watched how she comported herself, recognizing that she was working under circumstances that were quite challenging. Many turned to her for advice and assistance and saw her as a model of how to behave in a difficult situation. As of this writing, she continues to tirelessly work on behalf of her clients and her employees and is universally respected by her peers. Just like the individual I mentioned earlier in this section, her attitude became a self-fulfilling prophecy.

How to Complain

No matter how good an attitude we have, sometimes we need to complain. It may be because we want to right a wrong, it may be because our supervisor has been acting inappropriately, we may simply feel that we have to bring something to our supervisor's attention, or we may just have to vent. We are all human, and in the course of our careers, there are times when we have to let management know that something is bothering us.

This is not to say that you should go to management and complain every time something seems to be wrong. That would be foolish, since you would quickly get a reputation for being a chronic complainer. In every aspect of life, you need to pick and choose your battles carefully, and this is no exception. The appropriate time to complain is when an issue arises that must be addressed and that no one except your supervisor can handle.

If you are not sure whether you should bring an issue to your supervisor's attention, run it by one of your mentors or someone else in your network. It is always good to get a dispassionate opinion from a third party before going to management to complain about something. However, once you have concluded that you need to bring an issue to management's attention, you are likely to find that management will appreciate hearing about it, as long as you raise the issue in a proper manner.

By this I mean that you should discuss the issue in a nonthreatening manner so that you are not embarrassing or accusing your supervisor in the process. Far too often, I have seen employees angrily accuse a management official of making an inappropriate decision or chastise an official in front of other employees. Once you do that and put a management official on the defensive, you are undermining that person in front of his subordinates. How do you think you would feel in that situation? Not too good, I suspect, which is exactly the way every management official feels when this happens.

While mature managers can brush off such criticisms and let them roll off their backs, many cannot. A large percentage of supervisors will resent being put in such a position and will look for payback at another time—in many cases, using a more subtle approach than the complaining employee did.

For example, I've seen supervisors lower employees' ratings because they believed that those employees were not good team players. The reality was that they had reached this conclusion at least in part because the employees had publicly embarrassed them.

Now, there is nothing wrong with complaining publicly to management in an open forum. After all, part of the intent of such a forum is to glean the perspective of the employees. The point is that when you complain publicly, *you should never embarrass the boss.* Simply state the issue that you are concerned about in a mature and nonthreatening manner, and you will be fine.

As an example, I recall an employee publicly telling her division chief that she was concerned about a decision that he had made. Specifically, she told him that she was unhappy that he was restricting overtime availability to only a few people, and that she wanted to work overtime. He replied that he would have liked to include more people, but since he had a very limited amount of money available, he had offered it only to the people who historically had been the most productive. He pledged that as additional funds became available, he would include more people. While she still did not like the decision, she did not attack him and gave him the opportunity to present his rationale. In this case, an appropriate and productive dialogue ensued, ensuring that everyone understood where everyone else was coming from.

Open forums are good opportunities to complain about issues that are of interest to a wide range of people. However, with issues that are of a more personal nature, the best way to approach such concerns is one-on-one, and always in an area where no one else is privy to your conversation. Under these circumstances, simply state your concerns as clearly and concisely as you can, and then give your supervisor the opportunity to respond. Never attack her or anyone else. In most cases, if you handle yourself as a mature professional, you will receive the same treatment in return.

If you are not satisfied, you then have two options: Either drop the issue or pursue it further. If you decide to escalate the issue, give your supervisor the courtesy of knowing that you plan to go over her head. While she may not like it, at least she will not be caught off guard. Pursue the complaint as professionally and unemotionally as you can; simply state the facts, indicate why you feel aggrieved, and identify the remedy you are seeking.

Of course, if you are a member of the bargaining unit, you always have the option of having the union represent you in pursuing your complaint. Some of the things you should consider in deciding whether to have the union represent you include the following: (1) Do you need the union to speak for you, or do you prefer to speak for yourself? (2) Do you have the technical skill and ability to represent yourself and to navigate through the system in the event that you have to escalate the issue? (3) Once the union is involved, an issue tends to take on a higher profile than if the employee pursues it by himself. Are you prepared for this? (4) If you feel that the issue will not be resolved by management at any level and you believe that it should eventually be decided by an arbitrator, recognize that this is unlikely to happen unless the union represents you throughout the process.

Having the union represent you is your right, if you so choose. It is a personal decision that has its pluses and minuses. Simply take the issues mentioned here into consideration before deciding what works best for you.

PART 3

PLOTTING
YOUR
CAREER

(THRIVING)

CHAPTER 6

Looking Down the Road

NOW THAT YOU HAVE ESTABLISHED yourself with the government and hopefully built a good reputation for yourself in the process, it is time to start plotting your career in more earnest. While you need to stay in the present with respect to your current job, you should also begin looking down the road. It's been my experience that people who plan for success tend to achieve more than people who simply go with the flow. After all, if you don't know where you are going, you will never get there.

Where Do I Want to Be in Five Years? Ten Years? Twenty Years?

In looking down the road, you need to develop some sense of where you want to wind up. By this I mean that you should think about where you want to be in your career in the long term, the midterm, and the short term. You may decide that by the time you are 50, you want to be a senior executive, so by the time you are 40, you might want to be a division manager; and by the time you are 30, a supervisor. Or, you may decide that by the time you are 50, you want to be a well-respected trainer, so by 40, you might aspire to be a lead journeyman, and by the time you are 30, you would want to be an accomplished technician. Where you want to be is up to you. That is your choice and yours alone. The question is, once you decide where you want to be, how do you get there?

Before analyzing this question in more detail, notice that I started with the end state in mind (assuming that you plan to reach the zenith of your career by age 50), and then worked my way back to earlier states. That is because for planning purposes, it is much easier to envision an end state and then work your way backward than it is to do things the opposite way. Life rarely moves in a linear direction, so it is very hard to plan that way. To me, it makes much more sense to figure out where you want to be at the end of your career and then use rough guideposts along the way to see if you are on course.

This is not to say that you can't alter your course in midstream, or even change your ultimate destination at any time. Obviously you can; you are the one making the plans, so you are the one who can alter them.

I changed my plans on several occasions. Initially, I expected to work for the government only until I got a job in the fine arts. As I got a little older and realized that I was not going to be another Michelangelo, I decided to stay with the government, but to go to law school at night and become an attorney. However, once I learned that my wife was pregnant with our second child, I abandoned those plans and decided to pursue my government career. Up to that point, we had not been mobile, but as our family expanded and I set my sights higher, we agreed to move if it would enhance my career. So, as you can see, I changed my long-term plans several times, but each time I did so, I tried to adjust my other career benchmarks accordingly. In this way, I would always have a road map to guide me down my chosen career path.

Once you have that road map in your mind, you can refer to it periodically and determine if you are on the right path. For example, one of my goals was to get to the GS-13 level by the time I was 30. I felt I was right on target when I reached the GS-12 level at age 27, as the chief of employee and labor relations for the Bronx VA Medical Center. I knew that I didn't want to move up too quickly, because I needed several years to hone my skills before taking the next step up. That's why spending three years in this position before making my next move seemed like a good strategy.

I took this job knowing that it was located in one of the toughest areas of the country. I also took it knowing that my commute would be approximately two hours each way, going through some pretty rough areas. I did this because I was young, energetic, and highly motivated, and because I figured that this was an ideal spot to learn in. I also thought that it would serve as a springboard for the rest of my career. In retrospect, I was right.

This proved to be one of the best training experiences I ever had, since I faced incredibly complex and difficult situations (drug busts, thefts, alcohol and drug abuse, complex EEO cases, and so on) in which I had to both advise and later represent senior management. After three years in this position, I felt as though I had gained ten years' worth of experience.

I concluded that I now had the requisite skills to move up, but I realized that there were few opportunities to advance in that organization. In fact, for all intents and purposes, the only way that I was going to advance was if my immediate boss left, and this was not going to happen in the foreseeable future. Moreover, even if he did leave, there was no guarantee that I would get his job. Accordingly, I decided to look elsewhere, and I was eventually selected to be a personnel officer, at the GS-13 level, in another organization.

I did this because (1) I concluded that you should not sit in a job waiting for someone to leave, since that person may not leave, and even if she does, you never know who will be selected to replace her (unless you are perfectly content to remain in your current job), and (2) it was time for me to move on because I was ready, I did not want to stagnate, and I wanted a more responsible job that would position me for future promotional opportunities.

However, as I was trying to strike a balance between moving up and increasing my knowledge and experience base, I watched other people take the exact opposite approach. I recall one individual who spent years waiting for his boss to leave. All of a sudden, his plans were thrown out of kilter because I was hired to work alongside him. He deeply resented me because I was the new kid on the block, and because I was obviously bright and highly motivated. He was concerned that I was going to take the job that he had worked so hard to get, so he did everything he could to block my path.

I could see where he was coming from, but I chose not to compete openly with him; instead I focused on learning the job that was in front of me. I actually thought it was sad that his whole life seemed to be so focused on getting his boss's job. From my perspective, he was a short-sighted thinker, since even if he got that job, he really had nowhere else to go. He had spent so much of his career learning this one area of human resources management (HRM) that he had neglected to learn anything else, so he was basically pigeonholed. By the time I left the organization for a promotion to a different branch of HRM, he was still patiently waiting for his boss to leave, but happy with the knowledge that his chief competition was gone.

That type of approach was okay for him, I guess, but it would not have worked for me. I was simply more ambitious and had set my sights on a higher goal. I did not see my next job as the end of the rainbow; he did. I saw it as a stepping-stone on a larger career path; he did not.

Once I decided that management was in my long-term plans and that I wanted to become a senior executive, I realized that I would have to become mobile. I sat down with my family, and we all agreed that when the right opportunity came along, we would move. Fortunately, I did not move until I became a senior executive, since I was promoted to both the GS-14 and GS-15 levels in my same local organization.[1] However, this is more the exception than the rule.

Conversely, I have seen plenty of great people decide not to go into management and stay in one place, which is fine. Management is clearly not for everybody. You can have a terrific career and make a big difference without ever supervising another person. In fact, one of the biggest mistakes I've seen people make is to go into management when their hearts were really not set on it. In the end, they became miserable because they were not doing something that they were passionate about, and they wound up returning to their original positions, sadder but wiser individuals.

The key is to figure out what is right for you and then plan your career accordingly. Your personal situation will undoubtedly play a role in all of this (e.g., your spouse's perspective, whether you want to pull your children out of school in order to move, and other such considerations). As long as you keep the big picture in mind and make occasional adjustments, you will do just fine.

Do Not Focus Exclusively on One Career Path

Flexibility is an important component of any career. If you start with the government, find that you are in the perfect career field, and have no desire to explore any other path, congratulations; you are a lucky person. However, for most people, being exposed to a variety of career paths makes more sense. For one thing, how will you know that you are in the right career field if you have not tried anything else? In addition, if you simply proceed along one path, you may severely limit your options down the road, both during your government career and after you leave government. Finally, if you later decide to go into management, the more exposure you have to other career fields, the better able you will be to manage a broad-based operation. Let's look at these issues in a bit more detail.

Finding the Right Path

I was lucky that HRM was a great fit for me. I loved the work, and it offered multiple career paths, since each discipline within HRM was a mini-career path. I didn't particularly like some of these mini-paths, such as staffing, processing, and position classification, but I knew that I would have to learn enough about them to be able to do an effective job in my areas of interest: employee relations, labor relations, and EEO. Once I grew more proficient in these areas, I realized that I needed to know more about the internal clients I was representing: doctors, nurses, financial managers, medical records technicians, and others, and later about a new group of clients: claims adjudicators, loan processors, and vocational rehabilitation specialists. The point here is that no job exists in a vacuum, and the more you know about other fields, the better you will be able to do your job.

As I learned about these other fields, I found that some of them were quite interesting; on occasion, I even considered changing fields. Fortunately for me, Tom Lastowka, who later became one of my mentors, decided to expose me to other career fields. Tom placed management analysis, the budget, and our automated data processing under my jurisdiction, giving me the opportunity to learn areas that I would not have expected to know. It also gave me the chance to move out of HRM if I so desired and to go down a number of other potential career paths. This proved to be a marvelous opportunity, as it served as a springboard for me to later become an assistant director of a VA regional office.

Many other successful people have taken similar approaches. Some have moved between different government agencies in order to find the field and mission that was right for them. Others have switched from a field environment to an area or headquarters operation so that they could be exposed to a broader base of activities and potential career tracks. Still others have eagerly sought out details to different positions so that they could see whether the grass was truly greener on the other side. The one thing that is common to all of these approaches is a willingness to try something new, with the understanding that knowledge is power and that the more you know about the pluses and minuses of different career fields, the better position you will be in to make the best choice for you.

For example, on many occasions, I have seen employees switch jobs in the expectation that they will increase their perspective, learn new skills, have more career options, and be able to move up more quickly, and this is what usually happens. However, other people discover that they were actually happier working in their original positions and wind up returning to them.

From my perspective, both groups actually win from this experience: The first group uses it as a springboard to success, and the second group learns that sometimes there is no place like home. Either way, you learn from different experiences, which is why you should periodically seek them out.

Don't Limit Your Options

Conversely, I have seen many people stay in one field for too long, only to learn that it was not for them. In many cases, these folks chased after the quickest series of promotions they could get, instead of exposing themselves to different areas and finding the best possible career path for them. For example, I recall one woman who was always stressed out in her job. She was a very hard worker who did whatever it took to get the job done, but she always seemed to be unhappy. I found it a bit odd that she became a supervisor in that same field, since all this did was place even more pressure on her shoulders. Eventually, she decided that this was not for her, so she went to school at night and learned a different skill in a field that was much more to her liking.

I remember another individual who moved from job to job every six months or so. The good news was that he was exposed to many different areas; the bad news was that he spent so little time in each area that he never developed any real expertise. This is part of the challenge that you face in plotting your career. You want to learn one or more career fields so that you have the opportunity to move down several different paths if necessary. However, you don't want to bounce between jobs so frequently that you never have the chance to develop a specific skill set or demonstrate a strong and consistent work record.

To me, the ideal is to develop several skill sets, through carefully planned career moves, so that you don't have to be limited to one career path. If you don't do this, you can spend years waiting for one job or one of only a few jobs above you to become vacant, and then have to compete with many people, some of whom may already be in line for these positions ahead of you. Remember, the number of promotion opportunities above you becomes smaller and smaller as you move up the pyramid.

Trust me; it is not a lot of fun to wait for a position to become vacant, only to see it go to someone else. The better approach is to be able to follow any of several career paths, so that you have far more opportunities and flexibility, and are not stuck waiting for a narrow group of promotions to become available. Of course, another way to create additional opportunities is to move, but we'll discuss this issue in greater detail later on in the book.

Going Into Management/Getting Exposure to Multiple Fields

As you move up the ladder, the competition increases, the pressure for instant results grows, and your opportunity to learn new skills often diminishes. This is particularly true if you decide to go into management. If your goal is simply to become a first-line supervisor and manage the people who do the job you are technically proficient at, that should not be a significant problem. However, if you aspire to higher levels of management, you will find that the more broad-based your knowledge of various business areas is, the more effective you will be.

That certainly proved to be a challenge for me. As I mentioned earlier, I was an expert in HRM and pretty knowledgeable in many other administrative areas. Moreover, I knew the internal systems extremely well (metrics, productivity and effectiveness, budget, and so on), so by the time I went into senior management, I had a strong base of knowledge. However, once I became responsible for managing a large activity that administered a full program of benefits, my lack of expertise in certain areas hurt me. Certainly, I had division chiefs under me who were experts in their particular fields. Unfortunately, however, their overall skill sets varied, and if I had a particularly weak division chief under me, our operation sometimes struggled. In retrospect, if I had had more exposure to and understanding of these business lines, I would have been a more effective leader. That is not to say that you have to be a technical expert in all areas of the activities that you manage; you most certainly do not. What I am saying is that as you move up in the government, the greater your exposure to a wide variety of areas and business lines, the better the position you will be in to manage these activities successfully.

Conversely, I have seen technical experts struggle when they become leaders because they did not have the background that I had in HRM and various other administrative areas. It's especially tough to manage people when you don't have much expertise in HRM, don't understand how a budget is developed and implemented, and don't comprehend how the management systems relate.

It's also tough to manage multiple lines of business when you've spent your entire career in only one business line. I've seen plenty of folks move up in their careers and try to tackle this challenge, and it is not an easy thing to do. It's especially difficult when you've focused on one area for decades and suddenly have to shift gears and learn multiple areas.

No one enters a senior management position knowing everything; that is impossible. However, if you choose to go into management, the better you understand the different lines of business and administrative support programs that are under your jurisdiction, the more effective you are going to be. That is why the choices you make at the beginning of your career are so crucial.

Headquarters or the Field?

If you have never worked in your organization's headquarters, at some point in your career, you should consider moving there. This is not an easy decision to make, because moving, especially if you have a family, is difficult. However, there are many advantages to working in your headquarters that you should at least weigh. First of all, in most organizations, your headquarters is the center of power. This is where key decisions are made regarding policy matters, personnel issues, and other such things. By being exposed to the decision-making process at that level, you will have a much better grasp of what really happens and why. Moreover, you will hopefully develop contacts and allies who will assist you in moving your career forward.

When I worked in my organization's headquarters, I finally began to understand the pressures that senior management was under. Prior to that, I had the same basic attitude that most people in the field had about the folks in Washington, D.C. We generally felt that many of them didn't know what they were doing and were constantly switching priorities, and therefore making our jobs much more difficult than they needed to be. However, when I worked down there and saw the pressures that the people there were under, a different picture emerged.

I was amazed at how fast and furiously events seemed to unfold. One moment, the secretary wanted to change directions, the next moment, a congressman was calling to complain about something. There were always media issues to deal with, as well as demands from the Office of Management and Budget (OMB), the Congressional Budget Office (CBO), and various stakeholders. Throw in congressional hearings, Office of the Inspector General investigations, budget requests, intergovernmental committees, legislative issues, and a wide variety of field concerns, and you begin to have some idea of the pressure these people are under.

During my stay in Washington, D.C., I participated in countless meetings, briefed staffers from a variety of groups, worked with multiple elements from our headquarters and other departments, assisted the field on numerous occasions, handled a variety of complex personnel issues, wrote multiple policy statements, and conducted many training sessions. I also attended a variety of training sessions, conferences, and other business affairs. All told, my experience at the headquarters level almost seemed like a blur, although it was a great learning experience. I learned how and why things were done at the national level, and I developed a much greater appreciation for the forces that were at play. I also expanded my network, which is always a good thing to do.

Had I not already been a senior executive, I am confident that my time at headquarters would have led to increased promotion opportunities. That having been said, I turned down some very attractive offers to stay in Washington because I felt that the appropriate place for me at that time was with my family in Los Angeles.

Most people I have known who moved to our headquarters did so because (1) they wanted the experience, knowing that it would give them unprecedented insight into the way that government works, (2) they knew that working at headquarters would expose them to the people in power, and (3) they knew that they would meet a wide variety of people who could assist them later in their careers. In many cases, people moved there with the expectation that they would spend a few years learning the ropes, make their mark, get the promotion(s) they were looking for, and then move back to the field, hopefully to an area with a lower cost of living. From what I could see, most people who took this approach found it to be rewarding. In fact, on several occasions, I saw people who had been stagnating in the field move to headquarters and quickly receive several promotions, simply because there are far more opportunities at headquarters.

That having been said, some folks quickly learned that headquarters was not for them. For one thing, they found that in some jobs, the pace of work was quite intense[2] and required them to work long hours, something that they were not prepared for. Within a relatively short period of time, several of these individuals decided to return to their home offices, sadder but wiser employees. From my perspective, that was still a success because they had learned a lot and had come to appreciate the jobs that they had originally left.

A downside of working at headquarters is that you feel that you are removed from your customers. Whereas you often interact with your customers on a daily basis when you are in the field, you rarely have that opportunity in a headquarters environment. That is because you are so involved in developing and implementing policy, monitoring the field, and working with other parts of government and your stakeholders that you simply do not have time to interact with the people that you are being paid to serve. That can be very frustrating to people who want to see the direct and immediate impact of their actions.

On the other hand, people who work at headquarters have a greater opportunity to make a difference on a broader scale than people who work in the field. That is because the best way to improve performance in government is by working with Congress to pass a law or by changing an overarching policy; either of which can have a significant impact on our country. For example, the GI Bill is widely considered to be one of the most important pieces of legislation of the twentieth century. According to the noted historian Steven Ambrose,

> [The] GI Bill was the best piece of legislation ever passed by the U.S. Congress, and it made modern America. The educational establishment boomed and then boomed and then boomed. The suburbs, starting with Levittown and others, were paid by GIs borrowing on their GI Bill at a very low interest rate. Thousands and thousands of small businesses were started in this country and are still there thanks to the loans from the GI Bill. It transformed our country.[3]

It should be understood that the people at headquarters often don't feel that they are making much of a difference because their work has to go through so many different hands, takes so much time to be vetted, and gets changed so often. Often, they conclude that they are merely pawns in a bigger game, which is true to some extent. However, even though it may be years before their work comes to fruition, collectively the people at headquarters are usually the true movers and shakers.

By contrast, the people in the field merely implement laws and/or policy, and their impact is generally limited to their area of jurisdiction. That having been said, if they develop an approach that is creative, it could eventually be adopted by headquarters and be exported to the entire nation, state, or locality, as appropriate. For example, I recall when one of our offices implemented a novel program in which it trained its stakeholders to gather and submit evidence in support of claims for benefits. This resulted in the office no longer having to go out and request the evidence in many cases because it was submitted along with the claim, thereby reducing overall processing time. This program proved to be so successful that it was eventually exported to every office in the nation.

The point here is that there are pluses and minuses associated with both working at headquarters and working in the field. If you are perfectly satisfied with your current job and you have no major career aspirations beyond that, a tour at headquarters may not be for you. However, if you want to broaden your horizons and increase your chances for promotion, an assignment at your headquarters may be good for you.

Staff or Line?

Another thing to consider is whether you want to work in a staff or a line capacity. People in staff jobs support line managers. These jobs include management analysts, budget technicians, administrative officers, information technology experts, and HRM specialists. Line positions are connected with specific lines of business and provide more direct service to the public. Line positions include tax examiners, claims processors, physicians, police officers, and librarians.

There are pluses and minuses for each type of work, so let's examine them in a little more detail.

Staff Positions

I spent the first half of my career in a staff capacity. As an HRM official, my job was to provide advice and assistance to line managers. I really enjoyed this type of work because I had the opportunity to help the people who were in the trenches, doing the difficult day-to-day work that was required to serve our customers. It gave me insight into the pressures they were dealing with, and I grew to appreciate just how difficult their challenges were. My counterparts in finance, administrative services, the director's office, and other such areas seemed to have similar experiences.

From my perspective, we had the advantage of being involved in the action, but from the outside looking in, without all of the daily perform-ance pressures that the business lines had. Sure, we had our performance standards to meet, but they tended to be more general and less driven by numbers. Moreover, we didn't have anyone breathing down our necks, constantly reviewing our performance the way the business lines did. This is because support activities and positions do not focus on achieving an organization's direct mission; they exist to support the people charged with accomplishing the mission. As a result, they tend to receive far less scrutiny and operate under a lot less pressure.

On the other hand, because on most occasions they do not serve the public, workers in support activities generally do not have the same sense of accomplishment as those in line activities. They have to take their satisfaction from serving the line functions and knowing that their efforts contributed to whatever success these activities achieved.

Another thing to consider about support activities is that they are more vulnerable than line activities. Since they are considered to be "non-value-added" functions, meaning that they do not directly add value to the product or service being produced, efficiency experts invariably look to pare these functions down when money is tight. Over the past few years, we have seen multiple consolidations of HRM and other support functions, as administrations try to demonstrate that they have reduced the size of government. Furthermore, improvements in information tech-nology have automated many finance positions and reduced the need for clerical support, resulting in a slow but steady erosion of staff support positions.

Finally, because staff positions are secondary to a government organi-zation's mission, there is a smaller number of these positions as compared to line jobs. This means that from a long-term career perspective, there are fewer opportunities for staff people to progress within the same agency than there are for people serving in a line capacity. Conversely, line positions tend to be more specific to an agency's mission, whereas every organization needs staff positions. As a result, people in common staff positions often find it easier to move between agencies than people who are in line positions. For example, in my case, I worked as an HRM specialist for the Department of Defense, the General Services Administration, the Federal Energy Administration, and the Department of Veterans Affairs, because all of these organizations needed HRM support, and they all operated under the same basic personnel laws and procedures.

Line Positions

Line positions offer people the opportunity to serve the public directly. Customer contact specialists, nurses, claims processors, teachers, environmental technicians, and people in other such positions can all make an immediate difference and see the fruits of their labors. People who go into line work develop valuable skills that provide them with a profession and generally have multiple opportunities to grow within their organization. These are the folks who are the nuts and bolts of any government entity, the ones who get the job done.

To put this into perspective, a rating specialist working for a VA benefits office determines to what degree, if any, a veteran should be compensated for injuries or illnesses incurred as a result of military service. A typical rating specialist can grant benefits totaling roughly $750,000,000[4] during her 30-year career with the VA, meaning that she will have an enormous impact both on the lives of veterans and on the economy.

With the current push for accountability throughout both government and the private sector, people occupying line positions are finding themselves under more scrutiny than ever before. Stringent performance standards have been put in place for many, if not most, line positions in government, placing people who hold these jobs under more pressure than ever. However, I have not seen the same emphasis placed on developing performance standards for staff positions. The emphasis simply hasn't been there because the focus has been on the line activities.

Once I went into a line capacity, I certainly felt more pressure to perform. When I was in a staff capacity, I was evaluated primarily on my ability to give advice, which is a pretty vague and nebulous way of measuring someone's performance. However, once I became responsible for achieving bottom-line, measurable targets, the sense of urgency definitely increased.

The good news is that these jobs are generally more secure than staff positions. Since they are the bread and butter of any organization, line positions are the last positions to be eliminated as a result of budget cuts. Moreover, while you never know when a consolidation may take place, history indicates that line activities are less likely to be consolidated than staff activities, because they add value and are more politically sensitive.

So What Should I Do?

In my view, you should go into the activity that best suits your individual interests. If you are the analytical type, a staff position may be more up your alley. On the other hand, if you like working with the public, a line position may be right for you. My advice would be to try both areas if you can. I say this because the more exposure you get to different functions and activities, the more well-rounded an employee you will become. In addition, the more insight you gain into different areas of government, the better position you will be in to make the right career choice for yourself.

What About More Education?

This question primarily applies to people who have entered the government but wonder if they need more education in order to compete for future positions. From my perspective, there are two ways to look at this issue. The first way is: Will I need more education? The second way is: Do I want more education? Let's look at both questions.

Assume that you already have a good job with the government that has decent long-term potential, but you have only a high school diploma or less than four years of college. In my experience, the lack of a four-year degree will make you less competitive with others when you are first trying to get into the government, primarily because at that point, you are an unknown quantity. These days, government recruiters who are trying to hire people for administrative and technical positions that have promotion potential often target recent college graduates, particularly those graduates who have a grade-point average of 3.5 or better.[5] As a result, this is where having a lot of education helps you the most.

Once you get into the system, having one or more degrees will not help you as much, because selections for promotions are generally based on the person's work history and reputation. That's not to say that your education won't help you if you are competing with another employee who has an equal history and reputation; it may. However, once you become a known quantity, it will not help you as much as when you are unknown and are being evaluated in large part based on what you look like on paper.

During my career, I have seen people without any college rise to the level of senior executive. I have also seen people with a Harvard or similar degree stagnate pretty quickly once management got to know them and concluded that while they might have had a great education, they left much to be desired as employees. The point here is that education will get you only so far in your career; what will make or break you are your performance and your attitude.

That having been said, having a strong education can still help you in several ways. First of all, if you apply for a career field different from the one that you are currently in, your education may qualify you for this new field in a way that your experience does not. For example, people who are not college graduates often qualify for trainee positions if they have three years of general experience in a related field. They then develop the qualifications to move up because of the experience they get on the job. However, if they later want to take a lateral assignment in a different field, they will often be disqualified from consideration because they do not meet the minimum qualifications for the position.

On the other hand, an employee who possesses more education, especially a master's degree, may be able to qualify for the new career field because of his education, since an advanced degree often qualifies you for a GS-7 or GS-9 in the federal government.

Another way in which your education will help you within the government is if you apply to a different organization where you are unknown. Under these circumstances, your education will be a plus in much the same way that it was when you first applied for a job with the government. It may attract more interest to you than to another employee without your education, which could prove to be the difference between your getting the job and not even getting interviewed.

Finally, having a strong education can help you in the rating and ranking process. When you apply for positions for which there are multiple candidates, HRM officials have to rate and rank applicants in order to determine who the best-qualified individuals are. In many cases, people with better education will be ranked higher, and this could make the difference between being considered for a job and not making the final cut.

The more important question is, do you want more education? I do not recommend going back to school and investing your time, energy, and money in getting another degree unless this is something that you really want to do. It is simply too expensive and exhausting if your heart is really not in it. However, if you want to go back to school because it will make you a better, well-rounded individual and will also make you more competitive, then by all means do so. Having more education is always a good thing, and I encourage you to do that, if that is what you truly want to do.

I have seen many people go back to school for the right reasons and greatly improve their skills, their sense of self-worth and ultimately their careers. It is always gratifying and inspiring to see someone take this approach. For example, one of my former secretaries was always uncomfortable with the fact that she did not have a college degree, primarily because she wanted to be more educated and secondarily because she wanted to get ahead more quickly. Despite raising two children while working full-time, she went back to school at night, got her degree, and today is a high-level official with the government.

I recall another woman who also was uncomfortable with her education level. She was a highly motivated and successful employee, but she knew that her writing skills were holding her back. She went back to school and took several writing courses, and this improved her self-esteem. By the time she retired from the government, she was a division chief overseeing the work of many people.

Midway through my career, I considered making a significant change. While I already had a master's degree in fine arts, I decided that I wanted to be an attorney. I made this decision based on my experience representing the government before third parties, which I enjoyed immensely. I applied to law school, was accepted, and began reading several books in preparation for attending classes at night. However, as I started delving into this field, I began to get less excited about it, and I concluded that law was a bit too dry for me (it didn't help that my wife became pregnant with our second child at this time). As a result, I dropped out of law school before I ever really got started. In retrospect, this proved to be one of the best career decisions I ever made. My heart really wasn't in it, so I decided to put my energies into areas that I was more passionate about.

Ultimately, only you can determine whether going back to school makes sense for you. Carefully consider the factors that I have raised in this section, and then make a decision that will be in your best interests.

Switching Between the Public and Private Sectors

When I started working for the government in 1974, it was very unusual for someone to switch back and forth between the public and private sectors. Sure, I was looking to leave the government almost from the moment I started, but that was because I initially saw the government as a short-term employer. My thinking at the time was that I had no intention of staying with the government because my long-term goal was to become an artist. Once I decided that I was going to make the government my career, I never seriously thought of leaving the government until after I retired.

The driving force behind that decision was the federal government's retirement system at the time, known as the civil service retirement system (CSRS). The CSRS was an extremely attractive system that paid your retirement based on two primary factors: (1) your length of service with the federal government and (2) your high three, i.e., the highest average salary that you earned over a three-year period. Basically, you multiplied your high three times a factor (1.50 percent times your high three for the first five years of service, 1.75 percent times your high three for the next five years of service, and 2.00 percent times your high three for your remaining number of years of service). Thus, if your high three was $100,000 and you worked for 30 years, your retirement would be calculated as follows: $100,000 \times 0.015 = \$1,500 \times 5 = \$7,500; \$100,000 \times$

0.0175 = \$1,750 × 5 = \$8,750; \$100,000 × 0.02 = \$2,000 × 20 = \$40,000; \$7,500 + \$8,750 + \$40,000 = \$56,250.

Under this system, social security was not deducted from your paycheck, so you generally were not eligible to receive its benefits. As a result, there was little incentive to ever leave the federal government. You were able to retire at the following ages based on your length of service: age 55 with 30 years of service, age 60 with 20 years, and age 62 with 5 years of service.

As described earlier, that changed in 1983 with the introduction of the Federal Employees' Retirement System (FERS), which pays benefits based on a three-tiered system: (1) a government annuity, (2) social security, and (3) a thrift savings plan (TSP). This system was intended to be less costly to the government and to ensure that employees were not locked into working for the government because of the retirement program. Since two-thirds of the system is completely portable, meaning that your social security benefits and your TSP stay with you wherever you go, employees of the federal government working under FERS are in a much better position to transfer between the public and private sectors than their counterparts under CSRS.

There is no one system that covers employees at the state and local levels, since each state and local government has its own individual system. However, it is fair to say that in general, these systems are all pretty competitive and tend to look something like either CSRS or FERS. If you are working at either the state or the local level, the key is to determine whether your system looks more like FERS or more like CSRS. If your system is portable, i.e., more like FERS, then there is no reason why you should not at least consider switching to the private sector (or to a different level of government) if the opportunity presents itself.

By this I mean that if you can make more money, go into a job that stretches you beyond your comfort zone, or go into one that provides you with new and exciting challenges, why not at least consider these opportunities? You only live once, so try to make your business career as lucrative and/or interesting as possible.

Obviously, job security is always a consideration, so you want to at least factor that into the equation. Other things that you should also think about include how easy it would be for you to return to the government if you decided that the private sector was not for you. Also find out if your pay and benefits would be affected if you returned to the government. Let's look at these questions in a bit more detail.

Former employees of the federal government who served under a permanent appointment for three years or longer have lifetime reinstatement rights, meaning that they can be appointed to another federal job without going through the normal civil service procedures. This makes it a lot easier for such employees to move back and forth between the public and private sectors. For state and local civil service employees, the rules vary, and you need to become familiar with how they affect your particular situation. The point here is that in many cases, particularly at the federal level, it is not overly difficult to move back and forth, as long as someone is willing to hire you.

Concerning the pay and benefits, the big consideration is how your employer will set your pay if you leave the government and then return. In other words, let's assume that you leave the federal government while serving as a GS-12, step 6, earning \$67,329,[6] and then later you decide to return to the same position. There is no guarantee that you will be appointed at the same step. You may be appointed at that step; at a step 1, which would pay \$57,709; or at a step somewhere in between. That is a decision that is typically made at the local level, may be negotiable, and is usually based upon the pay policies of your particular organization. The same thing may hold true if you return to a job at the state or local level.

Regarding benefits, if you return to a job with the government, you can expect to have the same benefits as any other government employee, i.e., retirement, health insurance, life insurance, and so on. However, there are some nuances here that you may not be aware of. For example, if you leave the federal government and then return near the end of your career, you will find that you can't carry your health insurance benefits into retirement unless you meet the following criteria:

> **You must have been continuously covered by the Federal Employees Health Benefits Program, TRICARE, or the Civilian Health and Medical Program for Uniformed Services (CHAMPUS):**

- for five years immediately before retiring; or,

- during all of your federal employment since your first opportunity to enroll; or

- continuously for full periods of service beginning with the enrollment that started before January 1, 1965, and ending with the date on which you become an annuitant, whichever is shortest.[7]

Obviously, you want to make sure that you are aware of your rights and that you make decisions that are to your best advantage.

As another example, if you leave the government and then return, you will probably have to start from scratch with respect to your vacation time, and you may or may not lose the sick time you had previously earned, depending on the particular organization's policies. That is why it is important that you at least ask these questions when making important career decisions.

During my career, I have seen many people leave the government for the private sector or other branches of government. Some of them took more lucrative jobs, while others went into an area that was a better fit for them. Most of them did not return, at least to the same office, but a few did. I kept in touch with several people who did leave, and most of them did not regret their choice, since they had weighed their options carefully before making a move. That is the best advice I can give in this area. Be aware of the pluses and minuses of what you are considering, understand what your rights and benefits are should you wish to return, and then make a decision that is best for you and your family.

Find Your Niche: Learn How to Think Creatively and Competitively

Early in my government career, one of my greatest challenges was finding a way to express myself. I enjoyed the work, but I felt that I was a bit pigeonholed, since I was still at heart a creative artist. Slowly, I found avenues through which I could express that side of myself. Whenever somebody left the organization and we were looking to give that person a gift, I drew a sketch of that individual. It was always well received because I am a talented artist, no one else was able to do that, and it was highly personal in nature. My supervisors took note of this, and on several occasions they asked me to produce a work of art in support of the mission. For me, this proved to be very rewarding, as I found both an outlet for and recognition of my talents.

As time went by, I found other ways to express myself. I started developing videos highlighting the successes of my organization. I even developed a series of humorous videos depicting management meetings in which I did impressions of various members of senior management. All of these endeavors proved to be big hits, as people appreciated my insights and humor and recognized my talents.

Eventually, I found my voice in a concept that I referred to as visual management. I became the director of a VA benefits office that had the lowest customer satisfaction level in the nation. Even worse, our rate of granting benefits was 50 percent lower than the national average. Shocked and a bit desperate, I decided to redesign the interior of our office, since it was shoddy and run-down, and in no way reflected the grandeur of our mission. I thought this might at least support the cultural changes that I knew were desperately needed. Thus, visual management was born.

I started by putting up some pictures that portrayed the contributions and experiences of veterans. These photographs were so well received that one organization donated $33,000 to us to further this approach. I began to realize the power of visual displays in a work environment, so I doubled our efforts by transforming each lobby area into a history of America's wars. We later converted areas that had once housed public telephone booths into private reflection areas (a bunker, a field hospital, a Vietnam Veterans' Memorial, and so on), added television monitors that displayed performance and rewards information, built a series of war rooms, added patriotic music to every floor, and introduced many other unique and inspiring touches. As time went by, our customer satisfaction rate increased by 37 percent and our rate of granting benefits increased by 50 percent.

In recognition of this unique approach, our office received the OPM director's prestigious PILLAR (Performance Incentives Leadership

Linked to Achieving Results) Award, made the cover of several business magazines, and attracted dozens of visitors from both the public and private sectors. More information about this approach can be found in the book *Seeing Is Believing: How the New Art of Visual Management Can Boost Performance Throughout Your Organization,* by Stewart Liff and Pamela A. Posey (AMACOM, October 2004).

Developing visual management was perhaps the highlight of my career, because this concept was a perfect fit for my talents and passions, and it made a major difference in the lives of my heroes, America's veterans. Interestingly, while I was in the middle of perfecting visual management, I was asked to move to Washington, D.C., in order to manage the eastern part of our organization. This was a wonderful opportunity for me because it would give me the chance to work with dedicated, savvy, and inspirational leaders and to make an imprint on a larger scale. However, while I was considering the offer, I noted that I had a persistent knot in my stomach, which troubled me greatly. I knew that part of it was due to my reluctance to move my family. However, I also knew that another part of it was due to my desire to see visual management through, meaning that I had started something special and I wanted to see it ripen.

While I was agonizing over my choice, I conferred with one of my mentors, Bill Snyder, who gave me the best piece of career advice that I ever received. Bill simply said, "Go with your passion." I immediately realized that he was right and promptly declined the position. Instantly, the knot in my stomach went away, and I have never regretted that decision.

I have seen many other people take similar approaches during their careers. Some were creative types like me, who found opportunities to use their writing ability, their photographic talents, or other such skills within the broad context of their job. That may have entailed writing a brochure, putting together a poster for the government, or something similar. Others had a passion for helping people and found jobs that allowed them to make a difference in the lives of others. Some of these people were homeless coordinators, others were customer contact representatives; some were doctors and nurses, while others were social workers. The point here is that all of these folks found themselves by tapping into their passions, which made all the difference, as they were doing something that they believed in instead of going through the motions and simply working in order to collect a paycheck.

Another good example is Tom Lastowka, whom I mentioned earlier in this book. Tom is one of the brightest and most accomplished people that I have ever met. He has worked for the federal government for roughly 40 years, has received virtually every award possible in government, and was still going strong as of the writing of this book.

Tom has been the director of the VA's Philadelphia Regional Office and Insurance Center (VAROIC) since 1991. In this capacity, he has again showed that he is an outstanding leader, as the VAROIC has been recognized for its outstanding performance and received the VA's prestigious Carey Award. In a recent conversation with Tom, I asked him why he hadn't yet retired, since, from my perspective, he had no more worlds left to conquer in the federal government. His reply was telling. He said, "Stew, I am making improvements in our insurance program, and I want to see it through." Clearly, Tom is continuing to follow his passion.

CHAPTER **7**

Management

Is Management for Me?

In Chapter 4, I described some of the pressures that a supervisor typically has to deal with. Let's look at this issue in more detail, from both the positive and the negative sides, so that you can decide whether management is right for you.

A Government Supervisor/Manager: The Positive Side

There are a number of reasons why people go into management. They include, but are not limited to, advancement, power, becoming part of the management team, and the ability to make a difference. Let's look at each of these reasons.

As far as advancement is concerned, there is no question that going into management will advance your career, as long as you do a good job. While I have seen a few isolated instances where a supervisor had the same pay grade as his subordinates, that is very unusual. Managers are typically paid at a higher rate than the people they supervise because it is more difficult to manage people than to carry out a discrete job. In addition, managers invariably have more responsibility than their subordinates because they are responsible for the work of the entire unit they supervise.

In my particular situation, I joined the federal government when I was 23 years old as a grade GS-5. In three years I rose to a GS-11; two years later, I became a GS-12 supervisor; and by the time I was 30, I had been promoted to a GS-13 division chief. While the climb became more difficult after that because the opportunities were fewer and more competitive, I became a GS-14 division chief at 33, a GS-15 assistant director at age 35, and a senior executive at age 42. Many of my peers took similar routes to the top.

Another reason why people go into management is that they want to have more power. Obviously, the more you move up into management, the more power you will have, at least as it relates to making personnel and policy decisions. This can be a very good thing if you are wielding power wisely, i.e., using it to make the world a better place.

To me, the best managers are very cautious about using their power because they know how easily power can be misused. These individuals know when to use their power and when to refrain from using it. They see their role as building capability into the organization and developing other people to eventually take over. They do not try to hoard power for power's sake; they try to share it when appropriate. They are great managers in part because they are humble, not power-hungry.

In contrast, some people find power to be intoxicating and constantly try to build their power base. The more power they have, the more alive they seem to feel, almost equating power with their sense of self-worth. For these individuals, power is an end in itself, not a means to an end. As a result, these are people to be feared, or at least ones to keep an eye on, because they will do anything they can to retain their power, since that is all they have. People are not important to these individuals; power is. The problem for them is that once their power is gone, they are left with nothing—no friends, no close relationships, nothing—because their entire hold over people is based on power. In essence, it becomes a case of what goes around, comes around.

I recall one individual who spent much of his career hoarding power. If you disagreed with him, you were automatically deemed to be disloyal. He was an expert at "kissing butt" and at organizational infighting, and this enabled him to gain an almost unprecedented amount of power within his organization. As his power increased, he exercised it widely, and he was willing and able to hurt people who, in his view, did not display absolute loyalty to him. Along the way, he destroyed many, if not most, of the personal and professional relationships that he had built earlier in his life. On his deathbed, I wonder if he will conclude that having the power that he so desperately sought for a relatively brief period of time was worth losing those relationships.

I would be careful about going into management if you are motivated by power, because power is an illusion. No one retains his power forever—not the president of the United States, not the queen of England, nobody. If you want to go into management in order to have power, make sure you are doing so for the right reasons. If you want to have power so that you can change the world, make a difference, right some wrongs, and so on, by all means do so. People who go into management for those reasons are the ones who do make a difference.

Other people go into management because they want to be part of the management team. In effect, they want to become charter members of an exclusive club: the small group of managers who guide the organization they work for. In my view, there is nothing wrong with this, as long as you want to join a team that you respect and whose direction you want to follow.

One of the best things about being part of management is that you are much more in the loop than members of the bargaining unit. You get to attend most of the key management meetings, so you know what is going on before everyone else does. You also receive more detailed explanations of why things are happening, since you are usually called upon to implement key decisions. In many cases, you even get the opportunity to influence these decisions before they are made. If you are a regular worker, you rarely have the chance to do this, unless perhaps you are a key union official.

Since you are part of a small, elite team, you are generally treated better than nonsupervisors. This is because you play such an important role in performance management, human resources management, and many other areas that matter to senior management. You are their "go-to" people, and most senior managers recognize you as such. Of course there is a price to be paid for this, since senior managers always expect results from their subordinate supervisors. When things are going as planned, everything is great. You tend to be treated very well, and you feel as though you are on top of the world. However, when things are not going well, you are the first person that your boss will ask for an explanation, and she will expect you to turn things around quite quickly. Trust me, when performance goes south, being a first-line supervisor is not a lot of fun.

Another advantage of being part of the management team is that all of the key players get to know you, which is a good thing as long as you are respected and doing well. After all, if you are doing a great job, but no one outside of your immediate work area knows this, it will limit your opportunities to advance. This is because to get ahead in the government, you need to do a good job *and be recognized as having done so by the people in power.* When advancement opportunities arise, you are much more likely to be selected if you are already a known quantity.

Certainly, few people are better known than first-line supervisors, since they are always in the spotlight. Management knows who you are; so do the employees, the union, and your stakeholders. If you want the chance to demonstrate what you can do and to let upper management really get to know you, being a supervisor is an excellent way to go.

For example, I remember one young man who applied for a first-line supervisory position and got it because virtually no one else wanted it, since it was such a difficult job. He was highly motivated and a quick learner, and he was able to turn things around, much to the surprise of almost everyone. In recognition of the fact that he took a highly visible and difficult supervisory job and succeeded, management quickly promoted him to a third-line assistant division chief position.

For my money, wanting to make a difference is the single best reason for going into management. Members of management simply have more opportunities to effect change than regular workers do. They are responsible for the output of an entire work unit or section, so by definition, they have greater reach than the average employee. They can set and change priorities, instantly adjust to unusual situations, deal with the unique needs of their clients, and set policy, all of which are intended to further their organization's accomplishment of its mission.

They also have the opportunity to improve the performance of their team by acquiring the necessary resources, offering excellent training, providing the employees with a high-quality work environment, and ensuring that there is a good communication flow. Moreover, the supervisor has access to all of the team's key performance metrics, so she can make adjustments as needed in order to achieve the group's goals. Naturally, the more goals that are achieved, the more the team will make a difference in the lives of its customers.[1]

I recall one woman who was responsible for gathering evidence related to claims that were filed. This team was struggling because it was disjointed and had not been managed well. She reorganized the team so that it functioned more efficiently, ensured that everyone was focused on the same priorities, and, through savvy analysis, identified key roadblocks in the process and addressed them. The net result of her actions was that the evidence was gathered more quickly and accurately, leading to faster decisions and more satisfied customers.

Another way in which a supervisor can truly make a difference is in the lives of his employees. If he treats them fairly and consistently, and makes a good faith effort to help them do their jobs, most employees will appreciate his efforts. Employees want to achieve their goals, and if they see that their supervisor is working side by side with them to do this, they will become energized and be grateful for his efforts. After all, if the team achieves its goals, virtually everyone wins in one or more ways (performance appraisal, rewards and recognition, future promotions, sense of accomplishment, and so on).

By the same token, if the supervisor comes across a struggling employee and skillfully and compassionately tries to assist her, he can truly make a difference in that employee's life. One of the most gratifying things you can do as a supervisor is to take an employee who is having a hard time on the job and help her turn things around so that she becomes a fully functioning member of the team.

I recall one employee who was quite unhappy with his job. He tended to look at everything through a negative prism. His supervisor sat him down, resolved the issues that he was constantly worried about, and assured him that as long as he did his job, he had nothing to worry about.

The supervisor also noticed that this employee was a square peg in a round hole, meaning that his talents were not a perfect fit for his current job. The supervisor slightly reengineered his job to leverage some of his talents that weren't being used, which both helped the organization and made the employee happier and more useful. In addition, because the supervisor had reduced his anxiety level, the employee was able to do a much better job of performing the core tasks of his position. In this case, the supervisor had truly made a difference in the life of one of her employees.

A Government Supervisor/Manager: The Negative Side

As I described earlier, there are several downsides to being a government supervisor. For example, there are constant demands for excellent performance; you are often hammered by people above you, below you, and on all sides; there are always personnel matters to address; and there are a million other issues as well that always seem to require your attention. Since I've discussed some of these challenges already, I do not wish to repeat them. However, I would like to flesh out a few key points that were not previously addressed and that you should be aware of.

Most importantly, being a supervisor is not for everybody, as you have to have a pretty thick skin in order to survive. The problems come at you fast and furiously and often require you to make midcourse corrections. You frequently find yourself in the middle of battles, sometimes with management, sometimes with the employees, and sometimes with the public. On occasion, you may feel as though you are fighting everyone at the same time.

I remember one individual who was desperate to go into management because he saw it as the path to the top. In his particular case, he was not technically strong in any one area, but he had a good personality and was highly motivated. Once he became a supervisor, he struggled with all of the competing demands on his time. However, instead of successfully prioritizing things, he tried to do everything at once and wound up doing nothing well. He constantly complained that he had not received enough training and that he felt as though he was being set up to fail.

As the pressure on him mounted, upper management stepped in and tried to help him improve, but he tended to take every piece of constructive criticism personally, and both his performance and his attitude suffered. He turned inward, had trouble sleeping, went into a bit of a shell, and waited for the inevitable to happen, which it did. He was assigned to a nonsupervisory position. While this individual felt embarrassed and ashamed because he had failed as a supervisor, he also felt relieved, since he no longer had to carry the burden of being responsible for the performance of his entire team.

A big mistake that is often made is to promote a highly skilled technician into management, even though she doesn't have the people, analytical, and/or leadership skills required for the job. Invariably, the employee fails miserably because both she and her subordinates quickly realize that management is simply not right for her. When this happens, everyone becomes frustrated: the supervisor, because she is floundering and doesn't know what to do to turn things around; upper management, because it is unhappy with her performance; and the employees, because they can sense that their supervisor is uncertain and is unable to provide strong direction to the team.

For example, I remember seeing a highly respected long-term employee finally get promoted into management. He had never really wanted to become a supervisor, but he reluctantly agreed to take that position at the urging of upper-level management. Once he became a supervisor, he was unable to distance himself from his former coworkers, and he often fraternized with the group. He engaged in a lot of day-to-day banter that, while it had gone unnoticed when he was just one of the guys, suddenly took on a different connotation now that he was in management.

For example, several off-the-cuff comments regarding some of the female employees quickly got him into trouble. Moreover, his tendency to publicly vent about several less competent employees, which had been endearing when he was a member of the bargaining unit, now tended to grate on the other employees. Many employees began complaining about this individual, who eventually left management and took a leave of absence because of stress.

I've also seen people go into management who on paper seemed to have all the tools necessary to make a great supervisor. However, until someone actually tries the job and sees what it entails, you never really know what will happen. I remember a female employee who wholeheartedly went into management. She was universally viewed as an excellent employee. She was smart, was very knowledgeable about the job, outworked everyone, and seemed to have excellent people skills. In short, she seemed to be the perfect choice to become a supervisor.

However, once she took the job, her stress level skyrocketed. She felt personally responsible for everything that was happening in her work unit, and each failure, however minor, seemed to frustrate her and make her more anxious. Moreover, she found herself constantly being pulled in different directions by all sorts of people, which frustrated her even more. You could literally see her blood pressure climbing as the weeks went by, and it soon became apparent that management was not for her. While she was absolutely superb at performing a technical job, the same things that made her such a strong employee (her drive, her desire to succeed, her work ethic, her ability to focus, and so on) proved to be her undoing, and she reluctantly went back to her old job, secure in the knowledge that this was the best situation for her.

Perhaps the biggest challenge for most supervisors is personnel issues. No one likes to deal with conflict, but that is a significant part of the job for most government supervisors. Employees are often the biggest challenge because they always seem to have issues. These issues may range from requests for leave, with multiple people wanting to take off during the same time period, to performance problems, to disciplinary issues. All of these situations are uncomfortable, yet a government supervisor has to deal with them directly in a strong, empathetic, and fair manner.

Over time, the constant strain of dealing with these situations, especially when you have to take an action that involves a person that you see day in and day out, can take an emotional toll on the strongest of supervisors. In fact, the skill with which a supervisor deals with personnel issues will often dictate how successful that supervisor will ultimately be. Those who learn to treat everyone fairly and directly, and who do not let these types of problems linger, will generally prove to be excellent supervisors and progress upward in their careers. On the other hand, those supervisors who are uncomfortable dealing with such issues will simply watch them fester and metastasize, and their inaction will eventually come back and bite them in the butt.

For example, I was mentoring a young female supervisor who had inherited some difficult and challenging employees. Their problems involved both performance and conduct, and they clearly were having an adverse impact on the unit she was supervising. She knew that she had to deal with these individuals, and she did not back away for a minute. At the same time, she also knew that she needed some sound and dispassionate advice so that she could deal with these employees successfully. Accordingly, she turned to me for advice, and I walked her through the process, carefully outlining her options and the strengths and weaknesses of each potential approach.

She then chose the approach that made the most sense for her and the team, and dealt with each employee. One of them she wound up removing; another eventually turned himself around and became a successful employee. People respected her for dealing with each personnel issue head on, and today she is a division chief who was recently selected to be an assistant director trainee.

Conversely, I recall a different supervisor who constantly swept personnel problems under the rug. This individual was a good person, but he was uncomfortable dealing with conflict, so his approach was to do nothing and hope that each personnel problem would eventually go away—either by the employee's leaving or by his being rotated to another team. This strategy paid off in a narrow sense, because other people wound up dealing with these problems, so the supervisor did not have to do so. On the other hand, his career stagnated, since he developed the reputation of being unwilling and unable to successfully deal with personnel issues.

The lesson from all of these stories is that being a government supervisor is a tough and sometimes thankless job. In order to succeed in this position, you need to develop the necessary skill sets and be willing to deal with difficult personnel issues. In my view, if you want to go into management and you think you are ready, you should definitely apply for a supervisory position. That having been said, many people have concluded that the extra few thousand dollars they would make by being a supervisor does not outweigh the additional pressures and challenges they would face in management. Obviously, only you can answer that question. However, if your ambition is to go into management, you should definitely try it and find out if it is a good fit for you.

Preparing to Go Into Management

The first step in getting into management is to position yourself properly. By this I mean establishing your reputation as an excellent and reliable employee and building a solid relationship with key members of management. Once you have done this, the next step is to prepare yourself for a management position. You can do this in several ways: by watching other members of management and learning from them (both their good points and their bad ones), by reading books and articles on supervision, by taking advantage of opportunities to act as a supervisor or lead employee, and by attending classes that help introduce you to supervision. Let's look at each strategy in a bit more detail.

Watch Others in Management

You can learn an enormous amount about management by simply watching supervisors and managers in action. Ask yourself who are the best supervisors in your organization, and then try to watch them and learn from them. What do they do that makes them such good supervisors? How do they interact with the employees? How do they carry themselves? What are their core values? How do they manage their time? How do they delegate work? How do they deal with difficult issues? How closely do their management styles mirror your own, and how are they different?

As you ask yourself these questions, also try to analyze the causes and effects of these supervisors' actions. Does the way they treat the employees result in commitment, or merely compliance? Does the way they assign and distribute the work ensure that it is under or out of control? Do people feel that they are being treated fairly, and if so, why? Do the supervisors facilitate the way in which work is accomplished, or do they inhibit it? Over time, if you watch things closely enough, you will begin to see patterns emerge that will make sense to you. You will see that management is not organized chaos, and that things happen for a reason. You will learn that good managers succeed because of what they do and how they operate. You will see that they all share certain practices, such as treating employees with respect and dignity, communicating with them constantly, ensuring that the team is organized, and operating within and properly applying the management systems.

I suggest that you periodically sit down with the supervisors that you admire and ask them about the way that they manage. If they truly are good supervisors, they will be more than happy to talk to you, since they will recognize that one of their obligations is to help train the next generation of supervisors.

Conversely, you can learn just as much by watching bad supervisors in action. From them you will learn what not to do, which is an important lesson in and of itself. Bad supervisors tend to act on whims, not facts. They treat people differently, based on whom they like and dislike, not on the systems. They are inconsistent in their behavior, so their subordinates frequently do not know where they are coming from. They are often pessimists, and on many occasions they bring the team down rather than pulling it up.

In much the same way that good supervisors succeed for a reason, bad supervisors fail for a reason. They fail because their behavior and their actions tear the team apart rather than making it more cohesive. They fail because team members don't know their roles, don't know what's going on, and have no one to turn to for advice and assistance. They fail because they are disorganized and try to blame others for their problems rather than looking in the mirror.

Watching good and bad supervisors and learning from their actions, accomplishments, and failures is a great way to prepare yourself for management. There is no point in reinventing the wheel, so use this opportunity to understand what you need to do to become a good supervisor.

Read Books and Articles

You can never go wrong by reading; in fact, your entire lifetime should be characterized by a thirst for learning and growth. I have found that there are two ways to truly learn: through experience and through other learning opportunities (reading, classes, mentors, and so on). With respect to reading, it is important to read a wide variety of business books and magazines. Read some of the classics on leadership and supervision, such as *Leaders*, by Warren Bennis and Burt Nanus (Harper & Row, 1985); *On Becoming a Leader*, by Warren Bennis (Addison-Wesley, 1989); *Leadership A-Z*, by James O'Toole (Jossey-Bass, 1999); *Leading Teams:*

Mastering the New Role, by John Zenger, Ed Musselwhite, Kathleen Hurson, and Craig Perrin (Zenger-Miller, 1994); and *Teams at the Top: Unleashing the Potential of Both Teams and Individual Leaders,* by Jon Katzenbach (McKinsey and Company, 1998). Also read magazines such as *Government Executive* magazine, *Harvard Business Review,* and *Fast Company,* all of which will keep you abreast of what is going on in the areas of leadership and supervision.

Consider reading books and articles about related topics, such as human resources management (HRM), managing change, and time management, and works on more technical topics, such as statistics, budgeting and finance, and information management. Read self-help books such as *Man's Search for Meaning,* by Viktor E. Frankl (Washington Square Press, 1984). All of this reading will enhance your knowledge base and enable you to think more broadly.

Do not limit your reading to business books. Read as many biographies as you can, since that will give you greater insight into the minds of other individuals who were responsible for managing and leading people. You will learn that even the greatest leaders had more than their fair share of failures, and that it was these experiences, as well as a burning desire to learn and the drive not to give up, that helped shape them and ultimately made them successful.

Serve as an Acting Supervisor

Serving in an acting capacity is an excellent opportunity to see what management is all about. This type of assignment will provide you with real-world experience and will let you know almost immediately whether management is for you and whether you are up to the task. You will learn what it is like to try to motivate employees, to adjust to changing deadlines, and to be pulled in an untold number of directions. This is your opportunity to step onto the playing field while still keeping your other foot firmly planted on the sidelines.

One of the advantages of serving in an acting capacity is that it is short term, so you don't have the pressure to produce long-term results that a permanent supervisor has. Your role is primarily that of a caretaker in that you are expected to keep the work moving, respond to leave requests, implement policy, and perform other such tasks. You are not expected to make radical changes in the operation because you will serve for only a relatively short period of time.

Conversely, there are some downsides to serving in an acting capacity. For one thing, all of the employees know that you are there only temporarily, so they are unlikely to give you the same respect that they would give someone who was going to be there for the long term. In addition, it is never an easy thing to go from being one of the guys to being the boss, with the expectation that you will soon be one of the guys again.

Serving as an acting supervisor is a unique experience. Management gets the chance to see you in action, to see if you have the makings of a good supervisor. You have the opportunity to show your stuff, to demonstrate that you can run a unit that includes a diverse group of people and keep the work moving.

From your perspective, you get the chance to see whether management makes sense for you. You experience what it is like to attend management staff meetings, to deal with employee issues, and to address team-based workload concerns. You also find out whether you want to deal with the problems of supervision and whether you consider them to be challenges or merely hassles.

For example, I recall a terrific employee who was asked to serve as an acting supervisor. Although she had never really wanted to go into management, she had always been a bit curious about what it was like, so she accepted an acting assignment. Very quickly, she realized why she had not wanted to go into management, since she became embroiled in a series of complex employee relations issues. When her assignment ended, she happily returned to her old position, secure in the knowledge that management was not for her. In a sense, however, her serving as an acting supervisor was a success, since she learned that she did not like management, and it was better for her to learn that before she became a permanent supervisor.

Looking at a different example, early in my career, I had no desire to go into management. It simply wasn't my cup of tea, especially since at the time I still had aspirations toward being a fine artist. However, one day, I was detailed to the front office of another federal organization. This gave me the opportunity to both work with that organization's senior managers and observe them in action. I got to see what management was like, and I was hooked. I realized that while the challenges could be daunting, the potential payback was also high. Moreover, for the first time in my career, I felt that I was truly in the game. I was no longer just a worker bee doing what I was told. I was now working closely with people who made policy, made personnel decisions, and often determined what was going on. While these managers were always under a lot of pressure, from my point of view, it was definitely worth it. This assignment made me realize that management was for me.

Attend Management Classes

Taking classes is always a good thing to do, since you need to learn the fundamentals. The principle is the same, whether you are taking up a sport or learning to play an instrument. You need to master the basics before you can move on to the more complex tasks.

Virtually all government agencies understand that they need to aggressively engage in succession planning in order to replace the managers who will be retiring, moving up, or moving out of their organization. As a result, they frequently offer management training opportunities to employees who are not yet in management. This is an excellent approach, as it allows these employees to get ahead of the curve and learn about management before they are simply thrown into the job.

These classes expose you to current leaders, academics, and consultants who will share their experiences with you and discuss the fundamentals of management from many different perspectives. They give you the opportunity to interact with other people at your level so that you can explore ideas and build new relationships. They often give you some case studies to work through so that you will have the chance to try to deal with real-life types of situations. They may even give you the opportunity to complete a psychological profile such as the Myers-Briggs Type Indicator or the Herrmann Brain Dominance Survey, which will let you know where your management styles and tendencies lie.

It is important to understand that when you are taking these classes, your point of view will probably be somewhat limited because it is hard to put this learning into perspective when you have never been in management. Until you are actually down in the trenches, performing the day-to-day work of a supervisor and dealing with the constant swirl of problems, you may not be able to see how all the training fits together. That is why the more developmental experiences you have (watching other supervisors, reading, serving as an acting supervisor, and so on), the better, as they will round you out, make it easier for you to understand what is being discussed in the classroom, and help you relate it to your future role in management.

How to Become a Supervisor

If you follow the advice that I have given so far in this book, you will be off to a great start. If you demonstrate an excellent attitude, come to work on time and do a good job, take on the tough assignments, build a good reputation, and avail yourself of the many training opportunities that are available, you will no doubt be in a good position to go into management.

The next step is to start applying for management vacancies as they develop. In doing so, I recommend that you always look ahead, meaning that you should focus both on the job that you are applying for and on your next move after that. By doing this, you will give some shape to your career rather than strictly dealing with what is in front of you.

To get selected for a management position, you will probably have to compete with many other people who are also applying for the same job. Assuming that you meet the minimum qualifications, you will have to overcome two major hurdles in order to get selected. The first hurdle is that you want to be ranked high enough that your name will be referred to the selecting official for consideration.

This is the same basic process that occurred when you first applied for a job with the government, i.e., a panel will evaluate your knowledge, skills, and abilities (KSAs), and those of all other qualified candidates, against a predetermined rating schedule, and then assign an overall point score to each applicant. The highest-ranking candidates will then be sent to the selecting official.

You will be ranked based on the paperwork you submit, which, depending on the government agency, could include your résumé, your personnel folder, your appraisal, and/or your responses to a series of questions that are designed to assess your KSAs in greater detail. In order to give yourself the best possible chance of being selected, you need to make sure that you prepare a first-class application that addresses the job requirements in general and the KSAs in as much detail as possible. This means giving concrete examples that (1) clearly demonstrate that you have the requisite background and (2) distinguish you from the people with whom you are competing. Remember, the panel members will be reviewing multiple applicants, so you won't have much time to impress them.

Once you make it to an interview, you will need to prepare further. Review your strengths and weaknesses, and be ready to discuss them. Make a careful assessment of how others perceive you, and decide how you will rebut any criticisms that may be raised. Remember, you will probably not come to the interview as a completely unknown quantity. Be aware of your reputation, have a plan to address any possible concerns that may come up, and then do everything you can to show yourself in the best possible light.

Write down a number of challenging situations that you were involved in, and be ready to discuss two different scenarios: (1) those situations that you were successful in addressing, and (2) those situations in which the outcome was not successful and the lesson(s) you learned as a result. If you come across as never having been involved in a difficult situation and/or never having made a mistake, you will appear to be either naive or inexperienced, which will diminish your chances of being selected.

Make sure that you are familiar with all of the key management and political issues that affect your organization, and be ready to discuss them if asked. From my perspective, it is better to voice an opinion that your interviewer may disagree with than to have no opinion at all or, worse, to be unfamiliar with a key topic.

Be sure that you know the organization's key performance indicators, and be willing and able to offer a plan that will help improve performance. For example, I recall interviewing someone for the position of assistant division chief. This individual came to the interview confident and prepared, and he was very knowledgeable about our organization, even though he didn't work there. In fact, he articulated a logical and comprehensive strategy for improving our performance in several key areas. It was clear that he knew what he was talking about, had a good track record, and was ready. We knew that he was our man, and we selected him for the job.

If you have any prior supervisory experience, be ready to discuss it at the interview. Your interviewer is going to want to know what you have learned from the experience, so talk about it with confidence and insight. If you can honestly portray a prior supervisory experience as one that helped you to grow, it will surely increase your chances of being selected.

On the other hand, if you have never served in a supervisory capacity, emphasize what you have learned about management. Talk about the books and articles you have read, the classes you have attended, and other such preparation. Discuss your management style (e.g., are you a Theory X manager or a Theory Y manager?[2]). You want to come across as someone who has given a lot of thought to becoming a supervisor and will not be completely overwhelmed at the start.

Getting Into Upper Management

The best way to get into upper management is to do an excellent job as a first-line supervisor. If you show that you can lead people and produce results, everyone will quickly notice, and you will be on your way. It's almost that simple. Of course, you will still need to grow as an individual, build allies, and so on. However, if you demonstrate that you can do the job, are reliable, and are a good team player, your future should be bright.

The first year is usually pretty tough for a new supervisor. For one thing, you are now part of management, so your former peers will probably become a bit more distant with you. You are no longer responsible just for your own work; you are suddenly responsible for the work of your entire unit. Your whole world has been turned upside down, and you are dealing with things that you have never dealt with before. However, through training, experience, and hopefully some good mentors, the odds are that you will do just fine.

Learn About Organizational Design

Assuming that things go well for you as a first-line supervisor, at some point you will begin to think about moving up. Recognize that when you move beyond first-line supervision, the skills required again change. This is because you are no longer supervising direct labor employees; you are supervising several units or teams of employees *through* first-line supervisors who report to you. At this level, managing individual employees is less important than learning how to manage through systems. By this I mean all of the systems that are used to manage the organization, the employees, and the work, such as the structural system, the technical system, the decision-making and information system, the people system, the reward system, and the renewal system.[3]

At this point in your career, you should begin to learn about the power of organizational design and management systems and the way they can drive employee behavior and performance. As my mentor, Paul Gustavson, taught me, "Organizations are perfectly designed to get the results that they get." This means that all of the choices you make with respect to your systems (your organization chart, your work processes and work flow, your metrics, your performance standards, your rewards program, and so on) will influence the way your employees behave, the way they feel, and their overall skill sets, and will ultimately drive your organization's performance, one way or the other.

The better you align your systems so that they all transmit a clear and consistent message, the more your organization's energy will flow in the same direction. In addition, the more consistently you apply these systems in a fair and equitable manner, the better your employees will behave and the more they will perform according to your expectations. This is a very important role for higher-level supervisors: to understand the power of systems management, to adjust the systems when necessary, and to ensure that they are being properly applied.

If you can grasp this concept, it will make your life a lot easier and will enable you to make the jump to the next level of management more easily. You will stop trying to blame the employees every time a problem develops; instead, you will first look at gaps in your systems to find the solution. You will begin to understand the science of management, which will take some of the emotion out of the decision-making process, and you will start to operate on a higher, more professional level. The fog will start to lift a bit more, and you will begin to see the wisdom of the following adage: "If you always do what you have always done, you will always get what you always got."

One of the turning points of my career was being exposed to this concept. Prior to that, I tended to think that I could solve most problems by doing a better job of managing the people under me. However, as I began to realize that there were other important forces at play, I started to understand that I needed to look to my systems for many of my solutions.

For example, before this realization, whenever we had had employees who were struggling, I had always assumed that the problem could be solved by counseling the employees and then, if necessary, placing them on a performance improvement plan. While that may have indeed been the ultimate solution, my organizational systems training made me realize that I first needed to make sure that the problem wasn't caused by management.

I learned that before going after the employees, I needed to ensure that our training was sound, our instructions were clear, the employees had the necessary tools to do their work, their quality reviewers were treating them fairly, and so on. What I eventually came to understand was that many times the problems were not caused by the employees; they were caused by flaws in our systems. Perhaps one of our quality reviewers was calling a disproportionate number of errors; maybe our training manual was unclear. The point here was that if one of our systems was causing the employee performance problem, that problem was going to continue. Unless we addressed the systemwide problem, we would be spinning our wheels, pressuring the employees and causing bad feelings when it was not their fault. In essence, we would be getting the same results we always got because we were doing things the same way.

Expand Your World

Being a higher-level supervisor also means interacting with the world in a different way. At this level, you have to work more frequently with other high-level officials, both inside and outside of your organization.

You need to sharpen your political skills, and you frequently have to rely on personal relationships to get the job done. Also, you need to start looking down the road more often, not only in terms of your own career, but in terms of how best to get the work accomplished. In other words, you need to keep better track of the trends in government and the private sector, begin to benchmark with other best-in-class organizations, and take other such actions. At this level, your field of vision expands, and it should continue to grow if you want to keep on moving up.

Your network should also expand at this point. You should begin to meet a wide variety of people throughout the nation, state, or city, as appropriate, and you should start to meet people at the upper levels of government through day-to-day work opportunities, training classes, group assignments, VIP visits, and so on. Your reputation should be growing beyond your local organization, and you should assess your ultimate career goals.

In fact, this would be a good time for you to review all of the career development programs that are available within your organization. In many government organizations, there is a series of sequential programs that you can compete for, and if you get in, these programs will definitely increase the trajectory of your career. Examine them carefully, discuss the available options with your mentor(s), and go for it.

Also recognize that there is no reason why you have to remain with your current agency. Many organizations will hire people from another part of government at almost any level as long as they have the skills that are needed. I have even seen people stay with one organization for virtually their entire careers and then switch to another one in order to make it to the executive level. You do what you have to do to get ahead, as long as it makes sense.

The Challenges of Upper-Level Management
Mobility

As you move up the ladder, you will have to make some key decisions. For example, how frequently are you willing to move? Many government organizations make mobility a requirement for moving into a senior-level position. This is obviously a very personal choice that can have serious ramifications. While I will discuss this issue in greater detail in the next chapter of this book, it's important for you to recognize that mobility is usually one of the prices you have to pay for going into a senior leadership capacity.

In fact, many government organizations expect you to move a number of times because they believe that all of these moves will give you valuable experience, provide new perspectives, and keep you fresh and energized. Ask yourself what you are prepared to do with respect to mobility before committing yourself to this path.

Increased Pressures

I've discussed this issue before, but I need to reemphasize it, since the higher up the ladder you move, the more pressure you can expect to receive. Many people who have felt pressure at the first-line supervisory level have been surprised to find that the pressure only increases as you make more money and take on additional responsibility. They somehow expected that once they became an executive, they would be able to coast a bit and rely on their lower-level supervisors for results. In fact, the opposite happens, simply because you "don't get paid for nothing."

Perhaps the biggest revelation occurs when you go from being the number two person in an organization to being the number one honcho. It doesn't matter whether you are moving up to become a division chief, a service chief, a program director, or a field director. Once you make that leap, your whole world changes.

I remember being a young, inexperienced first-line supervisor in HRM. Above me were the assistant personnel officer, who was several years older than I, and the personnel officer, who was even older. The assistant personnel officer was the tough guy, the person who was constantly advocating that we take hard and sometimes extreme positions. The personnel officer was the more deliberate of the two and usually advocated a more nuanced and cautious approach.

One day, the assistant personnel officer scolded the personnel officer for taking a position that he believed to be too soft. The personnel officer responded, "You are always tough under my signature." The assistant personnel officer smiled but had no response, and the point was made quite effectively. It's a lot easier to be a tough guy when the ramifications of your actions do not fall directly upon your shoulders. However, once you move up and are responsible for a great many things, everything suddenly *does* fall on your shoulders. While you are the one who gets the credit when things go well, you are also the one who gets the blame when things don't go well—not your assistant, but you, because you are the one who is in charge.

I guarantee that if and when you find yourself in that position, your whole world will change. You will naturally become more cautious, weighing how things will play out. You will become more concerned about the political impact of your actions, because you will suddenly find that many more eyes are looking at you. The stakes will become higher because your actions will be more visible and will have a much wider impact.

I certainly found this to be the case in my career. When I first became an assistant director, I enjoyed the limelight and reveled in all the action. I had plenty of power, and for the most part, I was able to get things done my way. When things were going well in our organization, I didn't get credit directly; that was reserved for our director. However, since I was there at his side, assisting him, people acknowledged my contribution, at least in an indirect manner.

However, when things were not going well, he was the one who received all the negative phone calls and letters, not me. No one castigated me for our performance problems. I was only the number two man. While some negativity was reflected in my direction because I was associated with the problems, it was not enough to ever worry me, since I was not the one in charge.

In a sense, being the number two person is ideal, since you have a lot of power, but you really don't have the same pressures that the number one person has, and that is why many people choose to stop their careers at that point. Of course, the downside of that approach is that you are Avis and not Hertz, and that is the trade-off. You don't make the same money, and you don't have the same prestige. Again, you don't get paid for nothing.

The gap in pressure between the two positions has only increased during the past few years with the emphasis on accountability. Many government organizations now place their performance metrics on both their intranet and Internet sites, making every manager more exposed than ever before—both inside and outside of her organization. Moreover, with the increased sophistication of information management technology, performance data are at virtually everyone's fingertips, meaning that more and more people are instantly examining your performance and subjecting you to even more pressure.

Another challenge is that government leaders often do not operate on a level playing field, since some leaders work in low-cost areas, while others operate in high-cost areas. This means that those who work in high-cost areas will be recruiting from the lower part of the labor pool, have employees who work two jobs in order to survive, face higher turnover rates, and deal with more difficult personnel issues. These leaders will face greater performance pressures because their challenges are so much tougher. They will be making proportionately less money than their peers, be subject to more second-guessing and micromanagement by their supervisors, and receive little or no recognition of the challenges that they are facing.

Having spent most of my career in these areas, I am acutely aware of the challenges that leaders who take on these assignments face. I'm not sure that many of the people who oversee these activities, particularly those who have never managed an activity in an area with a high cost of living, appreciate what it is like. I recently had lunch with one such leader who confided to me that he was seeing a therapist to help him deal with all of the stress he was feeling. He was tense, he had difficulty sleeping, and his blood pressure was way up. Unfortunately, I have heard similar stories from other people who are in analogous situations.

My point here is not to scare you or to discourage you from going into senior management. After all, I spent many years in senior management, and, as I have already stated, I was generally happy with the opportunities I had, my ability to make a difference, my pay and benefits, the people I met, and so on. What I am saying is that if you decide to go into management, go into it with your eyes wide open, and be aware of both the opportunities and the pitfalls.

Dealing with Political Appointees

The higher you go in management, the more you will be affected by the political process. For most government employees, a change in administrations simply means a change in direction and policy. They expect that every four years or so, a new administration will come in and change the leadership at one or more levels of their organization. This will then filter down to them, causing some adjustments in the way they do business, but not really having a major impact on their lives.

However, once you become a high-level management official, you can no longer insulate yourself from the political process. You are now one of the leaders of your organization, and the political appointees will be looking to you to implement the changes they are expecting. Given the fact that political appointees have a very limited amount of time to make a difference, they tend to be very impatient and can be quite demanding of the career civil service leaders who are now under their supervision.

These appointees come into their jobs fresh from a successful political campaign and are determined to make good on their promises. Unfortunately, they often enter their new jobs without a full understanding of what those jobs entail, so they require a series of oral and written briefings from the senior civil servants. Inevitably, they come to realize that the task at hand is much more complicated than they had originally thought because of all of the forces that are at play. This leads them to become frustrated, and they often perceive the problem as being caused at least in part by the intransigence of the civil service leaders.

To further complicate matters, political appointees tend to be very skeptical of civil servants who were highly visible in the prior administration. They wonder how, if these employees were so dedicated to implementing the vision and approach of the last administration, they can now turn 180 degrees and support them. This is a legitimate question, not only for the political appointee to ask, but also for the career civil service leader to grapple with. Do you put all of your energy into supporting an incumbent political appointee and run the risk of being scorned by the next administration, or do you play it safe and go with the wind, never taking a stand that will get you into any trouble? This is the box that you may very well find yourself in if you rise high enough.

As stated earlier, I found myself in a similar box. I was highly supportive of a particular administration because I felt that the changes it was making were the right thing for our clients. I received a number of high-profile assignments to help implement these changes, was frequently recognized for my contributions, and was well known as one of the most influential members of that organization. On many levels, that was probably the best period of my career.

However, when the next administration came in, it was well aware of my history. I was viewed with suspicion, excluded from influential committees and important assignments, and basically shunted aside. It was quite unpleasant knowing that I was seen as being more loyal to the last administration than to the present one, especially since I was doing everything I could to successfully implement the changes that the new administration was demanding.

As I look back on this period, I have no regrets, since I always followed my conscience, yet stayed loyal to each administration. I was in a box, and I made my choice and then had to live with the consequences of my decision. Others chose different routes; many simply stayed under the radar screen, doing the best job they could, but never really going out on a limb, which was fine for them. A few actually became ardent advocates for both administrations, in part because they saw that as part of their role, and in part because they had strong political skills, were excellent infighters, and by taking this approach were able to advance their careers, which was good for them.

The point here is that when you become a high-level government manager, the political process can often put you in an uncomfortable spot and force you to make choices. That is not a bad thing; it is simply a fact of life. The more you are aware of this, the better you will be able to decide whether upper management is right for you.

CHAPTER 8

Balancing Your Work Life and Your Family Life

WHETHER OR NOT you go into management, finding the appropriate balance between work and the rest of your life is one of the most difficult things to do. This is especially true once you start moving up the ladder, since more and more demands are placed upon you. In my experience, far too many people become so consumed with their job that the rest of their life suffers, and they wind up paying a heavy price.

These people are so determined to get to the top, so hell-bent on achieving success, at least from a career perspective, that they fail to realize that there is more to life than simply their job. This is not to say that getting ahead at work is not important, because it surely is. However, from time to time, you need to step back and ask yourself how you define success. If you get the job you have always wanted, but you lose your marriage along the way, is that really worth it? If you work long hours and achieve the bonus you have been striving for, but you wind up overweight and with high blood pressure, what have you truly accomplished? The point here is that you need to define success on the job as part of a bigger picture—i.e., the success of your entire life—and make your decisions within that context. Otherwise, one day you may look back on your life and realize that you couldn't see the forest through the trees.

It's a Job

It's essential that you put your government job in its proper perspective. First of all, there is no doubt that your job is a very important part of your life for a variety of reasons: (1) it provides you with the means to help support your family, (2) it gives you the chance to help the citizens of our country, (3) it enables you to achieve your career goals, (4) it offers you the opportunity to meet other people, and (5) it allows you to have a comfortable retirement. A government job is a wonderful thing to have.

However, it is still a job, and it needs to be viewed as such. In one sense, a government job is like any other job: It is not permanent, and you will most likely change jobs on multiple occasions. The people you work for and with will come and go; there is no real continuity. People will get promoted, transferred, reassigned, or removed, or they will decide to retire or resign. Moreover, new employees will often be coming into the organization to replace the employees who have left. In essence, the only continuity is the organization. Everything else is in a constant state of flux.

You will also notice that loyalties frequently change. You may have busted your butt for one boss, only to have her leave and a new boss now demand that you be loyal to him. You may have given everything you have to a particular management program, only to see it all dissolve with the onset of a new administration; or you may see someone whom you have always supported suddenly turn on you for political reasons or for a reason that you will never know. That is simply the nature of work and the reality of working in any organization, be it government or the private sector.

That is also why you need to have some perspective and keep work in its proper place. If you do not, everything that happens to you at work, no matter how small the slight or the perceived injustice, will take on added meaning and will eat you up inside. When you look back on your career, you will see that all the issues that drove you crazy at work, all the problems that gave you angst, didn't "amount to a hill of beans in this crazy world."[1]

That is because these issues were transitory and were part of the normal challenges that everyone deals with on the job. This is the reason why a job is referred to as "work" and not as "play." Problems at work never go away because so many people are involved and there are so many variables at play (human resources management issues, computer systems, work-flow challenges, health problems, outside events, and so on). It's simply the nature of the beast. That is why the more important concern is how you react to all of these problems.

If you overreact and become easily frustrated, this is going to bleed into the other parts of your life and adversely affect your personal relationships. For example, if you continually take your frustrations out on your spouse, your children, and your friends, they will tend to withdraw from you because they will not want to become punching bags. Unfortunately, I have met many spouses of "highly motivated" employees who felt that their significant other's job was more important to him than they were. Far too often, this overfocus on the job would lead to extramarital affairs, divorces, alcoholism, and other such outcomes. It made me wonder whether those individuals' success at work was worth the price they ultimately paid.

If you are a supervisor who becomes angry over every problem that develops at work and takes out your frustrations on your subordinates, they will probably go into a shell, as they will not wish to incur your wrath. The downside of this reaction is that employees who try to avoid their supervisor will not give that supervisor bad news or problematic information.

If you become agitated every time something does not go your way, other people will notice, and you will develop a reputation for being immature and unprofessional. Such a reputation will definitely hurt you in the long term.

Early in my career, I was responsible for managing an office's labor relations program. This was a tough assignment, because relations between management and the union were quite poor. To complicate matters, shortly after I assumed this position, a new union president took over who was determined to give management a hard time. He filed more than 100 unfair labor practice (ULP) charges per year and a similar number of grievances, and this constantly kept me on the defensive. Third parties were often called in to resolve disputes, making it difficult to work things out on an informal basis. The union president was a professional agitator who was constantly baiting management, with the goal of trying to goad management into committing a ULP by denouncing the union.

While I was managing the labor relations program, I was also managing a personnel program, and I had more than a dozen people working directly for me. I must confess that there were times when I was so focused on dealing with the union that I did not spend enough time developing the people who worked directly for me. In later years, I learned that you must always find time for the people who work for you.

This ongoing battle with the union proved to be one of the most uncomfortable episodes of my career, since we were frequently involved in litigation on issues that were virtually meaningless. I used to go home at night angry and frustrated because I felt that I was wasting my time dealing with people who were intentionally hurting our office and the government. Quite frankly, there were times when I wanted to get even with them by firing them all. However, I knew I couldn't do that because it would be blatant retaliation for their labor activities, which was illegal. Moreover, deep down, I knew that it would be morally wrong. I used to vent about this situation to my wife, who would tell me, "What are you worried about? It's only a job. Do the best you can, and then take out the garbage."

Her reply always annoyed me, since it was not overly sympathetic concerning the problems I was dealing with. However, it also helped to ground me and made me realize that these frustrations were really not that important. What was more important was being good to my family and focusing my energy on the people that I loved, rather than on adversaries at work who were angry at the world. Eventually, the union president moved on, as did I, and all of those labor relations issues were replaced by new ones that were addressed by a different group of labor and management officials.

As I look back on this situation, I can see that it was one of the best learning experiences in my career. I became adept at dealing with a wide range of issues, and I slowly but surely learned to put them in their proper perspective. More importantly, I began to recognize that all of those issues would eventually get resolved one way or another, and that they were not worth losing any sleep over.

Eventually, I developed a personal philosophy for dealing with problems that developed at work. It was not a perfect philosophy, because I am not a perfect person. I still get frustrated just like everyone else. However, what it did was help me to keep these frustrations in perspective, which enabled me to stay calmer and on a more even keel.

Simply put, the following was my philosophy: "If my teenage daughter was in a good mood, I had a good day." This was my philosophy because I could see firsthand how difficult the teenage years were for her. More importantly, she was my only daughter and one of the true gifts that life had given me. By thinking about my day in that context, I was able to put things in their proper perspective and not overreact to all of the piddling problems that developed during the day. Moreover, when I shared this philosophy with others, they invariably laughed, since they understood what it was like to raise a daughter, and they often adopted the same approach.

This philosophy proved to be quite helpful to me, particularly during the last years of my career, when I had a lot of responsibility and was dealing with multiple issues. It enabled me to not sweat the small stuff and to retain a good balance in my life. However, on occasion, I still had to deal with some weighty issues that gave me a lot of trouble.

For example, I recall a situation in my office that caused me to become extremely worried. My office was charged with overseeing the work of a large number of conservators,[2] who were responsible for managing the estates of our incompetent clients. One of our conservators was brought to my attention when I received three congressional complaints about her. We looked into the matter and quickly discovered that she had mismanaged many of the estates that she was responsible for protecting.

I immediately appointed an employee to investigate her actions, and he uncovered additional problems. I then turned his findings over to the Inspector General for further review and relieved both the conservator and the individual who had been responsible for overseeing her work of their duties. I also ensured that we reviewed every single case that had been under her jurisdiction and did everything we could to reconcile her accounting and recover any money that we believed was missing. Lastly, I changed our internal procedures so that this would not happen again and gave periodic updates to our headquarters so that it would never be caught off guard.

To complicate matters, the *Los Angeles Times* had begun investigating California's conservator program right around the time that I had discovered problems with our conservator. It had heard the same concerns about her that I had, and was planning to do a front-page article describing the damage that she had done. I knew at that point that, despite my best efforts, I could be in trouble, since as a senior executive, you never want to find yourself on the front page of a major newspaper. Even though everyone in my organization appeared to be supportive of me, I recognized that if enough political pressure resulted from that article, I was disposable.

To make things even more difficult, the article was delayed for well over a year before it was finally published, so the prospect of it hung over my head like the sword of Damocles. It was without a doubt the most stressful period I endured during my career.

Three things got me through this period: (1) my family and friends, (2) my mentors, and (3) my attitude. My family and friends kept me grounded and made me realize that whatever happened, they were going to be there for me. They were my anchor in life, and I knew that I could always count on them.

My mentors helped me keep things in perspective, with one of them suggesting that I ask myself, "What is the worst thing that could possibly happen to me?" When I considered that and realized that the worst thing would be that I would have to leave, that helped keep me calm. After all, plenty of other people have lost their jobs and found other ones.

Lastly, I tried to stay positive, focus on the present, and be thankful for all of the good things in my life. I was confident that I had done the right thing once the problems with the conservator had been brought to my attention. Moreover, I had done everything I could to manage the potential impact of the article, so whatever happened after that was beyond my control.

When the article finally hit the newspapers, it did not have much of an impact within my organization. Everyone knew the issues and was prepared for the fallout. Fortunately, the reporters had concluded that we had made a good faith effort to address the problems, and their article was fair and evenhanded. It quickly became old news, and the issue went away.

I recognize that many jobs require you to put in long hours. That's the price of additional responsibility. They may also require a tremendous amount of energy, a commitment to continuous learning, and extensive travel. That was certainly my experience, especially during the second half of my career. However, I found that I could do all of these things while still spending time with my family and friends and having other interests outside of the job, as long as I made that a priority.

The approach I took was that once I came home, my job stayed where it belonged—at work. This meant that I didn't spend the rest of the evening worrying and replaying my workday. Once I got home, my focus was on the other, more important parts of my life. Sure, when I first arrived home, I would talk to my wife about how our days had gone, and occasionally I would think about the job when I was involved in a difficult situation, but I always tried to keep that to a minimum. To me, once I crossed the threshold, my focus had to be on other, more important things, such as my family and friends, my synagogue, the world around me, and my other interests, which were many.

Having a quiet dinner with my family after work, going to my kids' baseball games, riding my exercise bicycle while reading the newspaper, watching a good movie, working on an oil painting, or simply taking a walk, all took my mind off of the job and made me a more relaxed and well-rounded individual.

My weekends were always devoted to family, friends, and fun, along with the normal errands that we all perform outside of work. Saturday mornings usually involved shopping, going to the dry cleaner, and so on. The afternoons always had some type of sports activity, and the evenings normally included going out to dinner and the movies or the theater. Sundays were reserved for family outings, such as going to the park, a museum, or the beach.

We also tried to travel whenever we could; sometimes taking a cruise or a trip outside the United States, and other times simply going to another state or vacation spot. All of these activities ensured that my life was well balanced, which made me a happier individual who was eager to go back to work at the end of the weekend or my vacation.

By contrast, I recall an individual who once told me that he used to "think about work 16 hours out of every day." To me, this was an unhealthy and unbalanced approach to work and life, as it didn't leave much room for anything outside of work. He paid a heavy price for this approach, since he went through several divorces and did not have a good relationship with the other members of his family. Moreover, his focus on the job was so extreme that it adversely affected his health and made him very emotional at work, which inhibited his ability to build long-term relationships and make sound decisions.

The point here is that you can do well at work and still have a rewarding and well-rounded personal life. Ultimately, it all comes down to the choices that you make. If you find yourself in a job that is exhausting you, and you are not able to achieve any balance, first look at yourself and see if you can make adjustments in the way you are approaching the job. In my view, the solution usually lies within you. However, if the job is consuming you, and you conclude that lifestyle/attitude adjustments are not possible, then it is time to look for another job. Remember, the choice is yours.

Don't Treat the Job as if It's Life and Death

We've all heard the stories of people who worked themselves into exhaustion on the understanding that once they retired, they would finally start to live. The corollary to this story is that as soon as they retire, they die of a heart attack or a disease, with the ultimate moral being don't wait to live because you never know when your time will be up.

Unfortunately, this exact situation struck the person in life who was closest to me: my wife, Pat. Pat was an exceptionally dedicated teacher who decided to retire when she reached 55. It was her feeling that she had raised her children, and it was time to enjoy life. Shortly thereafter, we took a lengthy trip to the Grand Tetons, Yellowstone National Park, the Black Hills, and Mount Rushmore. We had a marvelous time, and we were planning many overseas trips, especially after I retired, which I was expecting to do 17 months later.

Six weeks after returning from that trip, Pat was diagnosed as having a malignant brain tumor and was given less than a year to live. After I got over the initial shock of her diagnosis and prognosis, I made arrangements with my employer to work at home so that I could spend this precious time with her. Interestingly, right before this occurred, I had applied for a job in a different part of our organization that would have been a welcome change, provided me with additional responsibility, and been an excellent addition to my résumé. However, even though I knew that this was a great opportunity and that I had a good chance of getting the job, I withdrew my application. My place was with my wife, and this was truly life or death.

She lived out that year with courage and dignity, and despite ongoing radiation and chemotherapy treatments, she still squeezed in two trips to Las Vegas and one to Mexico. Prior to Pat's death, she told me that she was at peace because she had raised her children and felt that she had led a full and active life. I also think she was quite happy to have had me by her side during this awful period.

From my perspective, I am at peace, knowing that I did everything possible to support my wife in her time of need and that I chose her over my job. That having been said, I sometimes wonder if I was too frugal during our marriage and if I should have made more of an effort to live for the moment, rather than saving money and putting things off for the future.

I vividly recall another individual who worked for the government for more than 60 years. He was a very nice man who always had a kind word for everyone. However, his entire life seemed to be wrapped up in his job, and during his last few years he struggled to make it to work. It seemed to me that his job was the center of his life, and he had never taken the time to find other interests or smell the roses.

In his last 20 years on the job, he was working for next to nothing, since his pension would have paid 80 percent of his salary and he would not have had retirement deductions taken out of his monthly check, would no longer have had to pay for commuting to work, and so on. He reluctantly retired only when the work he was used to performing was centralized at another office and he was given a different assignment.

Sadly, he died shortly after that. In his case, working for the government was a matter of life or death. What could he have accomplished had he used those last 20 to 30 years or so to really enjoy life? I guess we'll never know.

I know of an analogous situation where a woman in her seventies was really struggling on the job. Her memory was fading, her energy was diminishing, and her performance had declined significantly. Management tried to gently encourage her to retire, but she refused, so it was eventually left with no choice but to fire her.

She wanted to appeal her removal, but her family interceded, convinced her to face reality, and negotiated a settlement through which she retired with a clean record. Management was pleased with this because she had been a good employee, and no one wanted to see her end her career on a sour note.

More importantly, one of her family members actually thanked management for bringing this situation to a head, because they knew it was time for her to leave. I sincerely hope that she was able to spend her golden years enjoying a well-earned retirement.

My point here is that you need to view your job in the overall context of your life. Do not fall into the trap of making your job your life or of sacrificing your life or the life of someone who is dear to you for your job. In my view, that is incredibly foolish. I have seen people move across the country for a promotion even though a family member was desperately ill, and then live to regret that decision. I have also seen people literally sacrifice their health because they believed that they were irreplaceable on the job and couldn't take time off. The truth of the matter is that no one is irreplaceable, and you should never think of yourself as such.

Don't waste your life giving so much to your job that there is nothing left for you. Treat your job as important, because it certainly is. At all times, give it nothing less than your best. But don't confuse giving your best with giving your life. That is a major distinction that you should never lose sight of. Don't sacrifice your life or your family. It's simply not worth it.

A good rule of thumb when contemplating key decisions is the deathbed principle. If you have to make a key work/life decision, try to project ahead and determine what that decision would look like if you were looking back on it from your deathbed. Remember that the job you are anxious to get now may not look so attractive to you later on in life, especially if you and/or your family turn out to have paid a heavy price for it.

Obviously, there are times when we all have to make sacrifices for work. Simply make sure that the sacrifice is worth it.

Follow Your Passion

As I look back on my career, I realize that the happiest and most successful people I have known were those individuals who were passionate about what they did. Some simply loved their jobs and stuck with them, while others found ways to redefine their jobs by incorporating their passion(s) into them. For example, I witnessed a chief of an administrative division, who was passionate about construction, get heavily involved in the design of a variety of interesting and important space projects. His expertise in space management wound up influencing other offices and gave him a great deal of personal satisfaction.

I remember a senior executive who was passionate about computers and had many ideas for ways of tapping into their potential. He worked closely with his information resources management staff to design innovative computer programs that helped his customers and simplified the jobs of his employees.

Lastly, I observed a person who was managing roughly 200 people take a lower grade and transfer to a training job 3,000 miles away because he realized that his true passion was training people, not managing them. After he began his new job, people remarked that he suddenly looked 10 years younger.

The point here is that if you follow your passion, you will be a much happier, more motivated, and more energized employee. If you are passionate about your job or find a way to combine your passion with your job, great; you are ahead of the game. However, if you feel that you are stuck in a job that is boring or that is simply not right for you, look elsewhere until you find a good fit.

We spend so much of our adult lives at work that it would be an absolute shame to perform a job that we are not passionate about. If you currently feel that way, do not play the part of a victim. Either try to make some subtle changes in your current job or go out and find a new one. The choice is yours.

Maintain a Healthy Lifestyle

Another way to build balance in your life is to develop a healthy lifestyle. By this I mean establishing lifelong habits that will provide your mind and body with all the tools that they need to be strong, sharp, energetic, and resilient.

On its face, this sounds quite simple, yet it seems to be a challenge for many people in the workplace. Of course, when you consider that most people hold full-time jobs, are dealing with longer and longer commutes, and are facing more and more financial pressures, it is easy to see why so many people are struggling to maintain their health.

I recently spent some time with a friend, who has a high-level job with the government. I was struck by the fact that late into the evening, he was still receiving and responding to messages on his BlackBerry. It drove home the point that people are working more than ever, and in ways that our parents never even imagined.

Many people are now working while driving in their cars and using their cell phones, or working during lunch as they gobble down a sandwich, a bag of potato chips, and a Coke. People seem so stressed out they have virtually no time for themselves, so they develop poor health habits that eventually come back to haunt them.

The problem is often compounded by all of the pressures at work.

> Fear of job redundancy . . . increased demands for overtime due to staff cutbacks act as negative stressors. Employees who start to feel the "pressure to perform" can get caught in a downward spiral of increasing effort to meet rising expectations with no increase in job satisfaction. The relentless requirement to work at optimum performance takes its toll in job dissatisfaction, employee turnover, reduced efficiency, illness and even death. Absenteeism, illness, alcoholism, "petty internal politics," bad or snap decisions, indifference and apathy, lack of motivation or creativity are all by-products of an over stressed workplace.[3]

Look around at the people you work with. How many of them are overweight, smoking cigarettes, seeing a therapist, and/or taking medication to control one or more ailments? Unfortunately, I think the answer is far too many.

Why does stress cause so many health-related problems? "When your brain perceives stress, you get reactions from the stress-reactive area, and an elevation of stress hormones—cortisol and norepinephrine—increase in concentration in the blood," Dr. Bruce Rabin, M.D., Ph.D. (a professor of pathology and psychiatry at University of Pittsburgh Medical Center) tells WebMD.

> What happens next? "We believe that each person has different organ vulnerabilities. One person will respond with panic attacks, another with headaches," says John Garrison, PhD, director of the stress management program at Lahey Clinic in Burlington, Mass.
>
> While the impact of workplace stress varies from one person to the next, mounting evidence shows that stress can cause some very specific adverse health effects. For instance, stress may make it harder to control diabetes by raising blood glucose levels. This is related to the "fight or flight" response, which prompts your body to raise blood sugar levels to help boost energy in response to the stress. Stress may even raise cholesterol levels, immediately and long term.[4]

It seems to me that the only way to address this situation is to develop the self-discipline to live your life in a healthy manner. This means building a routine into your day-to-day activities that will promote all of the right habits that health experts have been advocating for years.

For example, keep a journal of your eating habits. If you are constantly eating food that is high in fat and full of empty calories, you may want to consult with a nutritionist, who can help you sensibly change your diet to one that features fruits, vegetables, and whole grains. Also, learn how to read the nutrition labels on the back of the food you buy so that you will become an informed consumer.

I remember personally meeting with a nutritionist and learning how unhealthy my diet was. She convinced me to switch to a low-fat, more balanced diet that helped me to reduce my cholesterol and keep my weight on a more even keel. These days, whenever my weight starts to drift a bit upward, I use a computer program called Dietpower that enables me to track my caloric intake versus the calories that I burn. It also allows me to track the percentage of fats, proteins, and carbohydrates that I consume and the amount of water that I am drinking. I have found Dietpower to be an excellent tool that helps me stay disciplined and informed.

Another key to maintaining a healthy lifestyle is exercise, which has always been a major part of my life. I have found that exercise keeps my body strong and supple and is a great stress reliever. When I was working full time and raising three children, it was tough for me to find the time to exercise. My eventual solution was to buy an exercise bicycle and some dumbbells, and to make sure that I exercised at least five days a week, usually about an hour after dinner. I also tried to play sports on the weekend, either tennis or basketball, which helped make me feel like I was 17 again, at least until the aches and pains started kicking in.

My biggest struggle in this area occurred when I developed a herniated disk in my back and had to undergo six back surgeries, including a spinal fusion. It seemed that for a two-year period, I was either undergoing or recovering from back surgery, which was extremely frustrating, as you can imagine. Fortunately, all of the exercise I had done regularly throughout my life gave me an edge, and I was able to recover from these surgeries. Today, I work out with a personal trainer and lift weights at least three days a week, am playing competitive tennis, and can still bend over and easily touch my toes.

Another area that is essential to good health is rest. Experts tell us that we should try to get at least eight hours of sleep each night. I try to follow this advice, and I generally go to sleep each night and awake each morning at roughly the same time. I do this because I perform at my best when I am relaxed and refreshed, so I have tried to build this into my lifestyle.

I have heard other people say that it is impossible for them to do this because they are always so busy. While this may be true, I suspect that it is more a function of poor time management than anything else. It seems to me that people who are scrambling to get stuff done late at night generally do not use their days to accomplish what they need to do. As a result, they are constantly working late into the night, in much the same way as a teenager puts off his work so that he can hang out with his friends and then finds himself always fighting deadlines.

Spend a week keeping track of your time. I suspect you will find that you waste an enormous amount of time lounging, watching television, or doing other things that don't contribute to your immediate tasks at hand.

If you manage your time well and do what you have to do when you have to do it, you will generally find that you can spend the last hour or two of your day winding down, rather than being in a mad rush to accomplish things. This approach will enable you to go to sleep without resorting to any sleep medications. Life will become simpler and easier to manage, because you will be doing a better job of managing yourself.

Lastly, do not drink an excessive amount of alcohol, and by all means avoid illegal drugs. Obviously, this admonition is pretty much a no-brainer, yet I'm constantly amazed at how many people try to solve their problems by going this route. If you find yourself in this situation, get help, and get it immediately. You are placing your career, your family, and your life in jeopardy.

In summary, you need to manage your body the way you manage all the other aspects of your life. The best way to do this is to take a good, hard look at your lifestyle and determine if there are ways in which you can make it better. Remember, you have only one body, and you aren't getting any younger. If you improve your overall health, you will look and feel better, have more energy, and probably have a better attitude, all of which will undoubtedly help your career.

When Things Are Not Going Well at Work

Do not be surprised if, at some point in your career, things take a downward turn. It may be the result of a change in leadership, the nature of your job, or outside forces, or you may simply be sick and tired of the job. The odds are that one or more of these things will occur, if for no other reason than that you are human and stuff happens. I'm not talking about the type of day-to-day problems that I referred to earlier in this chapter, which could be addressed simply by an adjustment in your attitude or philosophy. I'm referring to a deeper, more fundamental problem at your job that may cause you to feel that it is time to leave. The challenge here is that even if you decide you have no choice but to change jobs, it may take months or even years for you to find an acceptable position.

Under these circumstances, there are three strategies you can adopt: (1) manage your boss, (2) control your sphere of influence, or (3) reinvent yourself. Let's look at each one of these approaches in greater detail.

Managing Your Boss

If your problem is driven by your supervisor, which is often the case, your best bet is to try to speak with her at length and try to figure out what is driving her behavior. She may be dissatisfied with your performance, she may have been told that she needs to crack the whip, or she may simply be feeling unhappy herself. The point here is that if she is the source of your dissatisfaction, you need to find a way to patch things up.

If the issue is performance, try to see things from her perspective and understand what she thinks you need to do to improve. Once you have that information, give her your side and try to come to a meeting of the minds. After that, do everything you can to make the improvements she is looking for, keep her informed about your progress, and ask her for any help you need. The more she sees you trying to improve, the more supportive she will be.

If she is trying to crack the whip, try to get with the program and step things up. The odds are that other people will be resistant, but if she sees that you are ahead of the curve, she is likely to take note of that, be appreciative of your efforts, and cut you some slack.

If she is merely unhappy for reasons that aren't related to you, try to get her to open up by letting her know that you are always there to listen to her and to help her when you can. I once worked for a supervisor who was experiencing some personal problems. I let him know that I was empathetic to his problems and would be happy to listen and offer any advice I could. He really appreciated my taking an interest in him, and on occasion, he vented to me. This helped to keep him on a more even keel and improved our relationship.

Controlling Your Sphere of Influence

Sometimes, significant problems that you have no control over develop on the job. They come at you from left field, and there is nothing you can do about them. For example, early in my career, a new leader was appointed because our headquarters was unhappy with the way our office was performing. Virtually everything changed overnight, because his mandate was to shake the place up. This was difficult for me to handle, because I thought I was doing a good job, and I didn't want to see any changes in my particular area.

After much reflection, I decided to stop feeling sorry for myself and to face the situation head on. I concentrated on doing the best I could and made a point of not whining. I simply tried to control the things that were within my sphere of influence and to let go of the things that were not. It was not always easy, but it was a lot better than spending my time being angry over decisions that were not personal and that I could not control.

Eventually, this new leader came to see that I was making an important contribution to the office. He came to respect me because I was a serious individual who did a good job and was trying to get with the program. As time went by, he deferred to me more and more in my areas of expertise.

Reinventing Yourself

This is simply another name for renewal. As circumstances change at work, make sure that you find new ways to renew yourself so that you will stay, fresh, energized, motivated, and relevant.

In my situation, I found that writing is a wonderful way to express myself, help other people, and establish my legacy. As a result, I began writing books while I was still employed by the government. Writing gives me a sense of satisfaction and accomplishment, which is great. The funny thing is, I expected to be an artist, not a writer. Sometimes you never know how things will turn out.

Are You Willing to Move?

Speaking of reinventing yourself, one of the key decisions that you may have to make at some point in your career is whether you are willing to move. That is obviously a major life decision that can have serious ramifications for all aspects of your life. For example, what will be the impact on your spouse, especially if he has a job? How will a move affect your children? What about other family members and your friends? What is the real estate market like in the area in which you are living and in the area you will be moving to? How does the cost of living compare in the two locations? All of these things need to be factored into the equation and can be quite stressful.

There are many good reasons to physically relocate for another job. For one thing, sometimes the only way you can get ahead, or get ahead quickly, is to move because you will have far more promotion opportunities if you do not limit yourself to one part of the country or the state. Moreover, moving offers you different challenges and perspectives, especially if you work both in the field and at headquarters, which will make you a better and more well-rounded employee. Lastly, moving gives you the chance to meet additional people, which will make you better known and increase your personal network, all of which will benefit you in the long run.

In some agencies, the only way to reach the top is by being willing to sign a mobility agreement. Signing such an agreement means that you will move any time you are directed to. While this is a pretty high price to pay, many people are willing to pay it, especially since they understand that their organization needs the flexibility to move its human resources to where they are needed most.

Moving is not overly costly, since once you reach a certain level, the government will usually pay for your move (the broker's fee to sell your house, most closing costs, the cost of moving your family, and so on) and will even contract with a relocation company to help facilitate your move. Just make sure that you are clear about whether the government will pay for your particular move before going forward.

I have seen some people move 10 or more times in their career without any demonstrable issues, and I have seen others move only once or twice and experience significant problems. The ones who moved on multiple occasions came to accept this as a way of life, and simply dealt with each move as it occurred. As for the problems, they ranged from marital difficulties, especially when the husband and wife decided to live apart for a long period, to adverse reactions from the children, to extreme financial losses when the local market suddenly took a turn for the worse. The lesson from all of this is that each situation is different and that you have to make the best decision you can based on your own personal situation.

My only piece of advice here is to do the right thing based on the situation at hand and do not sacrifice everything for the job. Carefully weigh the pluses and minuses of a potential move, while including your family in the decision-making process, and you are likely to make the right decision. If necessary, consult with other people who have moved and try to learn from them. In my experience, most people who have moved have not regretted their decision and believe that it was the right thing to do. However, a small percentage of the people who moved deeply regretted that decision, either because they did not weigh all of the potential ramifications or because they were simply not aware of what they were getting themselves into.

For example, I watched a single mother drag her unwilling children across the country in order to take on a new assignment. The children were strongly opposed to leaving their friends and did not fit into their new school. All in all, they were very unhappy with the move, and they made their mother's life miserable. Moreover, because she was so preoccupied with her children's problems, she was unable to devote sufficient time to her new job. Eventually, she wound up moving back to her former position on the West Coast.

I have also seen a husband and wife live in different states for years at a time because they were each pursuing their own careers. While they both reached their desired career objectives, their marriage went down the drain. Only they can say whether the jobs were worth it.

As for me, my move from New York to Los Angeles went pretty well, since most of my family thought this was the right thing to do and I had a strong support network there. It was good to live in a different part of the country, meet a new group of people, and experience the California lifestyle. Moreover, it certainly paid off from a financial perspective and enabled me to purchase a lovely house with a pool.

The only person who was adversely affected by the move was my daughter, who was in the sixth grade at the time. She was at an impressionable age, and the move was quite difficult for her. She was not treated well by her new classmates and had a hard time adjusting. While she eventually came around, I regret that the move caused her quite a bit of angst.

Moving is not for everyone, especially people who are married and are responsible for many other people. However, it is often the best way to get ahead in government, and you should strongly consider it when planning your government career.

When and How to Retire

I did not have the opportunity to fully plan my retirement, as I left work the day my wife became ill.[5] However, since I had been looking ahead to retirement for quite some time, I was at least ready and able to retire from a financial perspective. The key to a smooth and comfortable retirement is careful planning from as many angles as possible.

The Financial Ramifications

Obviously, finances are very important, and as a government employee, you have an enormous advantage over most people. As described earlier, every level of government generally provides an excellent retirement package. If you are working under a system like CSRS, the factors driving the amount of your retirement are going to be your most recent salary[6] with the government and your length of service. If you are working under a system that primarily features some combination of social security, a 403(b) plan, and perhaps a small pension, the driving force will be how much money you can begin to save at a young age and how wisely you invest it. Regardless of the system you are under, you should look down the road when you are relatively young, figure out how much money you will need to live on during your retirement, and plan accordingly.

What you don't want to do is wait until you are 50 before even thinking about this issue. If you do, you will probably look at the numbers, find that you are unprepared, and realize that you will have to work into your late sixties or even your seventies before you have enough money to retire.

Sit down with a financial planner if you have to, but make sure you plan this part of your life very carefully. Take into account all of your assets, not just your government retirement plan, before deciding where you are and where you would like to be. Also, make sure that you carry all the benefits you need into retirement. For example, be certain that you will have health insurance (the federal government requires you to have health insurance through it for five years prior to retirement before allowing you to continue that insurance into retirement), ensure that you have adequate life insurance coverage, if needed, and look into acquiring long-term care insurance. Lastly, take care of your estate planning by preparing your will, including perhaps a living will, and considering a family trust. While doing this will cost you some money in the short term, it will help you protect your assets and ensure that they are transferred smoothly to your heirs upon your death.

What to Do When You Retire

From a different angle, try to envision what you want to do after you retire. Do you want to take another job, or do you simply want to stay home, relax, and play some golf? There is no right answer to this question, only an answer that is right for you. The important thing is that you know the answer to this question before you retire.

In my experience, the people who have known what they wanted to do after they retired have had the happiest retirements. Some retired only after they had found full-time jobs and started new careers, while others simply worked part-time in order to stay busy and bring in additional income. Some played golf almost every day and decompressed, while others did an extensive amount of travel to Europe or the Far East. Others volunteered their services to their church or synagogue, and still others decided to work out, sometimes with the aid of a personal trainer, and get in the best shape of their lives. Many, such as me, engaged in several of these activities, trying to make the most of their retirement.

The folks who had the hardest time in retirement were those who retired because they were unhappy at work and simply decided that it was time to leave. While they solved one problem by retiring, they created an entirely different set of problems by retiring without a plan. They suddenly found themselves with all sorts of time on their hands and nothing to do, which is a pretty difficult situation to deal with. People who had been active for thirty or more years and had spent eight or more hours of every business day interacting with other people now had only silence to deal with, no structure in their lives, and very little social activity during the day. Believe me, having been forced to retire before my time, I understand exactly what these people have to go through.

In my case, I had a purpose when I left work, which was to try to keep my wife alive. However, once she died, I was alone, without a direction and out of touch with many people. To complicate matters, I couldn't have gone back to work even if I had wanted to, since I was still dealing with severe back problems that ultimately required four more surgeries. The most difficult things for me to deal with were the lack of direction in my life and the fact that I couldn't get back into the world and be with people on a regular basis. When you are lying in bed for extended periods of time, you almost pray that the phone will ring, showing that someone still cares about you and wants to talk for a few minutes. It's pretty much the same thing for people who retire without a plan. They wander around aimlessly, desperately looking for something to do.

As my health improved, I began to rebuild my life. I had spent many years thinking about retirement, so I pretty much knew what I wanted to do from a business perspective. I wanted to write, teach, give speeches, and consult with other organizations in both the public and the private sectors. While it took me quite a while to develop myself in these areas, I made sure that I got back out into the world, marketed myself as much as possible, and reconnected with all of the people I cared about. As of this writing, I am planning my fourth and fifth books, have multiple speaking engagements lined up, and am bidding for several consulting contracts.

When to Retire

I pondered this question for a number of years, since for the most part, I loved my job and didn't think that I would retire until years after I first became eligible. I used to discuss this issue with the old-timers, i.e., both those who had already retired and those who were near retirement. What

I heard from them was that I would begin to see signs that would tell me when it was time.

For example, one individual told me that he knew he was ready to go when he went on a two-week vacation and did not look forward to coming back to work. While I'm sure that some of you who are years away from retirement may already feel that way about work, I suspect that this is more a function of your current job than of your overall attitude toward work. As this individual put it, toward the end of his vacation, he had always looked forward to getting back into the swing of things at work, so once the old desire was gone, he knew that it was time to move on to the next phase of his life.

Another individual explained to me that he knew it was time to leave when he looked around and noticed that all the people he had started his career with were gone. He realized that he was now dealing with a different generation of employees who had interests and experiences different from his, and that it was simply time for him to find a new group of people in his life.

A third person decided to retire simply because she felt that she had given over 30 years of her life to the government, and she wanted to do other things while she was still physically able to. She went biking throughout Europe and visited many people across the country whom she had not seen in years. In her spare time, she assists the elderly by doing their taxes free of charge.

Conversely, I know several people who are in their sixties and are still working for the government. Each of these individuals has over 35 years of service, and they are still working simply because they enjoy the work and have not been able to find an acceptable alternative. These folks have given their personal situations a lot of thought and have concluded that continuing to work for the government is the right move for them. To me, this makes perfect sense, as they are doing something that gives them satisfaction and makes them happy.

Only you can decide when the time is right for you to retire from the government. The key is to think things through and to retire on your own terms. Don't retire on the spur of the moment, out of spite or frustration. Rather, take your time, develop a plan, weigh all of your options, and then retire when it is most advantageous to you.

CHAPTER 9

Personal Development

ONE OF THE CHARACTERISTICS that distinguish the most successful people is that they continue to learn throughout their lives. No matter how much money they have, no matter how much power they have, they are never satisfied, and they constantly try to improve. I think this is an excellent lesson for all of us.

When I was growing up, I was struck by how accomplished some people were at a young age, whereas others were less mature and progressed at a slower pace. As I got older, I noticed that in many cases, the people who started out less advanced moved past the people who were initially perceived as being the greater successes. Looking back on those dynamics, I recognized that one of the reasons for the shift in fortunes was that many of the people who started quickly relied almost exclusively on their innate talents and simply did not develop much further. In contrast, a lot of the people who started out slower worked hard at improving, and ultimately achieved greater success than their more talented comrades. Once again, the tortoise defeated the hare.

Engage in Growth Activities

To me, the difference between the two groups seems to be largely a function of personal drive. The people who wanted to get better did whatever it took to improve, while the people who were satisfied with themselves simply coasted, and before they knew it, others passed them by.

While talent is obviously important in getting ahead, that is only one piece of the puzzle. Ultimately, the people who have the most knowledge, skills, and abilities, and who have a strong track record of success, are the ones who make it to the top. Nobody is born with all of these qualities; you have to add them to your personal arsenal one step at a time. If you don't, remember that there are plenty of people out there who are doing everything they possibly can to get better. As Satchel Paige once said, "Don't look back; something might be gaining on you."

These people may be going to school at night and/or on weekends, reading extensively, taking on new and challenging assignments, or engaging in other such actions. Most of them will eventually rise in government because they have a burning desire to get ahead, recognize that there is no substitute for hard work, and are willing to put in the time, energy, and effort to get better. It's that simple.

The people who feel that they are owed a good living, and who have done pretty well for themselves so far because of their talent, charm, and/or personal contacts, will get to a certain level and then see their careers slow down. This is because you can't fool all of the people all of the time. Everyone watches everyone else, and each employee knows which people are hard workers . . . and which are not. No matter how slick you may be, in most cases, if you don't grow as an individual, it will eventually catch up to you. Sure, there is the occasional exception to the rule; however, by and large, if you play with matches, you will eventually get burned.

Let me give you a good example. John (not his real name) was a very bright individual, and he knew it. He believed that he was smarter than almost everyone else, and as a result, he constantly tried to take shortcuts on his way to the top, feeling that he could think his way out of any problem. For example, he worked as few hours as he possibly could, since he truly believed that grunt work was beneath him.

Observing John over the years, I've been struck by the fact that he has never really changed as a person. In fact, he is virtually the same individual today that he was many years ago, albeit with less hair and a few more aches and pains. Let me be clear about this: I am not talking about his character or personality, since that remains the same for most people. Rather, I am talking about his interests and his view of the world, which to me seem to have remained relatively static.

He watches the same television shows and the same sports events that he always did. He rarely travels, but when he does, he invariably goes to Las Vegas, to an island, or to see members of his family. He hardly ever volunteers his time to worthy causes, and he has never coached a children's sports team. Perhaps most tellingly, he has not read a book in more than 30 years.

When he had surgery on several of his joints, he did virtually no follow-up exercise to strengthen the surrounding muscles. He said that the exercise was "too much work," and as a result, he continued to suffer from his condition. While exercise alone would not have solved his problem, if his muscles had been stronger, this certainly would have taken a lot of the strain off his joints. As a result, today he continually relies on Advil to relieve his symptoms, which I suspect will do him greater harm in the long term.

I'm not saying that he is a bad person or that he has led a less than desirable life. In fact, he is a very good person, has certainly had more than his fair share of laughs, and is more than entitled to live his life as he sees fit. What I am saying is that, at least in my own personal view, he has not tried to improve himself in many areas, and this has cost him dearly.

He rarely tries to learn new ideas; he has not done much traveling, which might have exposed him to new cultures and new perspectives; he has not taken any classes, which might have taught him new skills; and he has not joined any groups or clubs that could have introduced him to a different type of people from the ones he has been associated with for decades. He has simply stayed within his comfort zone and has not tried other things that might have made him uncomfortable in the short term, but would have made him a better and more well-rounded individual in the long term.

When an issue crops up that attracts his attention, he does not take the time to read about it and learn the facts. Instead, he asks someone else who has made the effort to grasp the key points to explain the subject to him in greater detail.

From a career perspective, his unwillingness to grow as a person has certainly harmed him. He left several jobs because he was unhappy, in part because he didn't like waking up early and working a 40-hour week, and in part because he felt that these jobs were beneath him. Moreover, he did not like working with government employees because he thought they were lazy and were not interested in doing a good job. I strongly suspect that when he came into contact with other, more successful individuals who might have been able to advance his career, they were able to see through him, concluded that he was not someone who engaged in personal growth opportunities, and so passed on helping him.

Let's contrast John's story with Bob's (not his real name either). Bob was just as smart as John, but he took a different approach to life, some of which was not of his own choosing. For example, he was drafted during the Vietnam War and spent several years in the military serving his country. He eventually received an honorable discharge, went back to school, and earned his bachelor's degree.

Bob had had a speech impediment while he was growing up, meaning that he had frequently stuttered in public. Imagine how difficult that must have been for a young child. He had spent many years working hard to overcome this problem, but he had finally done so. During this ordeal, he did not see himself as a victim, although I'm sure he felt a bit sorry for himself at times. Instead, he attacked the problem head on, with the support of his family and speech professionals, and he finally licked it. Today, if you were to meet him, you would never guess that at one time he used to stutter profusely.

After graduation, Bob went to work for the government, and he immediately distinguished himself as an up-and-comer. However, although he was quickly placed on a fast track, because management recognized his talents and abilities, Bob never relaxed for a moment. He continued to work very hard, took on all the tough assignments, and worked long hours when necessary in order to make sure that the job got done.

Bob also engaged in a wide variety of self-development activities. For example, he spent a good deal of time learning from senior members of management. He constantly asked them questions, trying to understand why things worked the way they did, and he frequently challenged their thinking, trying to find better ways to do things. When computers were introduced into the workplace, he immersed himself in the complexities of information technology. Eventually many people turned to him for assistance on working with their computer.

He read voraciously, plowing through books on everything from business to economics to home repair to a variety of self-help topics. When he watched television, he spent much of his time watching the news and the History and Discovery Channels. While he was driving to work each day, he generally listened to the Public Broadcasting System because he felt that this was a good way to receive more detailed information regarding the important issues of the day.

In his spare time, he coached a local soccer team. Since he did not have much of a background in sports, he attended coaching clinics and read several books on soccer theory. Eventually, he became a strong and innovative coach, and in one particular year, his team did not allow a single goal.

While Bob eventually became the youngest member of the senior executive service in his organization, his path to the top was not easy. For one thing, he had to take on increasing responsibilities while at the same time tending to a sick wife. She had a variety of emotional problems, which meant that he was frequently taking her to doctors and often had to take on a disproportionately large role in raising their children. When he was required to relocate in order to become a senior executive, he chose to live in the area that was best suited to his wife's condition, meaning that he had to commute much further to work than most other senior executives.

Because of his wife's condition, Bob was rarely able to travel with her. However, because he recognized the importance of seeing new places, he tried to travel every year, sometimes with a friend and other times by himself. He went to Europe, Canada, a national park, and so on, making sure to smell the roses, despite having a less than idyllic personal life.

Bob will be retiring shortly, having earned the respect and admiration of his peers, as well as a generous pension. Now contrast his situation with that of John, who will probably have to work for another 10 or 15 years. John had plenty of opportunities to better himself, both personally and professionally. However, he chose to live his life pretty much the way he had always done, focusing on his narrow interests instead of getting out into the world and developing himself. Today, he sees himself as a victim, someone who simply had a stretch of bad luck that prevented him from achieving his goals.

From my perspective, John's situation is a self-fulfilling prophecy. He chose comfort over personal growth and relaxation over hard work, and it eventually came back to haunt him. While life is certainly not fair, and John did experience his share of bad luck, most of us usually do. It's how we react to the bad times that ultimately distinguishes us. John chose to take shortcuts, the easy way out, and now he is paying the price.

On the other hand, Bob had his share of challenges as well, but the end result was quite different. The difference is that he worked his butt off and constantly tried to improve, and all his hard work paid off. John did not do so, and is now suffering the consequences.

In my particular situation, I tried very hard not to become too comfortable or predictable. In addition to engaging in many of the activities I mentioned earlier, I tried other things that I would not even have considered when I was younger. For example, I took several yoga classes and enjoyed its focus on the harmony of mind and body. Its use of movement, breathing, relaxation, and meditation in order to establish a balanced approach to life resonated quite strongly with me. I read about Buddhism and was struck by its philosophy: "Suffering ceases when desire ceases, and . . . enlightenment obtained through right conduct, wisdom, and meditation releases one from desire, suffering, and rebirth."[1] This view was quite different from what I was used to, since I had been raised in a Western culture, and it made me question some of my deeply held beliefs.

I took a creative writing course that taught me how to write from my deeper voice. It showed me how to not only report facts and information, but also convey the sights, sounds, and smells of a particular event so that the reader could almost feel that he was there. I intend to use the tools I learned from this class to write a family memoir, which is something I would never have envisioned undertaking a few years ago.

When I moved to California, I reconnected with my Jewish roots by joining a local synagogue and taking on a variety of assignments ranging from becoming a trustee to being the vice president of administration. As a result of this endeavor, I reread the Bible, watched numerous documentaries about religious issues, and am now planning a trip to Israel. As of this writing, I am also in the process of redesigning the interior of the synagogue, with the centerpiece being an 18-panel, 50-foot-long pictorial history of Judaism. I am very excited about this project, and have devoted many hours to its design and implementation, because I have found something that enables me to use my talents, give back to my community, and continue to grow as an individual.

One reason why I started doing all this was that I was inspired by other friends of different faiths. One of them is currently serving as the president of his church, while another spends some of his precious time in Europe helping his church redesign its worldwide activities. One cannot help but be impressed by the selflessness of these individuals and want to follow their examples.

Other friends of mine have also been doing amazing things. Several volunteer part-time in Africa, helping to teach young children or to bring needed supplies. Another works with the Desmond Tutu Peace Foundation "to support and promote the creation of a culture of peace throughout the world."[2] Many of them work tirelessly to raise money to fight cancer, with the goal of eventually eliminating it as a major health problem. The point here is that all of these individuals are making a difference, and in doing so are also growing as individuals.

I know of a woman who, while managing a large government office, went to school at night to earn her Ph.D. This helped make her a more informed and a better leader and positioned her for her next move after retirement. I know of several other individuals who have been working on books and screenplays; one of these people actually sold a pilot program to one of the studios and resigned from the government. I even know of a senior leader who spends virtually all of his vacation time backpacking in the national parks because it helps him become "one with nature."

All of the folks I have described here are accomplished people who constantly try to stretch themselves by engaging in growth activities, both inside and outside of their work lives. In fact, since they are all highly principled individuals, I think it is fair to say that they follow the same core values in every facet of their lives, which is one reason why they are so successful.

In my experience, most people's growth activities are driven from within; however, outside events sometimes force you to change your thinking, whether you would like to or not. For example, the deaths of my wife and my brother within a two-week period were life-changing events that I am still grappling with. In response, I saw a therapist to help me get through these twin tragedies. I recognized that there are times in life when you need help, and I was glad to work with a caring professional who has greatly assisted me.

I also read about a dozen books on coping with loss, and this helped me to understand the nature of grief and to put my feelings in perspective. The knowledge I gained from these books even helped me console other members of my family who were experiencing similar feelings.

Another approach I took was to talk with people who had experienced similar losses. Most of these consultations were helpful and taught me a lot about the human spirit. Interestingly, John, whom I discussed earlier, advised me that the best approach for dealing with grief was to simply "not think about my losses," which, in retrospect, I feel was poor advice.

Believe it or not, I even met with a medium, which was completely out of character for me. I did this on the advice of a dear friend whom I trusted, and because I wanted to remain open-minded, even about a subject on which I was certainly skeptical. That experience proved to be life-changing, since the medium revealed information to me that she could not possibly have known. I truly believe that I was able to communicate with my departed wife and brother through her, and this was incredibly comforting, although a bit disconcerting. Without a doubt, it has certainly altered my perceptions about death and the afterlife.

That having been said, I certainly made some mistakes while trying to cope with my grief. For one thing, I allowed myself to become too distracted by outside events and didn't give myself sufficient time to grieve. Moreover, I wasn't as in touch with my feelings as I had thought, and as a result, I sometimes went down the wrong path. However, throughout the process, I tried to learn from my experiences and to make adjustments along the way, and that certainly helped.

The point of this discussion is that success is a choice, and that day in and day out, accomplished people make the choice to constantly improve. That is why Michael Jordan, perhaps the greatest basketball player who ever lived, decided to strengthen his body midway in his career. He knew that as good as he was, he needed to get even stronger if he was going to withstand the pounding he was taking from his opponents and reach his goals. That is why Vladimir Horowitz, arguably the world's greatest pianist, was acclaimed for his rigorous practice regimen, regarding which he is credited with having said, "If I don't practice for a day, I know it. If I don't practice for two days, my wife knows it. If I don't practice for three days, the world knows it."[3]

If you want to make the most of your government career, then make the most of your time. Don't waste your time playing the role of the victim and feeling sorry for yourself, don't sit in front of a television for hours and hours vegetating and gaining weight, and don't do what you have always done, or you will get the same results you have always gotten. Get out in the world, try new and exciting things, and remake yourself into a better person. You'll be glad you did.

Study the Lives of Successful People

An excellent way to grow is to study the lives of successful people. If you do this, you will learn that virtually all great leaders have had their problems, their struggles, and their challenges. What ultimately made these people so successful was that they learned from their mistakes, kept growing as individuals, and continued to persevere despite incredible obstacles and setbacks.

Let's look briefly at the life of Abraham Lincoln, who overcame an amazing array of challenges in order to become perhaps our country's greatest president. For example, his mother died of milk sickness when Lincoln was only nine, and he was distant from his father for most of his life. His formal education consisted of roughly 18 months of schooling, but he educated himself throughout his life and became an avid reader.

Lincoln began his political career in 1832, at age 23, when he was defeated in an election for the Illinois general assembly. He later damaged his political reputation with a speech in which he said, "God of Heaven has forgotten to defend the weak and innocent, and permitted the strong band of murderers and demons from hell to kill men, women, and children, and lay waste and pillage the land of the just."

On November 4, 1842, Lincoln married Mary Todd, with whom he had a tumultuous relationship. The couple had four sons, but only one of them, Robert Todd Lincoln, survived into adulthood. Another son, William "Willie" Wallace Lincoln, was born in 1850 and died on February 20, 1862, during President Lincoln's first term.

Prior to Lincoln's election, seven Confederate states had seceded, declaring that they were a new nation. However, Lincoln refused to recognize the Confederacy, and the Civil War began shortly thereafter.

Before his inauguration, President-elect Lincoln evaded potential assassins in Baltimore. He arrived at Washington, D.C., in disguise and was mocked by the local media.

The war placed a great deal of strain and tension on Lincoln, and it prematurely aged him; for one thing, roughly 600,000 Americans died in a war that was waged entirely on American soil. One of Lincoln's greatest sources of frustration was his generals, who were either incompetent or unwilling to fight. This led to limited military success until late 1863, when Lincoln finally found the right leader: Ulysses S. Grant. As we all know, the North ultimately prevailed and the Union was preserved, with much of the credit rightly going to President Lincoln for his extraordinary leadership.

As I reflect on Lincoln's life, I'm still struck by how much he had to deal with and how much perseverance he showed despite overwhelmingly difficult circumstances. Here was a man who lost his mother early in life; had a strained relationship with his father, a limited education, and an awkward marriage; lost three of his four children; and had to guide our country through the Civil War.

One thing that is clear is that these difficulties helped shape Lincoln into a great man and a great leader. He did not sit back and feel sorry for himself, at least most of the time. Instead, he constantly learned and evolved, and he stepped up to the plate in a way that no other American ever did. The next time you are feeling down and angry about your plight at work, think about what Lincoln had to deal with. I suspect that you will find it comforting to know that your situation pales in comparison to Lincoln's plight, and that if he could ultimately overcome the challenges that were set in front of him, so can you.[4]

Ulysses S. Grant is another example of a leader who struggled throughout much of his life. He graduated from West Point with an undistinguished record. After the Mexican War, his pregnant wife could not accompany him to many of his military assignments because his salary was too low to support a family on the frontier. Grant eventually resigned from the Army, and rumors that he had been drunk on duty persisted. As a civilian, Grant struggled for years, failing at several business ventures. Finally, out of desperation, he went to work for his father as an assistant in his leather shop.

Once the Civil War broke out, the governor of Illinois assigned Grant to command an unruly volunteer regiment, and he quickly whipped it into shape. He was then appointed brigadier general of volunteers. From that point on, he quickly established his reputation as a skilled and determined military leader, winning important battles at Shiloh, Vicksburg, and Chattanooga. Grant's willingness to fight and win impressed President Lincoln, who eventually appointed him the general-in-chief of all the armies of the United States.

Grant's tenacity, skill, and willingness to fight a war of attrition ultimately led to victory for the North. In recognition for his efforts, he was given the rank of General of the Army of the United States, the equivalent of a four-star general in today's U.S. Army.

Grant was elected president in 1868 and served two terms. However, his administration was characterized by financial and political corruption on the part of his top aides, whom he protected when they were exposed. He is generally considered to be one of our country's worst presidents, and he was unsuccessful in winning a third term. He subsequently went into bankruptcy as a result of a series of bad investments, wrote his memoirs, which were enormously successful, and died of throat cancer in 1885.[5]

Grant, like Lincoln, had many challenges and many failures in his life. However, he continued to persevere and to fight for what he believed in. When the opportunity for him to excel at what he did best arose, he took advantage of it and cemented his reputation, although once the war ended, he failed again, and on a larger scale. The lesson here is that no one is perfect, and that failure is part of life. The key is to never give up, learn from your mistakes, and try to take advantage of your opportunities.

Many other successful people have similar stories. Harry Truman never graduated from college and went bankrupt during the recession of 1921. He sometimes spoke of Jews and African Americans in derogatory terms. He was a product of the Kansas City Democratic machine, led by boss Tom Pendergast, and he often felt like a failure. However, as he said, "I've had a few setbacks in my life, but I never gave up."

After he became president following the death of President Roosevelt, Truman's public opinion ratings eventually reached the lowest level ever recorded for any U.S. president. However, his persistence paid off, leading to his legendary upset victory over Thomas E. Dewey in 1948. Truman continued to persevere and dealt with such difficult issues as the atomic bomb, the Berlin airlift, the establishment of the United Nations, the recognition of the state of Israel, and the Korean War. Although Truman did not run for president in 1952, scholarly assessments of his presidency have been very kind to him, and today he is generally ranked among the top 10 presidents.[6]

Our founding fathers faced similar challenges. For example, the Revolutionary War went on for years, and George Washington had to struggle with all sorts of management problems ranging from lack of experience among the troops to a high desertion rate caused by low morale to weak leaders below him to supply concerns. Since the outcome of the war was in doubt for quite some time, he even worried about how it would affect his reputation.[7] Doesn't all of that hit home and sound pretty familiar?

It really doesn't matter whether you are a president, a general, a CEO, or simply a first-line supervisor of a government office; the challenges, the problems, and the headaches are pretty much the same—people issues, morale concerns, financial quagmires, supply limitations, and, of course, personal problems galore. The primary difference is simply the scope. During some of the most difficult periods of my life, I have found it very comforting to know that other people have dealt with similar and sometimes much greater problems than I have been facing, and have overcome them through perseverance, tenacity, and courage, even if they were not always confident of the ultimate outcome. Recognizing that even the most successful people have had more than their fair share of crosses to bear has made my personal burdens a bit easier to carry.

Who Is Going to Define You?

I think it is pretty clear that successful people tend to define themselves by their own behavior and actions. While they are all human and occasionally feel sorry for themselves, whenever they are knocked down, they all get up off the canvas and get back into the fight. They do not see themselves as victims who have no control over their personal situations; rather, they simply do their best to adjust to events and circumstances as they unfold.

It is this mind-set that often determines success or failure. Far too often, I have seen my coworkers decide that they are victims and then pretty much give up, because they feel that they have been wronged. While they may indeed have been wronged, so has everyone else at some time in her career and her life. Life is not fair, and successful people understand that. The difference is, they do something about it, while other, less successful people often give up and become cynical.

As part of your overall growth, you will need to make a choice about how to deal with these types of situations. Some people choose to cede all of their personal power to their supervisors and, as a result, allow their supervisors to define who they are as employees, and to a certain extent as individuals. Given that there are plenty of bad supervisors out there, if you allow this to happen, you will be making a major career blunder, in my view.

What do I mean when I say do not allow your supervisor to define you? Simply put, I mean do not blindly follow your supervisor and do whatever he wants you to do regardless of the consequences. Certainly, you should always comply with your supervisor's orders, as long as they are legal and do not place your health in jeopardy. That is a given.

What you should not do, however, is align yourself so closely with one particular supervisor that she will have an overwhelming impact on your personal life, such as dictating what jobs you should apply for, allowing your sense of self-worth to ebb and flow every time she says something good or bad to you or about you, and being so connected to her that you begin to emulate her and take on her characteristics and faults. If this happens, you will lose your independence, and before you know it, you will be viewed as just another one of that supervisor's personal lackeys. In a sense, that's what happened to Harry Truman when he was viewed as a product of boss Tom Pendergast, and he suffered from that label for years.

The point here is not to let your supervisor or anyone else define you, because if you do, it will most certainly stunt your personal growth. Maintain your balance, your independence, and your sense of self-worth, and establish the direction that makes the most sense for you. While you should always be a team player and you may sometimes have to go where your organization directs you, remain your own person and do not let your life revolve exclusively around the whims of people who are more powerful than you. Even if you are in a particularly onerous situation, in which you are constantly getting hammered by your supervisor or others, do not fall into that trap. Remember, no situation remains constant, and you can change jobs down the road. Always do the best you can, but make sure that you define who you are.

Let's look at a few people who worked for the same extremely difficult and demanding boss and see how they handled the situation. First of all, let me provide you with some context. This boss was the type who viewed his subordinates through the prism of personal loyalty. As long as they were completely loyal to him (as defined by him), he was supportive of them. However, if they did anything that he deemed to be disloyal, such as taking a job he didn't approve of, he took it personally and went out of his way to hurt them (i.e., by bad-mouthing them, ensuring that they weren't selected for a certain position, and so on). As you can see, he was a bit of a control freak, and he tried to use his power to control and define other people for his own benefit.

I recall one individual who often worked for this man and always did whatever he wanted her to. In fact, this person became so closely tied to his star that the two of them, to a large extent, became interchangeable. Many people who had once both admired and respected this person were both saddened and disenchanted by the way in which she began to act.

They noted that she began to act just like her boss: making things personal, micromanaging subordinates, and often making a mountain out of a molehill in order to put other people on the defensive and to make herself look good by comparison.

In the short term, this helped this person's career, since promotions and power quickly followed. However, by allowing her boss to be so controlling and by moving away from the core values that she had embraced earlier, I believe that this person at least figuratively sold out and will pay a price for it down the road. Remember, what goes around comes around.

Conversely, I can think of other individuals who did not so readily comply with every whim of that same supervisor. All of these individuals were honorable people, and they were always loyal to both the organization and the individual in question. However, none of them were blindly loyal, and on occasion they would voice an opinion that was different from that supervisor's, even though they knew that doing so would hurt them. They did this because they wanted to be able to look at themselves in the mirror each morning and know that they had tried to do the right thing. That was more important to them than losing a bonus or two, or some other perk that did not really mean much in the larger scheme of things.

Let me make it clear that these people did pay a price for maintaining their individuality. After all, it's not a lot of fun to know that your boss will get back at you for doing something that is inconsistent with his way of thinking. Many of these people experienced a lot of stress and agonized over the situation. However, in the end, they all concluded that they needed to "render therefore unto Caesar the things which are Caesar's; and unto God the things that are God's."

On a practical level, they also knew that this person's reign would eventually end, because all things, whether good or bad, eventually do. They were willing to wait for the storm to pass, knowing that the sun would eventually shine. They each decided that the most important thing to do was to maintain their integrity and take a few hits if necessary, rather than merely being a shill for someone else. They decided to let their character define them, not their job or a particular individual.

Unfortunately, many people become so wrapped up in their jobs that they define their own sense of self-worth almost exclusively by how they are doing at work. The problem with this way of thinking is that you are likely to make compromises with other parts of your life that you may regret later.

Your job is obviously important, but it is not everything. There is simply more to life than that. That is why, to me, personal growth sometimes means sacrificing your job ambitions, at least in the short term, for the greater good of your family. It may mean not accepting a promotion because pulling your child out of school in the middle of the school year may harm him. It may mean not applying for a higher-graded position because you are happy where you are and do not want to take on added responsibility and pressure at that point, or it may mean not transferring to another location because of the harm it will do to your spouse's career and psyche.

The point of this section is that you should be the one to define who you are. If you want to use your career as the only way you define yourself, that's fine, as long as it is a conscious choice and you understand the ramifications of it. Conversely, if you want to define yourself by a different standard, i.e., the type of person you are, you may wind up making some other choices. Neither path is easy, but I firmly believe that you will be a much happier person in the long run if you choose to define yourself by the way you live your life.

Smell the Roses

As this book comes to a close, I want to emphasize the importance of always taking the time to smell the roses. Sure, government employees operate under pressure and sometimes feel as though they are constantly swimming upstream. Unfortunately, that seems to be the nature of the highly pressurized world we are currently living in. On top of that, there are children to raise, bills to pay, health concerns to address, and so on. Keeping all of that in mind, I want to restate my firm belief that if you truly want to manage both your government career and your life successfully, it is essential that you slow down a bit each day and try to appreciate the good things in life.

As I've said before, because you are a government employee, you have the privilege and the opportunity to make a difference in the lives of other Americans. Why not take a few minutes and reflect upon that each day? I tried to do that when I worked for the Department of Veterans Affairs, and it literally changed my life.

For example, I remember getting personally involved in the case of a former prisoner of war from World War II. He was shot down over Japan, taken prisoner by the Japanese, and beaten to a pulp. When he was repatriated to the Untied States, he weighed only 80 pounds and suffered from a variety of physical and mental ailments. Despite this, when he applied to the VA for benefits, he was treated quite poorly, and he turned away from the agency in anger.

As you can imagine, he had a difficult and troubled personal life that included frequent bouts of alcoholism. Eventually, his situation was brought to my attention, which led to his finally receiving the monthly benefits that he should have been getting all along. We became friendly, he shared his personal story with me in greater detail, and he even donated some of his personal artifacts to our office's veterans' museum.

Knowing that I had made a difference in the life of this true American hero was very gratifying for me and made me feel that I was making a difference in the lives of others. It also made me more determined than ever to help as many veterans as I possibly could, and it ultimately led to my developing the concept of visual management, which I discussed earlier in this book. Lastly, it instilled in me an infectious passion for the VA's mission, which I've been able to share with others. In essence, this was my way of smelling the roses at work: Making sure that I took the time to appreciate the great job I had and the outstanding customers I was privileged to serve.

Many other successful civil servants have taken the same approach, whether they worked for the Federal Aviation Administration, the mayor's office, or the police department. For example, while teaching is a tough, demanding profession, it also offers the chance to shape young minds and truly change young people's lives. Several members of my family are or were teachers, and what attracted each and every one of them to the field was the chance to do something special. While there were many days when each of them was frustrated by the bureaucracy and the sometimes overwhelming nature of the job, there were many more days where they told me stories of how they had been able to have a positive impact on the lives of one of their students. Ultimately, this is what it is all about.

Keep in mind that when I say that you should smell the roses, I mean that you should do that in all aspects of your life. When you are at home, try to take a step back and make sure that you are truly appreciating your spouse. For instance, when was the last time you bought her flowers and told her you loved her? I know I wish I could do that again for my departed wife, and now I will never have that chance, at least not in this life. When was the last time you took a few moments to watch your children sleep, to appreciate the life you brought into this world, while recognizing that before you know it, they will be grown up and out of the house?

Are you taking the time to appreciate the beauty of a Vermeer painting, a Gershwin song, or a play by Shakespeare? Do you recognize the scientific genius of Albert Einstein or the exquisite way in which Roger Federer plays tennis? Have you gazed at the stars in the sky during the night and wondered about the size of the universe or stood in awe at the rugged splendor of one of our national parks? If you have, good for you; if you have not, why not get started and begin to smell the roses in every area of your life?

Ultimately, managing your government career is all about managing your life. If you are willing to live both your business and your personal life according to your core values, work hard, take no shortcuts, maintain a positive attitude, and find the right balance between the two lives, there is no reason why you can't be a happy and successful person. Good luck!

Notes

Chapter 1

1   The U.S. Bureau of the Census classifies local governments into the following major types: (a) county governments, (b) municipal and township governments, (c) special district governments, and (d) school district governments/public school systems.

2   The 1998 Federal Activities Inventory Reform Act requires federal agencies to maintain lists of all activities performed by federal employees that could be outsourced to private firms, as reported by the agencies. Activities that are considered "inherently governmental" are not included on these lists.

3   U.S. Office of Personnel Management, http://www.opm.gov/rif/employee_guides/career_transition.asp U.S.

> Agency plans must consist of three parts:
>
> (1) **Agency Career Transition Services**
> Each agency provides career transition services to surplus employees, giving them skills and resources to help them find other employment. These services might include skills assessment, resume preparation, counseling, or job search assistance. Agencies must also develop policies on retraining their surplus employees.
>
> (2) **Agency Special Selection Priority Under the Career Transition Assistance Plan (CTAP)**
> Agencies must give selection priority to their own well qualified surplus employees who apply for vacancies in other agency components in the local commuting area. Agencies must notify their surplus or displaced employees when they plan to fill these jobs. With a few exceptions, the agency must select those who apply and are eligible and well qualified before any other candidate from within or outside the agency.

(3) **Agency Reemployment Priority Lists (RPL)**
Each agency must also maintain a Reemployment Priority List (RPL) for each local commuting area where it separates employees by reduction in force. Employees can register for the RPL to tell their former agency that they want to return if the agency has vacancies. Before the agency can select a candidate outside its workforce, it must first check the RPL for that location.

Interagency Career Transition Assistance Plan (ICTAP)
Under ICTAP, employees must apply for positions in the local commuting area and include proof that they were displaced. ICTAP gives an eligible, well-qualified employee selection priority over almost any other applicant from outside the agency. For example, a Department of Defense employee with a RIF separation notice could apply for a competitive service vacancy in the local commuting area at the Department of Education. In most cases, Education must select this well-qualified person for the position before choosing another applicant from outside the agency.

4   New York State Governor's Office of Employee Relations, http://www.goer .state.ny.us/orientation/careers.html.

5   In general, government employees cannot appeal their termination during a probationary period unless they believe they were removed because of reasons related to prohibited discrimination (race, sex, national origin, and other such causes).

6   Seattle Civil Service Commission, http://www.cityofseattle.net/csc/.

7   Brian Friel, "Labor Pains," *Government Executive* magazine, October 1, 2002.

8   About AFSCME, http://www.afscme.org/about/aboutindex.cfm.

9   USAJOBS, "Working for America," http://www.usajobs.opm.gov/ei61.asp.

10 Ohio.gov, http://www.ohio.gov/stateemployee/.

11 Bureau of the Census, "Federal, State and Local Governments," *Census of Governments*, 2002.

12 Ibid.

13 This refers to the influx of people into the government near the end of the Vietnam War.

14 Corporate Leadership Council, January 2004, http://www.wapa.gov/news room/pdf/success.pdf.

15 USAJOBS, "Working for America," http://www.usajobs.opm.gov/.

16 U.S. Office of Personnel Management, OPM.gov, http://www.opm.gov/ses/.

17 Ibid.

18 Ibid.

19 Toward the end of the war, disabled veterans were given preference for fed-
    eral jobs. The act provided that

    > Persons honorably discharged from the military or naval service by reason of
    > disability resulting from wounds or sickness incurred in the line of duty shall
    > be preferred for appointments to civil offices, provided they are found to pos-
    > sess the business capacity necessary for the proper discharge of the duties of
    > such offices.

    U.S. Office of Personnel Management, "Appendix D: A Brief History of
    Veterans' Preference," *VetGuide*, http://opm.gov/veterans/html/vghist.asp.

20 U.S. Office of Personnel Management, OPM.gov, http://www.opm.gov/vet
    erans/html/vetsinfo.asp.

21 South Dakota Bureau of Personnel, http://www.state.sd.us/bop/jobs/
    jobs_applying.htm.

22 Military.com Benefits, http://www.military.com/benefits/veteran-benefits/
    utah-state-veterans-benefits.

23 Texas Veterans Commission, http://www.tvc.state.tx.us/vetpref.htm.

24 North Miami, City of Progress, http://www.northmiamifl.gov/cityhall/per
    sonnel/jobs.asp.

25 City of West Sacramento, Administrative Policy, December 12, 2001, http://
    www.cityofwestsacramento.org/cityhall/employment/veterans.pdf.

26 This means that they do not have to compete with the general public for
    positions announced under USAJOBS, nor do they have to follow the proce-
    dures that most members of the public have to follow.

27 U.S. Equal Opportunity Commission, "Interim Report on Best Practices for
    the Employment of People with Disabilities in State Government," October
    29, 2004.

28 Ibid.

29 Ibid.

30 U.S. Office of Personnel Management, "Federal Employment of People with
    Disabilities," http://www.opm.gov/disability/appempl_3–11.asp.

31 Ibid.

32 Studentjobs.gov, http://www.studentjobs.gov/firsttimers.asp.

33 Federal Jobs Net Career Center, *Government Jobs/Federal Jobs/Post Office
    Jobs*, http://federaljobs.net/student.htm.

34 Outstanding Scholar Program, *Government Jobs/Federal Jobs/Post Office Jobs*,
    http://federaljobs.net/oscholar.htm.

35 State of Illinois Job Opportunities, http://www.illinois.gov/jobs/index.cfm
    #intern.

36 Indiana State Personnel Department, http://www.in.gov/jobs/programs/
    internships.htm.

37 Yahoo Hot Jobs, http://hotjobs.yahoo.com/job-JIKBTVHFCDJ;_ylt = AiqL
    UzynbQjuHUxtiNu1SRz6Q6IX?search_url = %2Fjob-search-k-students-c
    -Government_Military.

38 At that time, teachers received deferments from military service.

39 Steven Barr, "Job Security Lures Young and Old to Government Work,"
    Washington Post, February 20, 2007, reporting on an as yet to be released
    Merit Systems Protection Board Survey.

40 Merit Systems Protection Board, "Merit Principles Survey 2005," http://
    www.mspb.gov/netsearch/viewdocs.aspx?docnumber = 251283&version =
    251556&application = ACROBAT.

41 Karen Rutzick, "Pay Gap: A Different Take," *Government Executive* maga-
    zine, May 18, 2006.

42 Congressional Budget Office, "Comparing Federal Employee Benefits with
    Those in the Private Sector," August 1998.

43 Congressional Budget Office, "Measuring Differences Between Federal and
    Private Pay," November 2002.

44 Stuart Greenfield, "Public Sector Employment: The Current Situation,"
    Center for State & Local Government Excellence (2007).

45 Steven Barr, "Federal Pay Scale Hampers Job Recruiters in Small Metros,"
    Washington Post, October 9, 2007.

46 Ibid.

47 The keystone of the Civil Service Reform Act of 1978, the SES was designed
    to be a corps of executives selected for their leadership qualifications.

48 Congressional Budget Office, "Comparing the Pay and Benefits of Federal
    and Nonfederal Executives," November 1999.

49 Ibid.

50 Ibid.

51 Congressional Budget Office, "Comparing the Pay of Federal and Nonprofit
    Executives: An Update," July 2003.

52 Institute for Policy Studies and United for a Fair Economy, "Executive Ex-
    cess 2006," August 30, 2006.

53 As of December 2005, the average senior executive earned $146,848 as com-
    pared to the average federal salary of about $63,000. Congressional Budget
    Office, "Characteristics and Pay of Federal Civilian Employees," March
    2007.

54 Mackinac Center for Public Policy, "What Price Government?" posted Feb-
    ruary 6, 2007, http://www.mackinac.org/article.aspx?ID = 8207.

55 Dave Swenson and Liesl Eathington, "Do Public Sector Employees in Iowa Earn More Than Private Sector Employees?" Department of Economics, Iowa State University, March 2005.

56 Oregon Business Plan: The Plan, http://www.oregonbusinessplan.org/pub lic_finance_review_compensation er ationale.html.

57 Program Evaluation Division, Office of the Legislative Auditor, State of Minnesota, February 3, 2000.

58 E. J. McMahon and Kathryn McCall, "Government Workers in New York: Empire State's Favored Class?" Empire Center for New York State Policy, September 1, 2006.

59 U.S. Office of Personnel Management, "Federal Human Capital Survey 2006."

60 On a somewhat ominous note, which probably relates to the issues of both pay and culture, only 43.5 percent felt that their unit was able to recruit people with the right skills.

61 U.S. Department of Labor, Bureau of Labor Statistics, "Career Guide to Industries," http://www.bls.gov/oco/cg/cgs042.htm.

62 Ibid.

63 U.S. Office of Personnel Management, "Federal Human Capital Survey 2006."

64 During this administration, my office received the OPM Director's PILLAR (Performance Incentives Leadership Linked to Achieving Results) Award, and I received the Presidential Rank Award and was prominently featured in both *Government Executive* magazine and the VA's *Vanguard* magazine.

65 Greenfield, "Public Sector Employment."

66 AICPA, "Federal and State Employee Retirement Programs," https://pfp.aic pa.org/Resources/Government + Benefits/Federal + and + State + Employee + Retirement + Programs/.

67 Steven H. Long and M. Susan Marquis, "Comparing Employee Health Benefits in the Public and Private Sectors, 1997," *Health Affairs* 18, no. 6, November/December 1999.

68 Obviously, some people move one or more times when they are growing up, so these comments don't apply to them.

69 Bureau of the Census, "Compendium of Public Employment 2002," *Census of Governments, Volume 3, Public Employment*, 2002.

70 Again, to some extent this is also driven by type of position. Certain types of positions, such as teachers, are more plentiful and therefore offer more opportunity at the local level.

71 Obviously, the converse can also be true. This same couple had made money when they bought and sold their previous house.

72   Tammy Flanagan, "CSRS vs. FERS," National Institute of Transition Plan-
     ning, March 31, 2006.

73   Employees who were under CSRS had the option of switching to FERS.

74   Flanagan, "CSRS vs. FERS."

75   In certain cases, you may be able to negotiate for a higher step on the pay
     schedule.

76   For example, if you leave a state agency and go to the federal government
     after 15 years of service, and then work 15 more years there and retire,
     you will be able to take and continue your thrift savings plan, if applicable.
     However, for the defined-benefit component of your retirement, which is
     usually based on earnings and years of service, your calculation will be based
     on 15 years of service, not 30.

Chapter 2

1   U.S. Office of Personnel Management, Veterans web site, http://www.opm
     .gov/veterans/html/vetsinfo.asp. Most state and local governments have pro-
     cedures similar to those of the federal government. However, because of the
     vast number of entities at those levels, it would be virtually impossible to
     list all of the variances in procedures for each entity.

2   For example, in the federal government, preference applies in *hiring* for vir-
     tually all jobs, but by and large, not for promotions. For further information
     on this topic, see U.S. Office of Personnel Management, Veterans, http://
     www.opm.gov/veterans/html/vetsinfo.asp.

3   For one thing, internal applicants already have an official personnel folder
     that contains a lot of key personal information. In some cases, this informa-
     tion is even in the computer system. State and local governments also use
     similar procedures for internal selections.

4   Obviously, there are other ways by which one can come into the govern-
     ment, such as internship programs, special hiring authorities, and so on,
     which were discussed in Chapter 1. However, the three routes discussed
     in this section are the main ways in which most people enter government
     service.

5   In my experience, the overwhelming majority of first- and second-line su-
     pervisor positions are filled from within. Only some higher-level supervisory
     positions that require an unusual degree of skill and experience tend to be
     filled from the outside.

6   Usually, it is fairly easy to switch agencies within the same level of govern-
     ment (e.g., within the federal government or within the same state govern-
     ment). However, when you try to move *between levels of government* (e.g.,
     between a state government and a local government, between the govern-
     ments of two different states, or between a state or local and the federal

government), you are treated as if you are simply a member of the public and have to compete with everyone else.

7   http://www.statelocalgov.net/.

8   http://jobsearch.about.com/od/governmentjobs1/Government_Jobs_Law_ Enforcement_Jobs.htm, which is a part of the *New York Times.*

9   From the GS-3 level, you can be promoted to a GS-5 after one year. Subsequent to that, for the next few years you can be promoted another one or two grades if you are qualified and selected, depending upon the job. If you do not get promoted for the first three years, you are likely to get a step increase plus a cost-of-living adjustment.

10 USAJOBS, Announcement 310-08-03, November 19–27, 2007.

11 U.S. Office of Personnel Management, "Salaries and Wages, Salary Table 2007, Philadelphia."

12

A.) A baccalaureate degree from an accredited educational institution authorized to grant baccalaureate degrees and B.) at least 24 semester hours (or equivalent) of study from an accredited institution of higher education in any of the following disciplines; accounting, business finance, law, contracts, purchasing, economics, industrial management, marketing, quantitative methods, and organization and management; or C.) a civilian employee in DOD, who occupied a GS-1102 position or contracting officer position with authority to award or administer contracts above the simplified acquisition threshold on or before September 30th, 2000 is excluded from the requirements of A & B above, but must meet the requirements identified in Public Law 101–510, section 1724. SPECIALIZED EXPERIENCE: One year of specialized experience equivalent to at least the next lower grade level in the normal line of progression. Specialized experience must have equipped the applicant with the particular knowledge, skills, and abilities to perform successfully the duties of the position to be filled.

USAJOBS Announcement DTC 08-494, November 20–27, 2007.

13 VRA stands for Veterans Recruitment Appointment, which allows the appointment of eligible veterans up to the GS-11 level or equivalent.

14 DVAAP stands for Disabled Veterans Affirmative Action Program.

15 USAJOBS, Announcement DTC-08-494, November 20–27, 2007.

16 When grades are announced with a slash (/) that means that the organization is willing to hire you at any normal promotion level from the trainee level up to the journeyman level, depending upon your qualifications, its needs, and where you are on the civil service register.

17 USAJOBS, Announcement 08PH3-SBE0088-512-5-11, November 26– December 16, 2007.

18   This job was located in New York City; however, it was announced for the Philadelphia area, since I scanned for jobs within 100 miles of Philadelphia.

19   This means that if your performance is acceptable, you will automatically be promoted two grades per year (some jobs have one grade interval promotions, while others have two) until you reach the journeyman grade of GS-11.

20   USAJOBS, Announcement PHJL-07-143476S0, June 12, 2007–June 9, 2008.

21   USAJOBS, Announcement DSCP-08-445, November 20–December 4, 2007.

22   Pennsylvania State Civil Service Commission, http://www.scsc.state.pa.us/scsc/cwp/view.asp?a = 11&q = 139639.

23   Ibid.

24   Pennsylvania State Civil Service Commission, Test Announcement 2006-764, issued June 9, 2006.

25   Ibid.

26   City of Philadelphia Personnel Department, *ExamNumber:*08Q37A01 *Announce/Closing Date:* November 5, 2007–November 30, 2007.

27   Ibid.

28   City of Philadelphia Personnel Department, *ExamNumber:*06Q39B03, *Announce/Closing Date:* November 21, 2005 (open continuous).

29   The federal government allows you to submit either a résumé or Optional Form (OF) 612, "Optional Application for Federal Employment." At the state or local level, the form or application to be submitted varies by the entity.

30   Group Qualification Standard, Administrative and Management Positions, excerpted from the OPM's web site, http://federaljobs.net/qualsam.htm.

31   Ibid.

32   Pennsylvania State Commission of Civil Service, "Veterans' Preference in State Civil Service Employment," http://www.scsc.state.pa.us/scsc/cwp/view.asp?a = 392&Q = 128236.

33   U.S. Office of Personnel Management, "Federal Employment of People with Disabilities," http://www.opm.gov/disability/appempl_3–11.asp.

34   Commonwealth of Pennsylvania, State Civil Service Commission, "Instructions for the Application for Employment/Promotion," http://www.scsc.state.pa.us/scsc/lib/scsc/scsc1.pdf.

35   City of Philadelphia Personnel Department, "Americans with Disabilities Frequently Asked Questions," http://www.phila.gov/personnel/eeo/index.htm.

36   For further information as to how the federal government determines basic eligibility, read Office of Personal Management, "Operating Manual Quali-

fication Standards for General Schedule Positions," http://opm.gov/qualifi cations/index.asp.

37 If you are found to be ineligible, you may have the chance to appeal that decision. However, it may be quite some time before you even find this out. If you do find it out, you decide to appeal that determination, and your appeal succeeds, the job(s) that you applied for will probably have been filled. While you may then be eligible for priority consideration for future vacancies, you will, at a minimum, lose months in your job search.

38 In the federal government, only a few positions now require a written test.

39 According to the VSR announcement,

> [A] VSR works within a team environment and serves as (1) a counselor or advocate for VA claimants providing information about a broad range of bene- fits and assisting with applications for VA benefits and services, (2) a legal technician gathering requisite evidence from medical, military, community, and other sources to support benefit determinations, (3) a decision maker weighing the evidence and applying the controlling laws and regulations, and (4) a computer systems user who enters appropriate data to generate accurate benefits payments, controls pending issues or schedules future actions, and releases complete, correct notifications of benefits determinations.

40 USAJOBS, Veterans Benefits Administration, Announcement VB162131, November 26–30, 2007.

41 According to the announcement, an Information Receptionist

> provides a variety of receptionist, office automation, and clerical support du- ties. He/she receives telephone calls and visitors to the office, controls access to the office and insures that only visitors properly cleared are authorized entry. She also notifies staff members of visitors and incoming telephone calls, uses and maintains multi-line telephone switchboard equipment and responds to inquiries, providing general information regarding office programs.

42 USAJOBS, Information Receptionist (Office Automation), Announcement 08-WDPA-02, November 19–December 3, 2007.

43 Nevada Employee Action and Timekeeping System, Training Officer 2— 07.524, Announcement 5670, posted November 30, 2007.

44 Even if you are a veteran, other veterans who have more severe disabilities may also apply and may go ahead of you on the civil service register.

45 Recruiting specialists typically set up interviews for some people who cannot initially be selected because of their location on the civil service register. They do this because they do not know which candidates on the register will still be interested at the time selections are made. By then, some may have

gotten other jobs, while others may no longer want to work for the organization.

Chapter 3

1 U.S. Office of Personnel Management, as described by Joe Gray, Labor Relations Specialist, Civilian Personnel Division, U.S. Army Medical Command.

2 By this I mean the public stereotype of what a government employee looks like. I am not implying that this stereotype is true. In my experience, many government employees dress professionally, although some do not.

3 Love to Know, "Tattoos in the Workplace—An Interview with Talar Herculian," http://tattoos.lovetoknow.com/Tattoos_in_the_Workplace_Interview _with_Talar_Herculian.

4 CBS, *The Early Show*, "Tattoos Becoming More Accepted at Work: As Dress Codes Become More Lax, so Are Rules About Body Art," New York, January 29, 2007.

5 Joe Thompson served as the undersecretary of the Veterans Benefits Administration from 1997 to 2001.

6 U.S. Department of Veterans Affairs, "The Veterans Benefits Administration: An Organizational History: 1776–1994," November 1995.

7 These individuals are different from the people who ask many questions because they *do not* do their homework, i.e., who simply try to get by on the backs of the people who made the effort to learn the job.

8 In fact, "most organizations don't have a defined policy addressing it." Society for Human Resource Management (SHRM) and CareerJournal.com, 2006 Workplace Romance. "Only 9 percent of HR professionals surveyed say dating among employees is prohibited, and . . . [most] did not have formal written policies." Kathy Gurchiek, "Most Organizations Lack Policy on Office Romance," SHRM, February 9, 2006, http://www.shrm.org/ hrnews_published/Archive/CMS_015775.asp.

9 About 80 percent of HRM professionals believe that this type of relationship "should be off limits—up from 64 percent in 2001, SHRM/CareerJournal.com found. Employees also feel such a relationship is inappropriate, though less strongly than four years ago—70 percent voiced this sentiment in 2001, compared with 60 percent in 2005." Ibid.

10 Ibid.

11 American Management Association, "Workplace Dating: 44% of Office Romances Led to Marriage, AMA Survey Shows," New York, February 10, 2003.

12 General Services Administration, Office of Government-wide Policy, "Model 'Limited Personal Use Policy' of Government Equipment," July 7, 1999.

13 U.S. Office of Personnel Management, "Retirement Systems Modernization, Coverage Determination Application," http://www.opm.gov/forms/pdf_fill/OPM1676.pdf.

14 Ibid.

15 Treasury Inspector General for Tax Administration, "Inappropriate Use of Email by Employees and System Configuration Management Weaknesses Are Creating Security Risks," July 31, 2006, Reference Number 2006–20–110.

16 Ibid. According to the Treasury Inspector General for Tax Administration,

> The large number of inappropriate emails places the IRS network at risk. For example, malicious software could be attached to these emails that could destroy data on the computer, enable unauthorized persons to access sensitive information, and disrupt computer operations by causing a denial of service attack.
>
> In addition to the security risks, the performance and efficiency of the IRS' computing network is degraded by the number and size of inappropriate email messages. Many of the sampled messages contained graphics, sound, video, and/or animations that significantly increased the sizes of the files. Inclusion of these unnecessary features in an email message often increases message's size from 10 to 50 times the size of a normal text message, causing the system to operate slower and less efficiently, and creates the need for additional storage capacity that can be costly.
>
> Offensive and inappropriate content in messages can also damage employee relationships and lead to adverse personnel actions or potential lawsuits. When forwarded to outside recipients, these messages could also invite high-profile media attention, damaging the IRS' reputation.

17 Trudy Walsh, "Workers Disciplined for E-mail Use," *Government Computer News*, December 6, 2007.

18 *USA Today*, "A Computer Disk Stolen," May 23, 2006.

19 *Federal Daily*, http://www.federaldaily.com/labor/relations.htm.

20 National Right to Work Legal Defense Foundation, http://www.nrtw.org/a/a_1_s.htm.

21 Ibid.

22 If you feel that you are being discriminated against by management for joining the union or becoming a union official, you may file an unfair labor practice charge.

23 Michael H. Cimini, "1982–97 State and Local Government Work Stoppages and Their Legal Background," *Compensation and Working Conditions*, Fall 1998.

24 Ibid. Ten states have granted their public employees a limited right to strike. Courts in several other states have also held that government employees have the right to strike (e.g., California, Idaho, Montana, and Colorado).

25 Ibid.

26 For example, in 2005, New York transit workers went on strike even though a judge declared the strike to be illegal (CNN, Tuesday, December 20, 2005). At the federal level, this happened most noticeably when the air traffic controllers went on strike under President Reagan.

27 Cimini, "1982–97 State and Local Government Work Stoppages." In states where collective bargaining rights laws were not in place, only one-fifth of the nonfederal civil service employees were represented by the union or an employee association.

Chapter 4

1 As an example, the federal government operates on a two-year budget cycle.

2 Other factors also played a role, such as decisions made by the Court of Veterans Appeals, but staffing was the primary reason for the increase in the backlog.

3 In many cases, employees must use a certain amount of vacation time by the end of the year or they will lose the leave. This is referred to as "use or lose." In the federal government, for most employees, if they have annual leave in excess of 240 hours that they have not taken by the end of the leave year, they will lose it.

4 A continuing resolution continues funding for a program if the fiscal year ends without a new appropriation in place. It usually provides temporary funding at current levels or less.

5 Tom Musbach, "What Employees Want for 2008: A New Boss!" Yahoo Hot-Jobs, Career Check-In, http://hotjobs.promotions.yahoo.com/careercheckin/survey_article.html.

6 The only possible exception to this rule would be if the employee had a serious health problem or had a family tragedy. Under these circumstances, most supervisors would be understanding, as long as they were aware of the problem and were periodically kept informed. However, the employee would still be expected to deal with the problem and perform up to his capabilities.

Chapter 5

1 In response to the oil crisis, the GSA attempted to reduce the energy used in federal buildings. Lights were shut off, thermostats were turned down, new policies were established, and other such actions were taken.

2   Wikipedia, the Free Encyclopedia, http://en.wikipedia.org/wiki/U.S._General_Services_Administration.

3   U.S. General Services Administration, "GSA Since 1949," http://www.gsa.gov/Portal/gsa/ep/contentView.do?contentType = GSA_BASIC&contentId = 23723&noc = T.

4   The power of veterans' service organizations tends to increase even more during a time of war because of all the media attention focused on veterans' issues.

5   *Star Wars Episode I: The Phantom Menace*, Lucasfilm, 1999.

Chapter 6

1   I was detailed to several other locations around the country, but these were on a temporary basis.

2   The intensity of headquarters work varies greatly. Some staff jobs are relatively easy and can be done in a typical eight-hour day. However, many other jobs are much faster paced and more demanding.

3   Online NewsHour: "The GI Bill's Legacy," July 4, 2000, http://www.pbs.org/newshour/bb/military/july-dec00/gibill_7–4.html.

4   This number was developed by a member of the undersecretary for veterans' benefits staff while I was working at the VA's Central Office in the late 1990s.

5   In the federal government, graduates with a grade-point average of 3.5 may be hired without going through the normal competitive process because they are considered to be outstanding scholars with excellent potential.

6   This salary comes from the base pay schedule and does not take into account any locality pay.

7   U.S. Office of Personnel Management, http://www.opm.gov/retire/html/faqs/faq9.asp#keep.

Chapter 7

1   Assuming that the goals are appropriately set from the customer's perspective.

2   A Theory X manager believes that the average person dislikes work and will avoid it if he/she can. Therefore, most people must be forced with the threat of punishment if they are to work toward organizational objectives, and the average person prefers to be directed, prefers to avoid responsibility, is relatively unambitious, and wants security above all else. A Theory Y manager believes in a participative style and that effort at work is as natural as work and play; people will apply self-control and self-direction in the pursuit of organizational objectives, without external control or the threat of

punishment; commitment to objectives is a function of the rewards associated with their achievement; people usually accept and often seek responsibility; the capacity to use a high degree of imagination, ingenuity, and creativity in solving organizational problems is widely, not narrowly, distributed in the population; and in industry the intellectual potential of the average person is only partly utilized. Douglas McGregor, *The Human Side of Enterprise, Annotated Edition* (New York: McGraw-Hill, 2005).

3 Paul Gustavson, "Designing Effective Work Systems for Greenfield Sites," *Expansion*, November 1988.

Chapter 8

1 *Casablanca*, Warner Brothers Pictures, 1942.

2 According to the Free Dictionary by Farlex, http://legal-dictionary.thefree dictionary.com/conservator, a conservator is "a guardian and protector appointed by a judge to protect and manage the financial affairs and/or the person's daily life due to physical or mental limitations or old age."

3 Canadian Mental Health Association, "Sources of Workplace Stress " Richmond, British Columbia (April 28, 2000).

4 WebMD, March 17, 2008, http://men.webmd.com/guide/work-stress.

5 I did not actually retire that day, as I was more than a year short of age 55. My organization graciously allowed me to work part-time, from home, so that I could retire at age 55. Fortunately, I had saved up enough vacation time and sick leave to be able to work roughly two hours per day and still receive a full paycheck until retirement.

6 The federal government bases your retirement on your three highest consecutive years of salary. Other levels of government sometimes use different formulas.

Chapter 9

1 The Free Dictionary by Farlex, http://www.thefreedictionary.com/Bud dhism.

2 Desmond Tutu Peace Foundation, http://www.tutufoundation-usa.org/.

3 About.com: Classical Music, http://classicalmusic.about.com/od/performer biographies/p/horowitz.htm.

4 This discussion of Lincoln's life is based on Wikipedia, the Free Encyclopedia, http://en.wikipedia.org/wiki/Abraham_Lincoln, and on Stephen B. Oates, *With Malice Toward None: A Life of Abraham Lincoln* (New York: HarperPerennial, 1994).

5 This discussion of Grant's life is based on a description in Wikipedia, the

Free Encyclopedia, http://en.wikipedia.org/wiki/Ulysses_S._Grant, and on "Biography of Ulysses S. Grant, The White House," http://www.whitehouse .gov/history/presidents/ug18.html.

6   This discussion of Truman's life is based on a description in Wikipedia, the Free Encyclopedia, http://en.wikipedia.org/wiki/Harry_S._Truman, and on David McCullough, *Truman* (New York: Simon & Schuster, 1992).

7   David McCullough, *1776* (New York: Simon & Schuster, 2005).

Index